Explaining
and Understanding
International Relations

Explaining
and Understanding
International Relations

MARTIN HOLLIS AND
STEVE SMITH

CLARENDON PRESS · OXFORD

Oxford University Press, Walton Street, Oxford OX2 6DP

Oxford New York Toronto
Delhi Bombay Calcutta Madras Karachi
Petaling Jaya Singapore Hong Kong Tokyo
Nairobi Dar es Salaam Cape Town
Melbourne Auckland
and associated companies in
Berlin Ibadan

Oxford is a trade mark of Oxford University Press

Published in the United States
by Oxford University Press, New York

First published in hardback 1990
First issued in Clarendon Paperbacks 1991
Paperback reprinted 1992

British Library Cataloguing in Publication Data
Hollis, Martin
Explaining and understanding international relations.
1. International relations
I. Title   II. Smith, Steven H. (Stephen Murray), 1952–
303.482
ISBN 0–19–827589–7

Library of Congress Cataloging in Publication Data
Hollis, Martin.
Explaining and understanding international relations/Martin
Hollis and Steve Smith.
Includes bibliographical references (p.
1. International relations—Philosophy.   I. Smith, Steve, 1952–
II. Title.
JX1245.H65   1990   327.1'01—dc20   89-72209
ISBN 0–19–827589–7

Printed in Great Britain by Biddles Ltd
Guildford and King's Lynn

Preface

Books which bring together International Relations and philosophy are rare enough to call for comment. This one has grown out of joint teaching which began in 1984, and out of many lively discussions in consequence. We would like to thank all the students who have taken Martin Hollis's Philosophy of Social Science course in the period, both those also studying international relations with Steve Smith and those majoring in other areas of social science or in philosophy. Their keen interest and their comments, especially those by Tim Dunne, have helped in many ways, not least by convincing us that issues which are fertile for the social sciences at large are well exemplified in the discipline of International Relations.

The book is aimed chiefly at those engaged in reflecting theoretically on international relations. We hope to show how many of the central questions in such reflection belong to wider debates in the theory and philosophy of the social sciences, and how the discipline can gain from setting them in this wider context. Very little has been written on this subject, the most notable exception being Charles Reynolds's 1973 book *Theory and Explanation in International Politics*.[1] Reynolds's absorbing study is not undermined by more recent developments in the philosophy of science, and its contrast between 'scientific' and 'historical' approaches remains instructive. But whereas his 'historical' explanations are always particular, we have sought to establish a dimension of 'understanding' which permits a range of hermeneutic disputes between individualism and holism. Yet we are not offering simple answers. Indeed, as we explain in the introduction and demonstrate in the dialogue of the final chapter, we are not even offering agreed answers. The theme foreshadowed by our title is that Explaining and Understanding are alternative ways to analyse international relations, each persuasive but not readily

---

[1] Charles Reynolds, *Theory and Explanation in International Politics* (Oxford: Martin Robertson).

combined. Although either can allow some scope to the other, one must predominate. We disagree about which.

This will emerge only after we have agreed about a great deal on the way. It is worth saying now, however, that the argument is not one between our disciplines. Had one of us taken a different line on his side of the house, there would have been no need for a final dialogue, and if both of us had, we would merely have ended on opposite sides of an argument still structured in the same manner. What follows is a joint exploration of a shared line of thought for most of the way.

Our differences of intellectual background are, however, reflected in the drafting of the book. Hollis wrote the first drafts of Chapters 3, 4, and 8, where philosophy is uppermost, Smith those of Chapters 1, 2, and 5, where International Relations is primary. Chapter 6 started out in the form of two separate contributions. Chapter 7, which has a longer history than the rest, draws on our joint paper 'Roles and Reasons in Foreign Policy Decision Making', which appeared in the *British Journal of Political Science* in 1986 and led us to believe that we had more to say.[2] Although neither of us claims expertise in the other's discipline, both have nevertheless had a large hand in all chapters, and the final draft has invariably emerged very different from the first. It is very much a joint work and one for which we take joint responsibility.

Steve Smith would like to thank Marysia Zalewski for her detailed comments, her trenchant criticisms and, above all, her invaluable support. Martin Hollis wishes to acknowledge Blackwell's permission to reprint the diagram on p. 51.[3] We would both like to thank Mary Robinson and Carol Forward for typing the final drafts of various chapters.

Martin Hollis and Steve Smith
School of Economic and Social Studies
University of East Anglia

[2] Martin Hollis and Steve Smith, 'Roles and Reasons in Foreign Policy Decision Making', *British Journal of Political Science*, 1986, 16(3), pp. 269–86.
[3] From M. Hollis, *Invitation to Philosophy* (Oxford: Blackwell, 1985).

Contents

1. Introduction: Two Traditions   1
2. The Growth of a Discipline   16
3. Explaining   45
4. Understanding   68
5. The International System   92
6. The Games Nations Play (1)   119
7. Roles and Reasons   143
8. The Games Nations Play (2)   171
9. Explaining and Understanding   196
   Guide to Further Reading   217
   Index   223

1

Introduction: Two Traditions

INSIDE AND OUTSIDE

The social sciences thrive on two intellectual traditions. One is founded on the triumphant rise of natural science since the sixteenth century. The other is rooted in nineteenth-century ideas of history and the writing of history from the inside. This book is guided by our belief that both traditions are fertile for the study of international relations, despite a lively tension between them. In international affairs, and throughout the social world, there are two sorts of story to tell and a range of theories to go with each. One story is an outsider's, told in the manner of a natural scientist seeking to explain the workings of nature and treating the human realm as part of nature. The other is an insider's, told so as to make us understand what the events mean, in a sense distinct from any meaning found in unearthing the laws of nature. Thus our title does not use two words where one would do. 'Explaining' is the key term in one approach, 'understanding' in the other.

The 'inside' story is the more familiar one. The media tell it whenever they present international relations as a dramatic encounter between world leaders who personify their countries. Think of the popular picture of US–Soviet relations as Bush-meets-Gorbachev, or of the US–UK 'special relationship' in the 1980s as a special personal relationship between President Reagan and Mrs Thatcher. The air of human drama and of history in the making is especially potent in times of crisis, when leaders can be shown locked in combat, for example Reagan with Gadaffi over the US bombing of Libya in April 1986. Reporters try to establish what the unfolding events mean to the principal actors concerned. They report their statements, analyse their actions, and re-create their thoughts, so as to convey the reasons which account for why each step was taken rather than any other. The actors themselves are generally keen to help, both in person and through the mouths of officials at the time, and (often telling a rather different tale) in tranquil autobiographies afterwards.

No one supposes that international relations can be fully understood just by assembling a patchwork of what the actors say was in their minds. Nor should the media habit of personalizing events and trends be taken too seriously. Drama is easier to convey than analysis, rather as the political decisions of kings and queens make for more comprehensible history in the schoolroom than do gradual shifts in economic and social patterns. All the same, the actors' view is a starting point and, advocates of Understanding will say, the only starting point. We must know how the actors defined the issues and the alternatives, what they believed about the situation and each other, what they aimed to achieve, and how. Only then can we ask more pointed questions about their clarity of vision, their underlying reasons, and the true meaning of the episodes.

There is a distinction to be drawn here between simplifications and assumptions. It is a simplification to banish all but the principal actors from the international stage. The pretence is that the White House spokesperson is the voice of the President; the reality is closer to being that the President is the voice of the White House and other agencies of decision-making. There are a thousand other actors in the wings and the official tale about the President's intentions and reasons is never full and rarely frank. Everyone is well aware that the considered official record is as much a simplification (even if of a different sort and for different reasons) as is the news story filed by reporters for press and television—the actors, the reporters, the academic researchers, and, one hopes, the public too.

The assumptions raise deeper questions. For instance, there is usually a starting assumption that individuals make history, at least by the sum of their actions and even if not quite as they intended it to be. In that case the simplification is warranted because it encapsulates a truth about what is going on. But the general proposition that human affairs must be understood from within does not require the assumption that *individuals* make history, except perhaps as a convenient device for identifying what calls for deeper understanding. Individualism is a possible, indeed common, trump suit in the search for the meaning and true interpretation of social events: but, we shall find in later chapters, it is by no means the only possible one. An 'inside' story can also be told in terms which subordinate individuals to some larger social whole.

At this stage, therefore, we shall say nothing about the range of theories which can be brought to bear on international relations, if one believes in working from the inside in pursuit of understanding. But it is worth pointing out one obvious hostage given by treating the 'inside' as a matter of the desires and beliefs of individual actors. It is that the actors' desires, beliefs, and resulting reasons for action may be generated in turn by external factors. In the jargon of social science, they may be intervening and not independent variables. Although there are 'inside' ways of trying to rescue the hostage, as we shall see, the point will serve to introduce the rival 'outside' story about explanation.

The 'outside' way of accounting for behaviour is modelled on the methods of natural science and is usually described as a search for causes. To explain an event or state of affairs is to find another which caused it. This bald statement conceals much dispute about the exact relation between a cause and its effect, about the right way to define 'cause', and about the nature of causality, both as a concept and in the world. So what follows is very preliminary. But the broad idea is that events are governed by laws of nature which apply whenever similar events occur in similar conditions. Science progresses by learning which similarities are the key to which sequences. That catches the familiar dictum that science explains particular events by generalizing and by making them cases of laws at work. To this is often (but not always) added an idea that a cause makes its effect happen, implying perhaps that to find a cause is to show why the effect had to happen as it did.

If these ideas are taken together, and if three centuries of physics and chemistry are taken as the model to emulate, it is tempting to suggest that it really does not matter what the actors on the international scene have in their minds. In the strongest version of this approach, behaviour is generated by a system of forces or a structure, external not only to the minds of each actor but also external even to the minds of all actors. In that case it is a basic mistake to reduce US–Soviet relations to the personalities of individuals. Bush and Gorbachev merely represent the forces which brought them to office and merely pursue an agenda so predetermined that its outcome could have been predicted in advance. If either were run over by the proverbial bus, his replacement would carry on as before. Similarly, the special relationship between Thatcher and Reagan was a meeting of ideologies, which in turn expressed congruent interests within a larger system of forces. To call it a personal relationship or to believe that the individuals contributed more than its pleasantries is an illusion.

It must be said at once that nothing remotely as strong as this is required by the proposition that to explain an event is to find its cause. That would mean crossing most brands of psychology and economics off the list of social sciences. Theories cast in terms of external structures and systematic forces are at the 'holist' end of a range of causal theories, just as theories which take actors as the final authority are at the 'individualist' end of a range of theories in search of understanding. What marks the 'explanation' range is the assertion of only the weak determinism involved in claiming that similar effects always occur in similar conditions. The rest is a matter of dispute, as we shall find in Chapter 3, and there is no objection in principle to a psychological explanation of international relations or to one cast in terms of individual behaviour.

All the same, there is still point in contrasting 'insider' and 'outsider' accounts. The point could be simply made if psychology modelled on the natural sciences were always 'behavioural' and concerned with the actors' brains rather than with their minds. But, in international relations as in economics, there is scope for applying scientific method to the beliefs and desires of individuals. The crucial move is to insist that every individual works basically in the same law-like way, with individual variations depending on systematic differences in, for instance, preferences and information, or, more broadly, nature and nurture. Admittedly the difference between understanding from inside and explaining from outside will seem to be pretty thin, if beliefs and desires can appear in scientific explanations. But we ask for patience until Chapter 4.

Meanwhile, the contrast is best made for introductory purposes by thinking about the middle of the range, where individuals take the stage in a social capacity, as, for instance, Prime Minister or Secretary of State. In Figure 1.1 we have represented the holism–individualism range on the vertical axis and the explaining–understanding contrast on the horizontal, with the actors in their social capacities located on the dividing line, where, one might say, structure meets action. *X* is an actor conceived in the spirit of

external structures
+ systemic forces.

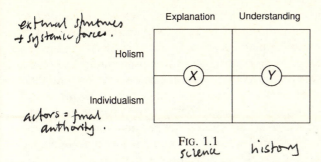

actors = final
authority.

FIG. 1.1
science   *history*

the scientific tradition, *Y* the counterpart in the spirit of the interpretative tradition. For both there is a pull in two directions. On the one hand, *X* and *Y* are human beings with beliefs and aims, *INDIV.* and we are interested in what is in their heads. On the other hand, their situation is structured, and ('holism' here standing for the *HOLISM.* idea that the parts of a whole behave as the whole requires) we are interested in the social constraints on their actions. Both pulls are strong and theories which purport to reconcile them tend to be fragile, even though they capture a stout commonsense conviction that, as Marx put it, 'Men make their own history but they do not make it just as they please; they do not make it under circumstances chosen by themselves.' But let us suppose that there are theories robust enough to hold the tension.

The contrast shows up in the different notions of 'social capacity'. Being part of the natural world and a proper object of scientific study, *X* is predictable on the basis of *X*'s preferences and information, which are in turn the result of *X*'s nature and nurture. There is a disputed question about the proportions of nature (psychology) to nurture (sociology), but, to keep *X* on the border between top and bottom boxes, both are important. Since no two mice are identical, let alone two human beings, replacing *X* would make a difference. Yet the situation is full of constraints and the difference is not as large as Mrs Thatcher, if she were *X*, might like to think. Social capacities are a useful source of *SCIENCE* predictions, since they greatly reduce the range of alternatives that an actor is likely to pursue.

The fabric of *Y*'s social world is woven from rules and meanings, which define relationships among the inhabitants and give inter- actions their purpose. Social capacities are normative or prescrip- *HISTORY.* tive, in that they include responsibilities for whose discharge the actor can be praised or criticized. Other actors are entitled to expect *Y* to live up to them, even if they would be wise not to count on it when temptations arise. In other words, *Y* is expected to pick an intelligent course through a variety of social engagements, to which actors bring something of themselves in exercising their social capacities. What this comes to will be clearer by the end of the book, but we need to mention both a normative element and a personal one, if *Y* is to be located neither above nor below the dividing line. The social world must be seen through the actors' eyes because it depends on how they see it and it works in whatever way social capacities are exercised. *social forces*

It may sound as if *Y* has free will and *X* does not. But that is too simple. Some philosophers maintain that to act freely is to do what one wants and to act rationally is to do what will best satisfy one's desires. In that case it is no obstacle to freedom that actions are predictable; indeed, free *and* rational action is possible only in a predictable world. By this test *X* is a free agent. Other philosophers argue that free agents need to be self-directed (or 'autonomous') and hence need to choose in a sense not cashable as the effective satisfying of desires. In that case *X* is not a free agent, but it is not yet clear whether *Y* is one. So we cannot characterize the difference between inside and outside in terms of freedom vs. determinism.

The crucial contrast between *X* and *Y* lies in the stuff of their social worlds. For *X* the social world, like the rest of the natural world to which it belongs, is an environment, independent and to some extent predictable. For *Y* it is a construction consisting of rules and meanings. This contrast brings with it different theories of social action and how to study it. It also implies different analyses of human nature. Hence, to give warning, we shall find no easy way to combine a natural science approach with an interpretative one. For the moment, we repeat that there are two plausible stories to tell, one from outside about the human part of the natural world and the other from inside a separate social realm. One seeks to explain, the other to understand. We are well aware that many have attempted to combine these two stories, for example Anthony Giddens in his work on the concept of structuration.[1] However, we believe that readers will come to

---

[1] A. Giddens, *Critical Issues in Social Theory* (London: Macmillan, 1979), ch. 2.

understand by the end of the book that combining the two stories is not as easy as it at first seems. Although it is appealing to believe that bits of the two stories can be added together, we maintain that there are always two stories to tell and that combinations do not solve the problem.

With this broad theme in mind we turn to the subject of International Relations and then to an outline of the book.

LEVELS OF ANALYSIS: 'TOP–DOWN' AND 'BOTTOM–UP'

The study of international relations deals with a peculiar area of politics. Whereas domestic politics occur within a political system which includes a government to make and enforce laws, the international system is anarchic. By this we mean not that it is chaotic but simply that there is no government above the states which comprise it. The individual nation state is often therefore presented as a self-contained unit, analytically prior to its international relations. It may turn out not to be the final or the only unit of analysis but, even so, to contend that it were would not be so wildly wrong as treating America as fifty states without mentioning the Federal Government.

Our approach to theories of international relations will be based on a distinction between system and units, and will make central what the literature calls 'the level-of-analysis problem'. This was originally posed by David Singer in 1961 as the problem of whether to account for the behaviour of the international system in terms of the behaviour of the nation states comprising it or vice versa.[2] We propose to extend the problem in two dimensions. One dimension concerns the identities of system and units for purpose of what is, on reflection, a very general problem indeed. Singer's question was about the international system and national units. One answer to it might be that there are systemic forces strong enough to propel the nation states through their orbits, rather as if they were planets in a solar system in dynamic equilibrium. In that case one might hope to account for the working of the system without enquiring into the internal organization of the units. But if

---

[2] J. D. Singer, 'The Level-of-Analysis Problem in International Relations', in K. Knorr and S. Verba (eds.), *The International System: Theoretical Essays* (Princeton: Princeton University Press, 1961), pp. 77–92.

it turns out that the units make an independent contribution, then there is a further level-of-analysis problem. Are we to account for the behaviour of the state in terms of the behaviour of its constituent bureaucracies (and other agencies), or vice versa? Then, if the answer requires us to take the bureaucracies as making an independent contribution, there will be yet another level-of-analysis problem. Are we to account for the behaviour of a bureaucracy in terms of the behaviour of the human individuals comprising it, or vice versa? At each stage the 'unit' of the higher layer becomes the 'system' of the lower layer. We shall distinguish the three layers just indicated, and on each shall contrast an analysis which proceeds 'top–down' (from system to unit) with one which proceeds 'bottom–up' (from unit to system).

That way of describing the level-of-analysis problem is markedly scientific in tone. Our other dimension concerns the contrast between explaining and understanding. There is also a level-of-analysis problem for theories which try to work from the inside. Again, there are three layers. The highest requires that we think of the international system as a set of norms or purposes which shape the process of history. If a fully systemic answer to the problem were to prevail, something very ambitious would be needed, for instance the positing of a World Spirit to guide human history, as Hegelians and Absolute Idealists have sometimes seemed to suggest. But we ourselves shall not tackle such grand theories. In what follows the interpretative dimension will come alive only on the next layer of the problem, where we ask whether social rules and institutions account for the performance of social roles, or vice versa. In other words, we think international institutions too fragile to permit a fully systemic answer on the highest layer and so incomplete that an answer which favours the international units must yield to curiosity about how these units work. But it is certainly possible to argue for a systemic answer in which nations or cultures or, to use a phrase from Wittgenstein, 'forms of life', account for what goes on within them. Equally, it is possible to deny it, and the lowest layer of the level-of-analysis problem is broached by asking whether individual actors construct institutional rules and roles, or vice versa.

The three layers of the level-of-analysis problem are set out systematically in Figure 1.2, with the debate on each being a matter of whether to proceed 'top–down' or 'bottom–up'. In the

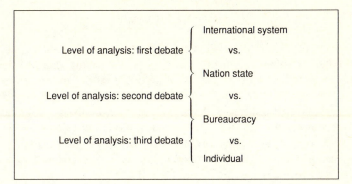

Level of analysis: first debate
International system
vs.
Nation state

Level of analysis: second debate
vs.
Bureaucracy

Level of analysis: third debate
vs.
Individual

Fig. 1.2

first debate, 'top–down' makes the international system wholly dominant and 'bottom–up' retorts that it is the sum of what nations do. It is possible to conduct this debate without either side maintaining that the internal organization of the units matters (witness what will be said about Game Theory in Chapter 6). In the second debate, 'top–down' sees the state as a single agent responding rationally to its situation, whereas 'bottom–up' sees the state's behaviour as the outcome of bargains (and other manoeuvres) among bureaucratic agencies. (It may be helpful to note a parallel dispute in economics about whether firms respond rationally to their market situation or need to be analysed in terms of how they are organized internally.) In the third debate, 'top–down' contends that bureaucratic demands dictate individual choices, whereas 'bottom–up' makes individual choices central to the analysis of collective decisions.

Then there is the other dimension, whether the aim is to explain or to understand. It will be seen that Figure 1.1, which introduced two individuals *X* and *Y*, is a case of the third debate. We began there, because the contrast between explaining and understanding is likely to be less familiar than the contrast between holism ('top–down') and individualism ('bottom–up'). Also, it takes an austere mind not to believe that the scope and limits of individual human action are an absolutely central theoretical crux for the social sciences. But, in principle, there are ways of understanding the social world which dispense with individuals, at least as prime movers, and ways of explaining it which rely on them.

SOME KEY TERMS

Leaving the theme to develop as we go along, we shall next specify our use of some key terms. Let us start by saying that we shall never use 'explaining' (or 'explanation') and 'understanding' interchangeably. When we want a neutral word it will be 'analysing' (or 'analysis'). Thus, the 'level-of-analysis' problem is conveniently neutral between a level-of-explanation problem and a level-of-understanding problem, as we have just stated. The senses which we attach to 'explaining' and 'understanding' will emerge more clearly in Chapters 3 and 4.

In speaking of international relations, we shall sometimes be referring to the international world and sometimes to the theories of that world which comprise the discipline called 'International Relations'. To avoid a muddle we shall use initial capitals— 'International Relations'—when we mean the latter and small letters—'international relations'—when we mean the former. Thus, International Relations is a discipline, where theories of international relations compete. These, for the most part, are theories about international relations (hence the small letters), although we may occasionally take note of theories about the conduct of the discipline itself (i.e. theories of International Relations).

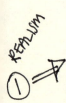

There are some key terms that are sure to cause trouble because they have different meanings in International Relations and in philosophy. The first is 'Realism', which in International Relations refers to a school of thinking opposed to 'Idealism'. Realism, given classic expression in Hans Morgenthau's *Politics among Nations*,[3] calls for the explanation of international behaviour in terms of national interests and without regard for the moral sentiments and hopes which nations profess or which observers may have in their heart. It is squarely in the scientific tradition and is a conscious attempt to apply scientific method to international relations. In philosophy, 'realism' (usually with a small 'r') is broadly the view that whether a thing exists is a question about the world independent of questions about how we could know it or what statements concerning the thing mean. Thus, on a realist view, there are truths about the past which are distinct from all present

---

[3] H. Morgenthau, *Politics among Nations: The Struggle for Power and Peace*, 1st edn. (New York: Knopf, 1948).

evidence and may therefore remain unknown to us. Similarly, a realist claim that electrons exist is a claim not about the instrumental observations or theoretical predictions of physics but about an independent world which physics investigates. This is the broad definition of 'realism' in the philosophy of science, theory of knowledge, and metaphysics, and it licenses talk of unobservable structures which cause observable behaviour. Sometimes, however, it has a more specific sense, when used by authors with a materialist view of nature and human history.[4] But since this use implies the broader one, which is all we need in this book, we shall not pursue it.

Correspondingly, 'Idealism' in International Relations names an approach concerned with the human will and institutional progress. Arising in the aftermath of the First World War, it took the view that disasters are due partly to failures of understanding and partly to the lack of suitable institutions to encourage co-operation. Hence it is often seen as primarily normative, in contrast to a more scientific Realism. But it also involves a descriptive account of human nature and institutions. Its liberal hopes of progress are grounded in the beliefs that human beings individually have reconcilable goals like peace, health, and prosperity and that institutions are a human construct, not always deliberate and, once created, having effects of their own on people's thoughts and actions. Philosophically it inherited something from the Absolute Idealism of the Hegelians and other nineteenth-century opponents of materialism, thus refusing to think of 'reality' as distinct from ideas of reality. Meanwhile, 'idealism' (with a small 'i') is a broad philosophical term for theories which work in terms of experience, conceived as 'ideas' in the mind. Hence, although the connections are not automatic and are not embraced by all who call themselves idealists, there is an affinity between Idealists, idealists and an interpretative approach, just as there is between Realists, realists and a scientific one.

The other term is 'positivism'. In the social sciences at large the word has often been used very loosely for any approach which applies scientific method to human affairs, conceived of as part of the natural order. Thus, it is not uncommon to find Comte, Durkheim, Marx, and Weber all described as positivists, even

---

[4] e.g. R. Bhaskar, *A Realist Theory of Science* (Brighton: Harvester, 1978).

though from many points of view they make strange bedfellows. But current usage tends to be more precise, perhaps influenced by the philosophical meaning. For philosophers, the epitome of positivism is 'Logical Positivism', the hard-headed empiricism of the Vienna Circle popularized in English by A. J. Ayer's *Language, Truth and Logic*.[5] Here the stress is on experience (on observation and testing) as the only way to justify claims to knowledge of the world, and hence on methods of verification as the key to the meaning of scientific statements. When 'positivism' is so construed, it is opposed to realism and insists that theory is a guide to prediction rather than a source of substantive hypotheses about what could not, even in principle, be observed. This makes it empiricist in a very sharp and disputable form, which has lately cost it allegiance even among most other empiricists.

But Logical Positivism has retained more influence in the social sciences. When economists speak of 'Positive economics' they mean a predictive science, governed solely by the test of experience. The empiricism here is not so tight that all theoretical terms and assumptions must refer directly to observables, but all substantive hypotheses must be able to be confirmed or falsified. Notions of real structure are at least suspect and often rejected altogether. In this, Positive economics is typical of other 'Positive' sciences, although perhaps clearer and more developed in its approach. In International Relations, however, a further step is usually taken, in that 'Positivism' tends to be associated with quantitative analysis. The connecting thought is that, since only behaviour can be observed and measured, only behavioural data can provide a proper scientific basis. Hence Behaviouralism, the version of a more general behaviourism specific to International Relations, which we shall meet in the next chapter, is commonly spoken of as a Positive approach and often contrasted with Realism on this score. Certainly Realists are inclined to a belief in the structures which a Logical Positivist would reject. But, from the standpoint of current usage in other social sciences and the philosophy of science, Realism aspires to be a Positive science and Behaviouralism is a particular version of it with an austere view of what is testable. Since this brings out what they have in common and shows them to be on the same side, we too shall use 'Positivism' to include the Realist approach.

[5] A. J. Ayer, *Language, Truth and Logic* (Harmondsworth: Penguin, 1971).

THE PLAN OF THE BOOK

The book falls into two main parts. The first, comprising Chapters 2–4, introduces the main debates in International Relations and the philosophical considerations which bear on them. Accordingly, Chapter 2 summarizes the growth of the discipline of International Relations, focusing on Idealism, Realism, and Behaviouralism as its principal phases. It will end with a brief survey of contemporary debates, including those revolving around the issue of whether the nation state is still the major actor on the international scene. But, without dismissing the claims of other actors such as transnational corporations or revolutionary groups, it will conclude that they do not affect questions about explaining and understanding, which are more clearly raised by considering better established theories that address the state. Chapters 3 and 4 explore philosophically the two traditions with which we began. Chapter 3, 'Explaining', asks what is involved in applying the philosophy of natural science to international relations and Chapter 4, 'Understanding', asks a similar question about international relations approached from the inside. The whole first part provides a framework for what we have just described as a level-of-analysis problem with three layers and two dimensions.

The second part, Chapters 5–8, conducts the three debates catalogued in Figure 1.2. Chapter 5 asks whether it is possible to develop a theory of international relations wholly at the level of the international system. We look at some of the main attempts to do so, spending most time on Kenneth Waltz's systems account.[6] Chapter 6 sets out the counter-case for an analysis in terms of the state, working 'bottom–up' from states to system. The vehicle chosen is Game Theory, which treats the state as a closed, utility-maximizing unit and so denies the need to 'open the box' to see how states are organized. In Chapter 7, however, we do 'open the box', by taking bureaucracy as a rival to the state in what is thus the second debate about the level of analysis. We use Graham Allison's Bureaucratic Politics model to see whether foreign policy can be convincingly portrayed as the result of bureaucratic bargaining.[7] If it cannot, that might mean victory for the state in

[6] The best source is K. Waltz, *Theory of International Politics* (Reading, Mass.: Addison-Wesley, 1979).

[7] The best source is G. Allison, *Essence of Decision* (Boston: Little, Brown, 1971).

the second debate. But, alternatively, it might mean that there is a further debate to conduct. Accordingly, in Chapter 8 we 'open the box' again and ask about the bureaucrats, the men and women who do the bargaining. Are they rational decision-makers of the kind proposed in microeconomics and Game Theory? Or are they mere voices of the bureaucracy (which, in this third debate, is the 'system')? A possible reply is that they are neither. That leads us to examine Wittgensteinian ideas of action and meaning, and to consider a very different notion of a 'game' in social life, where the actors are players of roles.

The debates will turn out to be less clear and clean than they seem in this outline. Argument on each layer tends to have half an eye to what is at issue on the others. Thus, objections to a full-blown systems theory such as Waltz's come both from those who think of the state as a rational closed unit and from those who think that its internal organization matters. Similarly, Game Theory faces objections both from systems theorists and from those opposing a Bureaucratic Politics model to every form of Rational Actor model. When, in Chapter 8, we reach what one might have hoped was, so to speak, the basement, we shall find that some arguments about the nature of role-play lead back up to the previous layer. To this extent our framework is artificial and offered only as an *aide-mémoire* for theoretical intricacies richer than we have made them. But we stand by our contention that the issues which we simplify are genuine, very much alive, and illuminated by philosophical treatment as well as by reference to the International Relations literature.

That the issues are very much alive becomes plainer still in the final chapter, Chapter 9, where we admit to disagreeing on them! The chapter begins by summarizing the common ground—that analysis can proceed 'top–down' or 'bottom–up' on all three layers and in the dimension either of 'Explaining' or of 'Understanding'. But, although the common ground is large and includes almost everything said in the first eight chapters about how to fill in the framework and conduct the disputes, unity then becomes too much for us. One of the pleasures of writing the book has been the attempt to settle an amicable debate of our own. We are not sorry that it failed and that, accordingly, Chapter 9 breaks into dialogue. Hollis (the philosopher) opts for 'Understanding' and a position just below the horizontal dividing line in Figure 1.1; Smith (the

International Relations scholar) for 'Explaining' and a position just above the dividing line. Stopping only to emphasize that this is not because we belong to different disciplines and that several other final positions are open to anyone from either discipline, we then leave readers to make up their own minds, or else to decide that there is no monopoly of wisdom to be had.

2

The Growth of a Discipline

International Relations emerged as a separate discipline in the aftermath of the First World War. For centuries previously the subject was a province variously of law, philosophy, history, and other disciplines, each with its own ways of seeing the world. The legacies of these origins have persisted and there has never been agreement on the nature of international affairs, on the proper methods for studying them, or on the range of elements which theories of them must take into account. International Relations began—and, many would say, remains—more of an inter-discipline than a discipline. But its seventy-year history has distinct phases and has been increasingly unified by a self-conscious aim on the part of its practitioners to make it a 'science'. This chapter will trace the rise of the leading approaches and show how disputes within the discipline have helped to create a scientific framework for it. We shall end with a brief survey of the fragmented current scene and a pointed reminder that International Relations is heir not only to a tradition of scientific explanation but also to one of historical understanding.

The chapter risks seeming ethnocentric in its focus on British and then, increasingly, on American works. We will stress now, therefore, that we are describing the growth of a discipline which, although helped by many contributions from elsewhere, has taken shape largely in Britain and America. Especially since 1945, American foreign policy issues have stood high on the International Relations agenda and its key debates have tended to reflect those within the American academic International Relations community. So, although we have of course taken a view of what has been significant, we deny that we have been ethnocentric in our choice of an Anglo-American focus. The focus is the discipline's own.

There is also a risk of making the story too pat. We shall open with an Idealist phase, followed by Realism, Behaviouralism, Neo-Realism and some current alternatives. That may make it seem as if we thought each had specific dates and a definite content. Ideas can never be packaged so conveniently. Each school of thought has enjoyed constant internal debate about assumptions and methods. Each has always had porous boundaries. Behaviouralism, for instance, has self-consciously hoisted its own flag and been sharply critical of Realism. Yet it has influenced both Realism and Idealism, while seeming to commentators (including ourselves) to be at heart a stricter version of Realism itself. Moreover, as this remark implies, the phases of the story do not end with the demise of their dominant school. Adherents of all of them are active in current debate, and the story is one of proliferation. New phases bring new dominant tendencies, but are not to be regarded as self-contained episodes. It is perhaps worth adding that the phases we have identified are the ones which the self-conscious discipline of International Relations itself regards as significant.

IDEALISM

The emergence of International Relations as a separate field of study was closely related to the approach that first captured thinking about the subject. To understand why Idealism became dominant in the early years one only has to think about the event that led to the establishment of the subject, namely, the First World War. Two points need to be kept in mind. First, there was a widespread view that the overwhelming lesson of the war was that military force could no longer achieve its objectives. If the reason for resorting to war had traditionally been to achieve territorial conquests, to obtain markets and raw materials, or to overthrow leaders of whom one did not approve, then the events of the First World War offered a corrective. Public perception of the war in Europe was of a senseless conflict fought out in the mud and filth of Flanders, with thousands killed each day for the sake of only a few yards of territory soon lost in the next offensive. The war, in short, achieved little tangible reward for either side, involved death *en masse*, and was a war not of manœuvre and conquest but of stalemate with little prospect of victory in the traditional sense. After this, what purpose could war ever serve again? The likely nature of any future war would, it was felt, be one of attrition and

massive deaths without the possibility of victory. War seemed to
have become an unusable tool of statecraft.

But, <u>secondly</u>, this was by no means the only important lesson of
the war. The lack of tangible reward for either side after the very
heavy losses suffered by both was compounded by the fact that it
was seen as <u>a war that no one had actually wanted</u>. This is not to
claim that the war was totally unintended, but that national leaders
had become caught in an irrational process which led inevitably to
war. War had resulted from the separate acts of various leaders,
none of whom wanted war as the outcome, and these separate acts
so reinforced mutual fears and suspicions that war became, in a
sense, unavoidable. The implication was that the slaughter had all
been in vain. The lesson of the casualties and the lack of any real
gains even to the victors was made harsher by this realization, that
for four years Europe had fought a war which no one had wanted.
The 1914 analogy remains potent in a nuclear age, where many
observers worry about a drift to war resulting from the increasing
automation of the battlefield and of command and control
systems.

The legacy of the war was a powerful one, both for politicians
and for the group of academics who were attempting to study the
phenomena of international relations. Four main conclusions were
drawn: first, war was a senseless act, which could never be a
rational tool of state policy; secondly, the 1914–18 war had been
the result of leaders becoming caught up in a set of processes that
no one could control; thirdly, the causes of the war lay in
misunderstandings between leaders and in the lack of democratic
accountability within the states involved; and fourthly, the
underlying tensions which had provided the rationale for the
conflict could be removed by the spread of statehood and
democracy. These views were expressed most succinctly by US
President Woodrow Wilson, in his famous Fourteen Points
proposal of January 1918.

The subject of International Relations grew out of this intellectual
and political setting; and it bore the birthmarks of its origins. First
of all, the discipline originated in two countries which were
essentially satisfied powers following the First World War. This
meant that the subject was developing in a specific type of state
with a specific view of the main features of international society.
The USA and the UK <u>were, crucially, status quo powers</u>, with

interests firmly committed to allowing as little change to the new international order as possible. One of the main problems for the subject in the inter-war period was that it became increasingly identified as a status quo subject.

Secondly, the imprint of the First World War, with its wholesale destruction and loss of life, stamped the survivors with a strong conviction that such a war must never happen again. It had been a 'war to end all wars'. Accordingly, the subject that studied such phenomena took on a strongly normative, prescriptive character. International Relations had to be concerned with devising ways to prevent such wars from occurring.

Thirdly, the way the war had broken out stamped the assumptions of the subject. Just as generals always seem to be planning for better ways to fight the last war, so the study of international relations has often reflected the concerns of the previous generation. The accepted view was that, since the war had occurred through misunderstanding, the task of International Relations was to devise ways to reduce misunderstandings in the future. This had implications for the organization of both domestic and international societies. Domestically, it was necessary to prevent 'sinister interests' from dominating the political process— the world that had been made safe for democracy had to be kept safe by democracy. Internationally, the emphasis was on developing mediation processes and organizational structures within which leaders could perceive more accurately the (non-aggressive) aims of their potential adversaries. Together these alterations in domestic and international societies would make wars like the First World War impossible.

Underlying this approach was a liberal view of human nature; good men and women would never want war, which must therefore result only from either mutual misunderstanding or the dominance of uneducated or uncivilized minds in the political process. Individuals were rational, and war was not a rational tool of foreign policy, since it could no longer be used to achieve the goals traditionally associated with it. Hence, the First World War had simply been dysfunctional. The new subject of International Relations must find the best ways of making leaders aware of the dysfunctional nature of war, or, if it failed in this, appeal directly to the populations concerned. The subject had a mission, just as the international organization that was created by the peacemakers, the League of Nations, had a mission to the international political system.

This first approach to studying international relations has become known as Idealism, although this was not a term that the academics working in the subject at the time used themselves. As Hedley Bull has commented:

> The distinctive characteristic of these writers was their belief in progress: the belief, in particular, that the system of international relations that had given rise to the First World War was capable of being transformed into a fundamentally more peaceful and just world order; that under the impact of the awakening of democracy, the growth of the 'international mind', the development of the League of Nations, the good works of men of peace or the enlightenment spread by their own teachings, it was in fact being transformed; and that their responsibility as students of international relations was to assist this march of progress to overcome the ignorance, the prejudices, the ill-will, and the sinister interests that stood in its way.[1]

Accordingly, the subject during the inter-war period concentrated on issues like the outlawing of war and the establishment of an international police force, until the events of the 1930s challenged its basic assumptions. Its response to these events was to see the sinister interests represented by the challenge to the international order as being peculiar to the revisionist states, Italy, Japan, and Germany. At this point the interests of powers such as Britain, France, and the United States were identified with those of humanity as a whole. Thus, in the mid-1930s, the discipline was once again identified with representing the interests of the status quo powers in the international system.

REALISM

This identification was one factor which provoked a major attack on the practice of International Relations which helped usher in a new way of thinking about the subject. This attack was mounted by the British historian E. H. Carr in a book published in 1939.[2]

[1] H. Bull, 'The Theory of International Politics, 1919–1969', in B. Porter (ed.), *The Aberystwyth Papers: International Politics 1919–1969* (London: Oxford University Press, 1972), p. 34.

[2] E. H. Carr, *The Twenty Years' Crisis 1919–1939*, 2nd edn. (London: Macmillan, 1946).

The Twenty Years' Crisis was a sustained critique of the way in which utopian thought had dominated international relations in the inter-war years. As Carr commented, utopianism

took its rise from a great and disastrous war; and the overwhelming purpose which dominated and inspired the pioneers of the new science was to obviate a recurrence of this disease of the international body politic. The passionate desire to prevent war determined the whole initial course and direction of the study. Like other infant sciences, the science of international politics has been markedly and frankly utopian. It has been in the initial stage in which wishing prevails over thinking, generalisation over observation, and in which little attempt is made at a critical analysis of existing facts or available means. In this stage, attention is concentrated almost exclusively on the end to be achieved . . . The course of events after 1931 clearly revealed the inadequacy of pure aspiration as the basis for a science of international politics, and made it possible for the first time to embark on serious critical and analytical thought about international problems.[3]

Idealism, then, simply did not look as if it had much to say about the major events in international relations in the 1930s. In its place, Carr proposed an approach that saw international relations as they were, rather than as they might be. This approach had to be able to explain the way in which events since 1930 had unfolded—a matter, said Carr, of analysis rather than normative commitment. He wrote:

The impact of thinking upon wishing which, in the development of a science, follows the breakdown of its first visionary projects, and marks the end of its specifically utopian period, is commonly called realism. Representing a reaction against the wish-dreams of the initial stage, realism is liable to assume a critical and somewhat cynical aspect . . . it places its emphasis on the acceptance of facts and on the analysis of their causes and consequences. It tends to depreciate the role of purpose and to maintain, explicitly or implicitly, that the function of thinking is to study a sequence of events which it is powerless to influence or to alter.[4]

The approach became known by the term coined by Carr in the quotation: Realism. He was clear that International Relations was a science, brought into existence by a perceived need to rid the international system of an evil—war—but dominated by a concern with eradicating the evil before it had been properly understood.

---

[3] Ibid. pp. 8–9.   [4] Ibid. p. 10.

What was needed was a dispassionate focus on the root of the problem, and this meant that the subject had to lose its normative character.

Realism, claimed Carr, is a well-established way of thinking about the world: witness, for instance, Machiavelli, 'the first important political realist'.[5] He argued that Realism is based on three foundation stones, all to be found in the writings of Machiavelli. They are, first, that history is a sequence of cause and effect, whose course is to be grasped not by imagination but by intellectual effort; secondly, that theory does not create practice but is created by practice; and thirdly, that politics is not a function of ethics, but rather, that ethics is a function of politics, and morality is the product of power.[6] Carr used these three foundation stones to construct an attack on the utopians, contending that their faith in a timeless moral code merely reflected the specific interests of one set of satisfied powers after the First World War. In this light, Idealism embodies only a particular notion of morality, reflecting not even the interests of particular nations, but more specifically the interests of a particular class within the states concerned. Carr commented that 'as soon as the attempt is made to apply these supposedly abstract principles to a concrete political situation, they are revealed as the transparent disguises of selfish vested interests.'[7]

Although Carr produced the most sustained attack on the assumptions of Idealism, it was Hans Morgenthau who did most to popularize the new approach of Realism. In his textbook, *Politics among Nations*, first published in 1948,[8] Morgenthau proposed that international relations be studied by means of a Realist scientific approach. He reduced this approach to six principles, which make a good summary of the essentials of political Realism. Although there are many other strands involved in Realism generally, Morgenthau's work has been so influential that it seems sensible to start with it.

Morgenthau begins with a sentence worth pausing to consider: 'This book purports to present a theory of international politics.'[9] For Morgenthau there are two ways in which politics can be approached. One stresses that a rational and moral order can be

---

[5] Ibid. p. 63.   [6] Ibid. pp. 63–4.   [7] Ibid. pp. 87–8.
[8] H. Morgenthau, *Politics among Nations: The Struggle for Power and Peace*, 5th edn. (New York: Knopf, 1973).   [9] Ibid. p. 3.

created from a universally valid set of moral principles. This view is premissed on the essential goodness of human nature, seeing all failures to live up to this goodness as attributable to defects in the way that international society is arranged. The second and opposing view treats political events as the result of forces inherent in human nature. To understand international relations it is necessary to work with these forces, not against them. Morgenthau argues, as did Carr in his critique of Idealism, that universal moral principles do not apply to the analysis and practice of international relations. The Realist approach, he remarks, gets its name from precisely this point: that it deals with human nature as it is and not as it ought to be, and with historical events as they have occurred, not as they should have occurred. Moreover, the approach was trying to create a science of international relations. This made it an essentially Positivistic way of analysing events, since it relied on a notion of underlying forces producing behaviour. Although somewhat hazy about the precise nature of these forces, Morgenthau was clear that the subject needed to be elevated to a science; otherwise its radical message for American policy would be undermined by the wishful thinking of those wanting to return to a pre-war policy of isolationism.

Here we must pause to acknowledge that Morgenthau does not always advocate a scientific approach as he did in *Politics among Nations*. Elsewhere he writes of the need to oppose those who see politics as a science, which would let Reason transcend the political. This has led some writers to place him within the interpretative tradition. Yet *Politics among Nations* is the book which made him a major figure in the discipline and its message is as we have described it. Its core is a claim that there are forces determining international relations, and his thesis falls apart if this claim is removed. Although he relies on assumptions about human nature, he seeks to treat its inherent tendencies scientifically. Meanwhile, the discipline itself, especially in the United States, has resolved to regard him as a leading advocate of scientific method and by subscribing to this interpretation we have at least avoided causing confusion. But readers may wish to be aware that there is more room for dispute than our sketch suggests.

Morgenthau's science of international politics reflected three factors historically specific to the USA just after the Second World War. First, there was the emergence of the USA as the major world power. American politicians were turning to the academic community to provide the intellectual justification for confronting Soviet power. This was no easy task, given America's recent history of non-involvement in international affairs. Secondly, there was the general reverence for science in the USA, especially in the academic community. Science had guided the USA in 'conquering' nature; so why could not scientific method help it control international society? The social sciences took up the challenge and, importantly for the development of International Relations, paraded economics as an exemplary application of scientific method to human affairs. Thirdly, it happened that virtually all of the Realists in the early years were immigrants from Europe. They shared a common concern to explain the events that had changed the lives of themselves and their families, and came from an intellectual tradition that stressed causes and the analysis of social events at the macro level. The time was ripe for an approach that promised to apply the methods of natural science to the international environment.

Morgenthau's Realist theory was, as we have said, based on six principles, outlined in an introductory chapter added only in the second edition of the book; this fact may explain why the six principles do not deal explicitly with two of the three concepts that are central to the remainder of the book, namely 'national interest' and the 'balance of power'. The six principles, though, do outline the basis of his theory. The first of these was that politics was governed by 'objective laws that have their roots in human nature . . . The operation of these laws being impervious to our preferences, men will challenge them only at the risk of failure.'[10] This implied that it was possible to construct a rational theory based on these objective laws. As Morgenthau put it: '[Realism] believes . . . in the possibility of distinguishing in politics between truth and opinion—between what is true objectively and rationally, supported by evidence and illuminated by reason, and what is only a subjective judgment, divorced from the facts as they are and informed by prejudice and wishful thinking.'[11] The laws governing politics, says Morgenthau, have not changed through the years, and they enable the Realist to ascertain the rational thing for a national leader to do in any circumstances. In short, objective laws

---

[10] Morgenthau, *Politics among Nations*, p. 4.   [11] Ibid.

of human nature, combined with an assumption that actors are rational, can give us a map for explaining international relations.

Secondly, Morgenthau says that what is needed to find our way ②
by this map is the concept of interest, defined in terms of the concept of power. The concept of international power demarcates international politics as an autonomous sphere of action, and implies that ethical considerations are of little use in understanding the actions of states:

We assume that statesmen think and act in terms of interest defined in terms of power . . . That assumption allows us to retrace and anticipate, as it were, the steps a statesman—past, present, or future—has taken or will take on the political scene. We look over his shoulder when he writes his dispatches; we listen in on his conversation with other statesmen; we read and anticipate his very thoughts. Thinking in terms of interest defined as power, we think as he does, and as disinterested observers we understand his thoughts and actions perhaps better than he, the actor on the political scene, does himself.[12]

The concept of power, then, enables us to understand the actions of all statesmen and women, regardless of their views and intentions. 'A realist theory of international politics, then, will guard against two popular fallacies: the concern with motives and the concern with ideological preferences.'[13] Motives are very difficult to uncover, and, even if we could know them, they would reveal little about the likely course of foreign policy. Ideological preferences are similarly of little use, since they may simply be the way in which politicians present their views in order to gain public acceptance. Yet Morgenthau grants that actual foreign policy behaviour will not always be as rational, in the sense of self-interested, as the second principle assumes. This does not worry him, since he takes political Realism to be a limiting case whose usefulness has less to do with describing the actual conduct of foreign policy than with providing a way of explaining it. 'Far from being invalidated by the fact that, for instance, a perfect balance of power policy will scarcely be found in reality, it assumes that reality, being deficient in this respect, must be understood and evaluated as an approximation to an ideal system of balance of power.'[14] He thus seems to doubt the realism of his own Realism— an apparent quirk which we shall return to in Chapter 4, when

---

[12] Ibid. p. 5.   [13] Ibid.   [14] Ibid. p. 8.

discussing the relation of realistic description to methods of understanding by means of ideal types.

 Thirdly, Morgenthau contends that the form and nature of power are not fixed but vary with the environment in which power is exercised. The key concept, then, is really interest, the perennial component of politics, and the one which is unaffected by time and place. Treating power as a fluid category allows Realists to envisage different forms of international relations, and even the ultimate transformation of the states-system. The objectivity of interest can serve as a universal starting point for understanding events. Here too there are suppressed assumptions about the proper methods of science which will concern us in the next chapter.

 Fourthly, Realism accepts that political acts have moral significance, but only in a sense which relates to the interests of the political agent and which has more to do with prudence than with traditional ethics. 'Realism maintains that universal moral principles cannot be applied to the actions of states in their abstract universal formulation.'[15] While an individual may have a duty to act in the defence of moral principles, the same cannot apply to the state, since the state's action has to be judged by a different criterion: that of national survival.

There can be no political morality without prudence; that is, without consideration of the political consequences of seemingly moral action. Realism, then, considers prudence—the weighing of the consequences of alternative political actions—to be the supreme virtue in politics. Ethics in the abstract judges action by its conformity with the moral law; political ethics judges action by its political consequences.[16]

Fifthly, Realism denies that there is a single shared morality applicable to all states, as Idealism had maintained. States formulate their policies in a moral language only when it suits them and only in whatever form best cloaks and serves their interests. Behaviour which is hard to explain, if one is looking for moral consistency, makes underlying sense, if one thinks in terms of power. Questions about the distribution and change of power can be answered objectively by reference to a model of power relationships, which also has implications for the rational choice of foreign policies.

 Sixthly, Morgenthau is adamant about the autonomy of the

<hr />

[15] Morgenthau, *Politics among Nations*, p. 10.   [16] Ibid.

political sphere. By defining interest in terms of power, Realism gives primacy to political considerations. Economists may think of the interests of nations in terms of wealth, and lawyers in terms of adherence to legal rules working to one's advantage. Such approaches have their uses. Indeed, even a moralistic approach, as in Idealism, may have something to contribute. But in Realism all must be subordinate to a political analysis. Just as an economist can grant that religious beliefs have a bearing on market behaviour but will not allow that they are a primary force, so Realism insists that power is the key. According to this view, Idealism had made the mistake of subordinating political considerations to moral considerations.

Overall, the crux of this six-point programme is the claim that Realism is a *scientific* way of thinking about international relations. The second chapter of *Politics among Nations* is devoted to explaining and justifying this claim. Realism aims to 'detect and understand the forces that determine political relations among nations, and to comprehend the ways in which these forces act upon each other and upon international political relations'.[17] It is worth distinguishing between Morgenthau's general view of the proper conduct of a *science* and his specific account of international relations, conceived scientifically. There has been much criticism of Morgenthau on the latter score, as we shall point out in a moment. But his general view of science is also open to challenge and, in our view, any student of international relations needs to think very deeply about the nature of science, as we shall make clear in later chapters.

Realism can fairly be called *the* dominant theory in the history of International Relations. It became known as 'the power-politics model', because of its stress on the power-political situation of a state as the central determinant of its interests. Its dominance was not confined to the academic world; indeed, it became the intellectual creed of US foreign policy in the late 1940s and 1950s. As Robert Rothstein has commented, Realism was popular with politicians because it 'encapsulated what they took for granted, especially after the failures of the 1930s and during the height of the cold war'.[18] Crucially, Realism provided a justification for the

[17] Ibid. p. 16.
[18] R. Rothstein, 'On the Costs of Realism', *Political Science Quarterly*, 1972, 87(3), p. 348.

kind of foreign policy which the leaders of the USA felt that they had to undertake in the period immediately after the Second World War. There was a need to keep the US public involved in great power politics, in marked contrast to what happened after the First World War. Realism offered a way of showing why the USA had to be so involved. To quote Rothstein again, Realism became 'the doctrine which provided the intellectual frame of reference for the foreign policy establishment for something like twenty years . . . it did determine the categories by which they assessed the external world and the state of mind with which they approached prevailing problems'.[19] The great advantage of Realism was that it could justify both accommodation and the building up of armaments in the name of a balance of power. As such it was, claims Stanley Hoffmann, 'nothing but a rationalization of cold war politics'.[20]

BEHAVIOURALISM

Realism has held sway in International Relations for the last forty years. This remark will seem preposterous to many who work in the subject, because Realism has been the target of severe criticism and most scholars now claim to be working with another approach altogether. Before justifying our claim, however, we wish to say something about the main criticisms levelled at Realism. To understand them it is necessary to recollect that the period immediately after the publication of Morgenthau's book was one in which a new behaviourist wave of thinking about the social sciences was sweeping the US academic community. When it surfaced in International Relations in the mid-1950s, its advocates called themselves 'Behaviouralists'.

Realism was anathema to Behaviouralists, because their view of how to create theory broke with the particular brand of Positivism that underlay Morgenthau's Realism. For Behaviouralists, the path to knowledge was via the collection of observable data; regularities within the data were to lead to the framing and testing of hypotheses, from which theories would be constructed. These theories were to be constructed inductively, without relying, as

---

[19] Rothstein, 'On the Costs of Realism'.
[20] S. Hoffmann, 'An American Social Science: International Relations', *Daedalus*, 1977, 106(3), p. 48.

Realism did, on a priori assumptions. Specifically, Realists relied on a priori assumptions about human nature, and human nature was beyond all possible observation. For Behaviouralists, the path to theory started with what was observable, and strict Behaviouralists held that there should be no non-observable elements in the theory at all. The guiding light in the search for theory was the methods of natural science (usually equated with physics), construed in strictly observational terms. The social sciences were conceived as a realm of enquiry to which the transfer of these methods was essentially unproblematic. Embarrassment at the lack of results was brushed off by pointing out that the social sciences were new, and therefore could not be expected to achieve the theoretical power of the natural sciences straight away.

Behaviouralism criticized not only the role of untestable assumptions in the Realist view of the world, but also the Realist desire to make normative statements about the international scene. Behaviouralists drew a sharp distinction between normative and scientific statements, and made it the hallmark of science to avoid the normative. It thus seemed as if there was a significant dispute between the Realist and Behaviouralist camps, and for much of the 1950s and 1960s this dispute was carried on in the pages of the professional journals. Indeed, those in the Behaviouralist camp saw themselves as working within an intellectual framework altogether different from that inhabited by the Realists.

The central criticisms levelled against Realism related to its definition of terms, especially the three terms that did most work—power, the balance of power, and the national interest. In essence, the problem was that none of these terms could be defined 'objectively'. The debate on the definition of power is a long-running one in the social sciences, and we shall not go into it in detail here. The point is that Morgenthau needed to be able to define the terms 'objectively'; otherwise there was no way in which the power-politics model could be applied. If power was so defined that the observer had a subjective latitude in applying the concept, then there could be no neutral standard whereby the observer could judge the actions of statesmen and women. Morgenthau could not rest content with defining power in a way consistent with the rest of his theory, because the theory needed anchoring by means of an objective definition of its key concepts. Similar arguments apply to the other terms and, at bottom, unless there is a way of uncovering the objective laws of human nature, Morgenthau's approach loses the essential scientific quality which he claims for it.

Morgenthau's approach was also criticized for ignoring the domestic environment of states, for failing to specify whether human nature was the determining or merely one potential cause of political action, and for being unable to account for mistakes (if human nature is based on objective laws, then how can individuals make mistakes?[21]). An early challenge to the Realist view came in 1957 from Morton Kaplan.[22] Kaplan offered an alternative conceptualization of the international system, one without Morgenthau's reliance on the unobservable but crucial notion of a fixed human nature. This might be called a constructive attack, since it implied that Morgenthau's notion of a determining system might be strengthened by dropping the contentious and unprovable notion of human nature. A more radical attack came with the work of Snyder, Bruck, and Sapin, who claimed that Morgenthau had adopted an overly rational account of human behaviour.[23] To understand the behaviour of states, they contended, it was necessary to re-create the views of those who took the decisions. Reconstructing the participants' definition of the situation would allow the analyst to explain their reasons for action, and this would be far more realistic than an assumption that the actors acted rationally. In fact this criticism, which was very powerful in undermining the claims of Realism, was open to a retort that it missed the point, since Morgenthau claimed only that rationality assumptions were being used as economists use them, to establish a limiting case or ideal type by which actual behaviour could be evaluated.

Criticisms such as these were so widely deemed effective that by the middle of the 1960s Realism was popularly held to have been superseded as the dominant approach in the discipline. Yet the attacks conflated a difference in methodology with a difference in theoretical assumptions. Thus Realism was strongly attacked by

[21] See, for example, S. Hoffmann (ed.), *Contemporary Theory in International Relations* (Englewood Cliffs, NJ: Prentice-Hall, 1960), and I. Claude, *Power and International Relations* (New York: Random House, 1962).

[22] M. Kaplan, *System and Process in International Politics* (New York: Wiley, 1957).

[23] R. Snyder, H. W. Bruck, and B. Sapin (eds.), *Foreign Policy Decision Making* (New York: Free Press, 1962).

the Behaviouralists, but almost exclusively on methodological grounds. For example, a famous debate, which started with an exchange in the pages of the scholarly journal *World Politics* in 1966,[24] was ostensibly an across-the-board one between Behaviouralists and Realists (or Traditionalists as they were there called). Yet, although both sets of protagonists had much to say about how a scientific theory should be constructed, neither said much about the substantive assumptions that underlay inquiry or the types of questions with which the study of international relations in particular should be concerned. This was not a debate between theories, but one within a single theoretical orientation and about how to conduct enquiry within that approach. The two main protagonists, Hedley Bull and Morton Kaplan, shared a more similar view of the international political system than their location on the two opposing sides of the debate would suggest.

This confusion has been examined by John Vasquez in a book entitled *The Power of Power Politics*,[25] in which he claims that the Behaviouralists never really challenged the theoretical assumptions of Realism. Vasquez argues that the work carried out by Behaviouralists was based on three central assumptions of Realism, which together put them in the same broad camp.

(a) Nation-states or their decision-makers are the most important actors for understanding international relations.
(b) There is a sharp distinction between domestic politics and international politics.
(c) International relations is the struggle for power and peace. Understanding how and why that struggle occurs and suggesting ways for regulating it is the purpose of the discipline. All research that is not at least indirectly related to this purpose is trivial.[26]

Vasquez looked at a large sample of Behaviouralist work in International Relations and found that the vast majority of it worked within these three key assumptions. As was argued in an earlier research report by Vasquez and others:

---

[24] For the basic arguments of the so-called 'Great Debate' see M. Kaplan, 'The New Great Debate: Traditionalism vs Science in International Relations', and H. Bull, 'International Theory: The Case for a Classical Approach', in K. Knorr and J. Rosenau (eds.), *Contending Approaches to International Politics* (Princeton: Princeton University Press, 1969), pp. 39–61 and 20–38 respectively.

[25] J. Vasquez, *The Power of Power Politics: A Critique* (New Brunswick, NJ: Rutgers University Press, 1983).   [26] Ibid. p. 18.

Reviewing the literature of the 1960s, we find a number of schools which appear to challenge the Morgenthau paradigm because they use different concepts. However . . . all . . . must be considered elaborations of the initial paradigm . . . In effect the international relations literature of the 1960s was a set of variations on the Morgenthau paradigm.[27]

For this reason, Vasquez called his argument the 'coloring it Morgenthau' thesis.

Even if Behaviouralism in truth attacked Realism for its method rather than its assumptions, the attack did nevertheless have serious consequences for the development of the subject, making its practitioners at least much more conscious of the importance of methodological issues; and this has been reflected in continuing debates about methodology since the mid-1950s. The focus on studying behaviour also led to much dispute over the appropriate level at which to try to explain that behaviour. It was one thing to accept the assumption that the state was the dominant actor, but quite another to agree to how best to explain that unit's behaviour. This was most famously pointed out in an article by David Singer, 'The Level-of-Analysis Problem in International Relations', published in 1961.[28] Singer introduced International Relations to a vexed topic, familiar to other social sciences, to do with relating explanation couched at the systemic level (the international system) to explanation couched at the unit level (nation states). This will be a central concern of Chapter 5. Meanwhile, the general point stands that Behaviouralists, for all their dramatic talk of a 'Behavioural Revolution', were really arguing only about method within a basic theoretical approach shared with Realism. That is why we feel justified in saying that Realism has held sway for the last forty years. Up to the start of the 1970s, there had really been only two approaches: Idealism and Realism.

TRANSNATIONALISM AND INTERDEPENDENCE

The 1970s, however, produced a third approach: Transnationalism, which claimed that the state was no longer the dominant actor it

[27] J. Handelman, J. Vasquez, M. O'Leary, and W. Coplin, 'Color it Morgenthau: A Data-Based Assessment of Quantitative International Relations Research', unpublished manuscript, Syracuse University, 1973, p. 31.

[28] J. D. Singer, 'The Level-of-Analysis Problem in International Relations', in K. Knorr and S. Verba (eds), *The International System: Theoretical Essays* (Princeton: Princeton University Press, 1961), pp. 77–92.

had once been. This challenge to the state-centric outlook shared by Idealism and Realism (and Behaviouralism) was not a novel one, but the world of the 1970s gave it a new strength.

Before the 1970s, the dominance of the state had undergone three distinct challenges. First, there had been the challenge posed by the calls for an international working-class opposition to the First World War. According to this view, the working classes had more to unite them than divide them, and the separateness of states was a piece of mystification which helped to perpetuate capitalism. This claim was thoroughly undermined by the events of 1914, however, as in state after state the working class rallied to its national flag and volunteered to fight the Great War. Internationalists had their explanations for that, of course, but these failed to carry conviction in the face of the facts.

The second challenge came in the 1950s, when it became fashionable to speak of the demise of the nation state as a result of the development of nuclear weapons. These, it was argued, had exploded the state's claim to be able to protect its population. According to the leading proponent of this view, John Herz, the nation state was being undermined by four factors: its susceptibility to economic warfare; the rise of international communications and the consequent permeability of national frontiers; the development of air warfare, which could take war directly to a nation's population; and nuclear weapons, which threatened the very survival of states and their populations.[29] The state was therefore, he argued, unlikely to remain the dominant unit of international society for the future.

Yet in an article published a decade later, Herz reassessed his claims and retracted his thesis that the state was on the way out.[30] The increasing number of states, and the rising legitimacy of states resulting from the increasing democratization of governments (as it appeared in 1968) were important reasons for this development, but the major reason was the new impossibility of actually using force in international relations. Nuclear weapons were so destructive that those states which possessed them had to be very careful about getting involved in any conflicts, whether with other nuclear

---

[29] J. Herz, *International Politics in the Atomic Age* (New York: Columbia University Press, 1959).

[30] J. Herz, 'The Territorial State Revisited—Reflections on the Future of the Nation-State', *Polity*, 1968, 1(1), pp. 11–34.

states or with their allies. Force, which had long been used to conquer territory and to gain markets and raw materials, could no longer be used for these purposes. With force becoming less attractive, the states-system was likely to stay in place, since the available means to overthrow it were too destructive to use.

The third challenge was posed by moves towards economic integration, especially in Europe from the early 1950s. There had been earlier moves towards international integration, but the 1950s saw a new impetus and with it a new school of thought emerging to claim that the sovereignty of the state was being eroded. This view was most closely associated with the work of Ernst Haas, who proposed a 'neo-functionalist' approach to understanding international integration.[31] Essentially, states could no longer ensure economic growth unless they integrated with other similar economies. Success in one area of integration would spill over into others, and eventually there would be a need to co-ordinate and collectively govern the hitherto separate economic organizations: so economic integration would lead to political integration. This view had clear implications for the state as actor, but the events of the 1960s showed that it had made a false assumption. Leaders turned out not to be willing to give up sovereignty over 'low-level' political issues; nor, when they did, were they thereby more inclined to integrate in 'high-level' politics.

The challenge of the 1970s, then, had its precedents; and it too failed to prove the necessary demise of the state as the dominant actor, at any rate in the immediate future. But it did offer a rather different view of international relations, based on the two related themes of transnationalism and interdependence. Transnationalism makes the point that there are actors other than states which play a central role in international events, the obvious examples being multinational corporations and revolutionary groups.[32] Interdependence makes the point that the increasing linkages among national economies have made them more than ever sensitive and vulnerable to events in other countries.[33] Together, these two

---

[31]   E. Haas, *The Uniting of Europe* (Stanford: Stanford University Press, 1958).

[32]   See R. Keohane and J. Nye (eds.), *Transnational Relations and World Politics* (Cambridge, Mass.: Harvard University Press, 1972).

[33]   See, for example, E. Morse, *Modernization and the Transformation of International Relations* (New York: Free Press, 1976) and R. Cooper, *The Economics of Interdependence* (New York: McGraw Hill, 1968).

points suggest that the state is losing its control over events. Furthermore, the state-as-actor view of international relations is called into question by the involvement of other actors in the conflicts of the 1970s. The international environment therefore cannot be explained by looking at states alone. Transnationalism and interdependence challenge the three assumptions of Realism noted by Vasquez. States are not the only actors; the distinction between domestic and international societies is less clear-cut than before; and international politics looks to be influenced increasingly less by military factors and more and more by economic issues. Some authors writing in this vein have spoken of a fundamental change in international politics resulting from the rise of these 'new forces in world politics'.[34]

Not surprisingly, a counter-attack has come from those who believe that the state is still the dominant actor in international relations. Northedge claims that the transnationalist approach is simply an 'American Illusion', the result of developments in the USA's international situation.[35] In the crucial areas of international relations the state still dominates and will continue to do so for the foreseeable future. Hedley Bull argues that the state has demonstrated a formidable capacity to withstand challenges from other types of actors, and that it will continue to be able to withstand them.[36] This is because the state is expanding as the unit of international society, and is being called on to take responsibility for the welfare of its citizens in a wider range of areas. Furthermore, the state can still rely on the loyalty of its population, and still possesses the monopoly of legitimate force in international society. Finally, the state sets the rules of the international system, and all other actors have to work within them.

There has thus been a significant debate about the extent to which the state still dominates in international relations. We shall not take sides here. But we do wish to point out how sharply the transnationalist challenge breaks with the other approaches that have dominated the subject. It introduces non-state actors and so

---

[34] The phrase comes from the title of S. Brown's book, *New Forces in World Politics* (Washington, DC: Brookings Institution, 1974).

[35] F. Northedge, 'Transnationalism: The American Illusion', *Millennium*, 1976, 5(1), pp. 21–7.

[36] H. Bull, *The Anarchical Society* (London: Macmillan, 1977), part iii.

belongs to a new pluralism in International Relations. Admittedly, the events of the 1980s have renewed a concern with the military aspects of inter-state relations and so re-emphasized the state. None the less, the state may have to pay a price to get its own way. Transnational actors and growing economic interdependence result in a world where states retain their legal sovereignty but at the price of a loss of autonomy. According to Mansbach and Vasquez, power politics have been replaced by 'issue' politics, where actors group and regroup at the intersections of political and economic issues.[37]

NEO-REALISM

The transnational view undeniably has a point, as do other recent views which we shall mention in a moment. But before taking stock of the current scene, we shall introduce one more variant of Realism. It is known as Neo-Realism. Although it is partly a response to the claims of transnationalism and hence of recent birth, Neo-Realism belongs firmly to the Realist tradition, as its name suggests. The key text is Kenneth Waltz's *Theory of International Politics*, published in 1979.[38] Although it is too early to say what impact it will have on the discipline, it has stimulated a powerful line of thought, and one which will concern us in later chapters.

The essence of Neo-Realism is a more theoretically refined systemic or structural account of international relations. As its name implies, it has affinities with Realism, while rejecting its simpler canons. There are two main areas of concern. The first is an attempt to rectify Realism's inability to deal with economic issues. Writers such as Robert Keohane, in his 1984 study *After Hegemony*, and Stephen Krasner, in his work on international regimes and in his 1978 book *Defending the National Interest*, argue that a modified version of Realism, or what Krasner calls 'structural Realism', can help in explaining international economic

[37] R. Mansbach and J. Vasquez, *In Search of Theory* (New York: Columbia University Press, 1981).

[38] K. Waltz, *Theory of International Politics* (Reading, MA: Addison-Wesley, 1979).

issues.[39] Morgenthau has long been criticized for ignoring or underplaying economic factors. Notions of 'hegemony' and 'regimes' are introduced as a corrective. Neo-Realists see states as able to control international economic transactions in a way that restores explanatory power to Realist assumptions about the role of the power-maximizing state. International economic regimes are embodiments of structural power in the international system, and their existence allows states to control one area of the international agenda that eluded Realism.

The critical mechanism employed by Neo-Realism is termed 'hegemonic stability' ('hegemony' meaning 'domination', from the Greek *hegemon*, a leader). If an economic power can sufficiently dominate the international economy, it can provide a hegemonic stability which enables other states to co-operate with it and with one another. This suggests an answer to a question which has troubled international political economists since the early 1970s: what happens when the hegemon needed for hegemonic stability begins to decline? The answer is that the stability will persist in the form of regimes which continue to promote the economic interests of the hegemon (specifically the USA), as, for example, in areas such as telecommunications and finance. Realism thus becomes able to address issues of international economics after all: hence 'Neo-Realism'.

The other main concern of Neo-Realism is the development of a more thoroughly and rigorously structural account of international relations. Kenneth Waltz in particular has proposed a new, uncompromising 'systems' account. Waltz contends that Morgenthau and all the other so-called systems theorists were not truly basing their accounts on systems but rather on the capabilities of the units comprising the system. To use the term common in the literature, they were 'reductionist' accounts. Waltz insists on explaining the behaviour of states solely at the level of the international system. There is to be no appeal to the intentions or capabilities of states, or to the human nature of their leaders. This

---

[39] R. Keohane, *After Hegemony: Cooperation and Discord in the World Political Economy* (Princeton: Princeton University Press, 1984); S. Krasner, *Defending the National Interest: Raw Materials Investments and US Foreign Policy* (Princeton: Princeton University Press, 1978); and S. Krasner (ed.), *International Regimes* (Ithaca, NY: Cornell University Press, 1983).

stark view of what really matters has touched off a spirited debate[40] and will occupy us in Chapter 5.

THE CURRENT SCENE

International Relations at the start of the 1990s is thus a subject in dispute. There is no dominant theory. Instead, there are several schools, each with its own set of special assumptions and theories—international political economy, foreign policy analysis, strategic studies, peace research, and integration studies, among others. But, despite this fragmentation, strong shared assumptions exist about the character of the discipline overall and we shall risk claiming that they yield only three distinctive approaches.

These three approaches are usually called Realism, Pluralism, and Structuralism, or, to put it more graphically, the billiard-ball, cobweb, and layer-cake models. This classification has become widely accepted in the discipline, and virtually all discussions of the subject deal with this trio.[41] Each has a different notion of the actors, of the processes, and of the outcomes involved. The Realist perspective remains broadly the one described in this chapter. It defines the actors as states and sees the main processes in international relations as constituting a search for security. States are monoliths with interests, and the main interest of each is the maximization of its power. A world in which these actors and processes are at work is marked by a constant struggle for dominance. The result is an international system where war is an ever-present possibility, held at bay by a mixture of international law, informal conventions, and the operation of the balance-of-power mechanism.

In the view of the Pluralists, the state remains an important actor, but must increasingly deal with a world where other, non-state, actors penetrate its territory and reduce its autonomy. These other actors, subnational, supranational, and transnational, have

---

[40] R. Keohane (ed.), *Neorealism and its Critics* (New York: Columbia University Press, 1986).

[41] See, for good discussions of these approaches, M. Banks, 'The Evolution of International Relations Theory', in M. Banks (ed.), *Conflict in World Society* (Brighton: Wheatsheaf, 1984), pp. 3–21 and M. Smith, R. Little, and M. Shackleton (eds.), *Perspectives on World Politics* (London: Croom Helm, 1981), especially their introduction, pp. 11–22.

specific areas of interest, where they can challenge the dominance of the state. The resulting processes are very different to those postulated by the Realists. The very notion of a foreign policy process changes, as the issues and actors involved challenge the distinction between domestic and international environments. The processes are characterized by a wide range of policy concerns with no obvious hierarchy of dominance. Foreign policy becomes less to do with ensuring the survival of the state, and more to do with managing an environment composed of newly politicized areas and a variety of actors. This results in an international system where there is no obvious hierarchy, no dominant issue, and a shifting set of relevant actors. It is commonly called 'the mixed actor system'. The focus is on managing the effects of interdependence by the construction of institutions, formal and informal. This international system has multiple centres of power and states are increasingly sensitive and vulnerable to the effects of interdependence.

The more recent Structuralist perspective looks at international relations from the perspective of the less-developed nations. Indeed, its main proponents have come from outside the Anglo-American academic communities, often from Latin America or Africa, and from the peace movement and development studies parts of the subject. According to the Structuralists, the state is still a dominant actor in international relations, but in a very specific sense, which is that of representing a set of economic interests. This recalls the Marxist theme that the state is the tool of the dominant economic class in society. But the role of the state is limited or conditional, since the dominant class will cease using it if it cannot manage their interests. Hence there are actors other than the state, and their precise role in international society depends on the interests of international capital. The real actors are classes, and the location of the state within the global network of capitalism is crucial. This is usually discussed in terms of centre–periphery relations, both within and between states. It is the structural nature of centre–periphery relations that explains the nature of international politics and economics. The processes characterizing international relations are those of exploitation, imperialism, and underdevelopment; the outcomes are essentially those of the continuing exploitation of the poor by the rich. The Pluralist concern with management is, for the Structuralist, simply another means of ensuring the continued dominance of the rich. The only way in which this could be changed is by a revolution in the system of global inequality. Yet, according to Structuralists who adopt a historical approach, notably those associated with the world-system approach of Immanuel Wallerstein,[42] the central feature of the international capitalist system has been its capacity to maintain patterns of economic domination.

At the start of the 1990s, then, International Relations offers a number of competing views on how to explain the central events of the international system. They are not simply comparable, since they describe rather different worlds. Each approach sees certain problems as the most important, because there are different types of actors and processes involved. Each differs in the outcomes which it selects as the most important ones to be studied. Just as the First World War set the stage for the development of International Relations as a separate discipline, so now the subject is studied in a way which reflects an implicit view of what are the most important events and trends. As we noted at the start, the policy concerns of the country in which academics work are an important factor in determining the kind of International Relations that they will study.

Attempts are made to compare and contrast the different perspectives, but there is no agreement on which is the most powerful theoretically. A recent survey of the international relations literature in the English-language academic journals conducted by Alker and Biersteker revealed that the vast majority of those articles were based on Realist (including Neo-Realist) assumptions.[43] About two-thirds of the articles were Realist, with only some 10 per cent falling into a 'structuralist' (or, as they called it, 'dialectical') category. The subject in the USA is, therefore, still implicitly dominated by one major theoretical perspective, and given the dominance of US scholars in the literature at large, Realism can be said to be *the* major current approach. But this shows only that International Relations has become an American

[42] See I. Wallerstein, *The Modern World System: Capitalist Agriculture and the Origins of the European World-Economy in the Sixteenth Century* (New York: Academic Press, 1974) and I. Wallerstein, *The Modern World System II* (New York: Academic Press, 1980).

[43] H. Alker and T. Biersteker, 'The Dialectics of World Order: Notes for a Future Archeologist of International Savoir Faire', *International Studies Quarterly*, 1984, 28(2), pp. 121–42.

dominated discipline, and readers should firmly make up their own minds about the best way to understand and explain the international scene.

CONCLUSION

This chapter has traced the main phases in the history of International Relations as a discipline and has thereby set an agenda for the rest of the book. The agenda might be termed 'classical' in the sense that it addresses problems raised by Idealism, Realism, and other approaches whose focus is on the state as the crucial unit in the international system. That may seem perverse, given what we have just said about the current scene, especially since we do not ourselves believe that states are the only important actors in international relations. But we have both a general reason for setting a classical agenda, and two particular ones.

The general reason is that the book aims to show why a philosophical question about Explaining and Understanding matters for theories of international relations. For this purpose we need a set of developed and well-articulated theories to work with. That means looking to the mainstream history of the discipline, rather than to current alternatives, which are at present partial and incipient. We do so without embarrassment, since the mainstream theories are still flourishing and occupy the bulk of the current International Relations literature.

The particular reasons are more contentious. The first is that we do not see how states could possibly be regarded as merely one kind of actor among several on the international scene. In specific issue-areas there may be other more important actors, such as transnational companies, some of whose budgets are larger than those of many states, or international financial institutions. But the theoretically distinctive feature of international society is its anarchical structure, as we remarked at the start. This feature relates solely to the characteristics of the states comprising the membership of international society and is essential to explaining and understanding the international arenas where non-state actors operate. However powerful or disruptive other actors become, the theoretical framework is still set by what states decide about guidelines or, in a systems perspective, what states are pressured into deciding by the demands of the system.

Secondly, the central problem which we want to discuss, being common to all social sciences, is not avoided by demoting states from their position as principal actors. The problem is that of Explaining and Understanding and it applies no less to transnational companies, world finance, and revolutionary groups. Whatever the unit, its activities can be explained from without or understood from within. Every unit has a decision-making process. Those making the decisions are influenced from outside and from inside. Influences are a matter both of level, with top–down theories at odds with bottom–up theories, and of approach, with scientific explanation at odds with interpretative understanding. If this is granted, then we need labour no further to justify a focus on the most studied and, anyway, unavoidable actor, the state.

The central problem emerges readily from this chapter. Idealism saw the international world largely from within. Its message was that wars occur through misunderstanding, ignorance, and foolishness, all preventable if leaders and citizens will only reflect on the likely unintended consequences of their actions. Even if not everyone means well, leaders of goodwill can organize their relations so that goodwill prevails. There are, no doubt, structural questions too, for instance about the workings of a balance or imbalance of power, but they arise from the combined effects of national decisions and can be controlled by organization and agreement. Idealism, then, was an account that focused on how to maximize the free flow of information and remove barriers to accurate perception. As Chapter 4 will make clear, Idealism as a theory relies on Understanding.

Realism rests squarely on a contrary view, both in substance and for purposes of method. Recall Morgenthau's six principles. Politics is governed by objective and timeless laws, with roots in universal facts about human nature. The moving force is power, in a variety of forms, all of which relate to 'interests'. There is no similarly universal morality, if that means moral principle, since the 'morality' of states is, and indeed can only be, an expression of their interests. Politics is an autonomous realm, to be studied by the methods of science. Behaviouralist critics, who found these principles inconsistent, responded by pressing what they took to be the claims of scientific method, thus moving still further into Explanation and away from Morgenthau's residual gestures to human nature as an interpretative posit. That is why we could treat them as more Realist than the Realists. The underlying structure of the international system, crucial for Neo-Realism, is offered as an *explanation* of behaviour so strong that it no longer matters how, or even whether, the actors understand the world about them.

Since this last point can also be made about some of the 'billiard-ball', 'cobweb', and 'layer-cake' approaches now current, for instance where the demands of 'capitalist accumulation' are taken to be impersonal and determining, it is fair to describe the mainstream story as one from outside. There is a dispute about which units matter, or even whether units matter at all except as dependent variables. But there is large-scale agreement that the aim is explanation by applying the methods of natural science. Idealism apart, this long chapter has made strikingly little mention of individual motives or decisions. In contrast to historians' accounts of international events, or indeed the actors' views of their own contribution as recorded in their autobiographies, International Relations theories have usually put most emphasis on impersonal units and forces. Yet the obvious question stands: do the men and women who formulate the policies, make the decisions, and try to implement them really matter so little?

The two kinds of reason for saying that they do not matter need to be kept distinct. Theorists who aspire to make International Relations a 'science' have no reason to exclude historical actors. But they admit individual agents only on the terms on which a natural scientist admits individual and particular objects. What quite this comes to is a topic that will be addressed later, but it is safe to say now that they are not terms suited to actors' autobiographies, nor terms easily accepted by historians. Although we have tried to express these scientific impulses fairly, we hereby give notice that we intend to question them in later chapters.

The other kind of reason is the substantive one. The demands of science, however conceived, can never be the ultimate reason for a system-centred or state-centred approach to international relations. The final reason for ignoring human actors can only be that they do not matter. Here a system-centred version of Realism is in conflict with one which retains Morgenthau's propositions about human nature. In so far as economics is offered as a model of explanation, a theory of individual behaviour is likely to be a component of International Relations theories as much as of theories of microeconomics. For the moment, however, we adjourn discussion until we reach the topic of Bureaucratic Politics in Chapter 7. Meanwhile, we give notice that we mean to bring the individual actors back from the wings later, because we believe that states and systems do not account for everything important in international relations. As noted in the introduction, we are not fully agreed about how much these actors matter, or why. But we make common cause in attaching more significance to them than do the theories (except perhaps for Idealism) discussed so far. We also believe that the issue is one that leads to a number of problems that are fundamental to the social sciences.

3

Explaining

The growth of International Relations as a discipline has been much influenced by ideas of science. Realism, as described in the last chapter, is essentially a call for the application of scientific method. Carr and Morgenthau rejected the prescriptive and utopian elements in Idealism for the sake of a science which sees the world as it is. A shared concept of scientific explanation is a unifying theme among Realists (and Neo-Realists) who are otherwise divided on, for instance, whether to pitch the explanation at the level of the system or its units. When Behaviouralists objected to the presence of unobservables in Realist theories, they did so in the name of science and the same basic idea of what science demands. (That is why we refused to treat them as a separate school.) Even current theories, which break with the mainstream over non-state actors, usually retain the claim to offer *scientific* explanations.

This potent theme needs exploring not only for its past influences but also because it affects what sort of theories are thought worth considering in current debates. At the same time we must stand back from it. The shared concept of scientific explanation was always contestable and has of late been radically contested. What 'science' demands is a very open question, and we need to be as clear about it as we can before broaching the claims of 'Understanding' in the next chapter. In this chapter we shall trace some leading ideas in the history and philosophy of science and shall identify those most influential in International Relations. Then we shall stand back and ask what notion of scientific explanation best suits the attempt to apply the methods of natural science to the world of international relations.

THE SCIENTIFIC REVOLUTION

By applying scientific method, Realists hoped to locate causes and laws of behaviour which Idealists were too starry-eyed or

woolly-minded to detect. Morgenthau's six principles are instructive from this point of view. Some of them are substantive: for
instance, that politics is an autonomous realm where universal
interests, rooted in human nature, take particular forms connected
with the distribution of power. But some depend on a specific view
of science, notably that there are objective and timeless laws at
work and that normative considerations are to be excluded. This
view is commonly known as Positivism and, in its heyday, was so
widely diffused among social scientists that to spell it out would
have seemed a mere statement of the obvious. But its heyday is
over, at least for philosophers of science, and we promise that its
merits will no longer be obvious by the end of the chapter. We shall
lead up to it by starting where the modern world began, with the
scientific revolution.

When people speak of 'science', they usually mean the sciences
of nature, especially physics, chemistry, and biology, in line of
descent from the scientific revolution of the sixteenth and
seventeenth centuries. The starting point is Sir Isaac Newton's
discovery of the laws of gravity and his formulation of the laws of
motion to explain the movement of bodies in response to forces.
This is a symbolic starting point. Newton was not the first or the
only great scientific thinker of the time. By the test of later
reflection his idea of explanation was confused and his findings
have been at least modified by the theory of relativity. But,
symbolically, he inaugurates three centuries of amazing progress
in explaining how nature works and in harnessing these discoveries.
We may have mixed feelings about scientific triumphs which have
included nuclear weapons as well as electric light but we cannot
deny the comprehensive debt we owe to the emergence of
scientific method.

At their broadest, leading ideas of the scientific revolution
divide into a substantive picture of how nature works and a set of
methodological rules for filling it in. The Newtonian picture was of
nature as a mechanical system of causes and effects, driven by
invisible forces and governed by ineluctable laws. This mechanical
system was not directly presented to our five senses. For instance,
there are no yellow daffodils in the underlying system of mass in
motion; daffodils appear yellow to us because of the effect of
suitable wavelengths (or corpuscules in a rival theory) of light on
human sense-organs. So there was a need for a method of getting

behind 'appearances' in order to detect the reality which caused them. In a typical seventeenth-century image, the world was likened to a watch whose face is presented to our five senses but whose real workings are governed by springs and wheels, hidden from sight behind the back. Science was a method for prising the back off the watch with the aid of mathematics. Through science we can detect the necessities—the unalterable forces—which cause the appearances.

This picture broke with the past by dispensing with the idea that everything in nature has a purpose or proper function, which explains why it behaves as it does. That was not obvious at first. Witness the image of the watch: it remained easy to think of the system as having a grand purpose built into it. To explain a watch we need to realize both how its springs and wheels (or, nowadays, microchips) work and that its purpose is to tell the time. But the larger and more complex the system, the further one can get by studying its workings. Provided that each state of the system results from the previous state in accordance with known causal laws, its behaviour can be explained and, in principle, predicted without worrying about what the system is for. Although notions of purpose ('teleology') still have a place in biology, they have dropped out of the physics and chemistry which have become our model sciences.

It is worth noting, however, that teleological explanations are still common in biology, most grandly in theories of the evolution of species. The idea that organisms or even whole species adapt in order to survive is a useful explanatory hypothesis to account for the acceptance or rejection of small genetic mutations. Analogously, the social sciences have often employed notions of equilibrium and of what is functional or dysfunctional for achieving and maintaining equilibrium. Thus, Morgenthau's use of the balance-of-power mechanism is related to the maintenance of the system; and recent Structuralist theories contend that patterns of international inter-action reflect the needs of capitalist exploitation. Similarly, ideas of self-interest or of 'real interests' often give explanations a teleological character. At the same time, however, all such explanations are contentious, as we shall see. Meanwhile, so as not to break the thread of our story, let us just remark that any 'purpose' involved is internal to the agent or system and not that of a hidden hand. Modern teleology too breaks with the past.

Newtonian science, as epitomized by physics, thus yielded a picture of nature as a mechanical, inanimate, purposeless system of forces acting on matter in a way governed by inevitable laws of cause and effect. Luckily perhaps for those who believe in human free will, however, this was not the complete and only picture on offer when the social sciences began to take shape at the end of the eighteenth century. If the five senses do not give us knowledge of reality (as opposed to appearances), what does? The seventeenth-century answer was 'Reason', meaning the kind of analysis which mathematics offers to the enquiring mind. This was not at all a foolish answer, if one supposes that geometry describes the properties of space and that occupancy of space is the basic property of matter. Truths of geometry can be proved, and so known not only to be true but also to be *necessarily* true. For instance, Pythagoras' proof that the sides of a right-angled triangle are related by the formula $a^2 + b^2 = c^2$ shows more than the mere fact that all right-angled triangles do have this property. It shows that they *must* have it and that an exception is not improbable but *impossible*. This is an example of a necessity in the fabric of space, typical of the necessities which govern motion. If, moreover, 'the senses reveal no necessities' (to quote an old tag), then our mental grasp of it is not given by the senses.

Here lies what was later deemed a confusion between two ideas of necessity. The premisses of a proof in logic or mathematics *entail* the conclusions: causes *compel* their effects. It is not plain that knowledge that x entails y is a suitable model for knowledge that bodies attract one another with a force in inverse proportion to the square of their distance apart. Meanwhile, however, there is a much more radical objection to the whole presumption that science is the search for necessities. It is that our knowledge surely starts from what our five senses tell us and can extend beyond this direct experience only to generalizations of what we know by experience. At any rate, this line of thought was explored in the eighteenth century, notably by David Hume in *A Treatise of Human Nature* (first published in 1739) and has come to be termed empiricism. Hume's *Treatise* set out to lay the foundations for 'a complete system of the sciences' relying ultimately only on 'experience and observation'—an ambition which empiricists all share. Science cannot know anything of the kind of necessities with which causes *compel* effects and does not need to suppose that there are any.

Hume's centrepiece was his analysis of causation, the relation between a cause and its effect. From the standpoint of 'experience and observation', what do we actually know about the forces which one billiard ball transmits to another, when compelling it to move after a collision? In essence, we know only that there is a regular and predictable series of events, whenever the same conditions hold. (To be precise, there are four Humean conditions to satisfy, if we are to be sure that *c* caused *e* on some occasion, namely: *c* preceded *e*; there was no intermediate event; events like *c* are always followed by events like *e* in those conditions; and we are in the habit of expecting the sequence.) Yet this is enough. Provided that we can identify the regularities in nature, then we need nothing more in order to predict and explain what happens. The idea that there are forces and necessities in nature is spurious, a piece of mysticism which we can do without.

This brilliantly simple thought continues to reverberate. (It will be found in Volume I of Hume's *Treatise* which should be read at first hand, as we are not trying to do it any justice here.) It sets up a continuing argument about the proper character of scientific method, which 'Realism' has not resolved. To see how deep the argument goes, think about this remark from *A Sketch for an Historical Picture of the Human Mind* (Tenth Stage) by the Marquis de Condorcet, written in 1794:

The sole foundation for belief in the natural sciences is this idea, that the general laws dictating the phenomena of the universe are necessary and constant. Why should this principle be any less true for the development of the intellectual and moral faculties of man than for the other operations of nature?

Notice first that Condorcet, writing in the spirit of the Enlightenment, proposes to apply the methods and assumptions of the natural sciences to the study of human beings. This will produce the same triumphant progress only if 'the intellectual and moral faculties of man' are not of a deeply peculiar sort which makes the social world radically unlike the natural. Notice secondly that the general laws governing nature are said to be 'necessary and constant'. This phrase is crucially ambivalent between the idea that they are constant because they are *necessary* and the idea they are necessary only in the tenuous sense that they are reliable because *constant*. The ambivalence would be easily dealt with, if

Hume were right in his analysis of causation. But, as we shall see next, attempts to translate an austerely simple empiricism into an austerely simple scientific method do not yield a satisfactory account of explanation. There is more to 'cause' than a constant and predictable correlation between events.

POSITIVE SCIENCE

'Realism' in International Relations inherited both the presumption that the methods of natural science are the key with which to unlock the social world and the ambivalence about 'necessary and constant'. The 'necessity' sought was not that of Newton's grand mechanical scheme of iron laws and inescapable forces but was strong enough to sustain the thought that the international *system* is more than the constant and regular behaviour of its parts. On the other hand, a neat, simple, and not implausible scientific method can be offered using no more than constancy, and 'Realism' coincided with a distinguished attempt at this. The attempt was inspired by the work of the Logical Positivists in the 1930s, notably Rudolph Carnap, Carl Hempel, and Ernest Nagel,[1] and prompted very many social scientists to believe that scientific method could be boldly distilled in diagrams like Figure 3.1.

This diagram is taken (slightly simplified) from R. E. Lipsey's *Introduction to Positive Economics*, which remains a standard textbook and whose title includes the key word 'Positive'.[2] Its rationale is very neat. To detect the regularities in nature, propose a generalization, deduce what it implies for the next case and observe whether this prediction succeeds. If it does, no consequent action is needed; if it does not, then either discard the generalization or amend it and try out the fresh implications. The process continues until a solid body of successful generalizations has been

[1] Rudolph Carnap, *Der Logische Aufbau der Welt* (*The Logical Structure of the World*), trans. R. A. George (California: University of California Press, 1967) and *Logical Foundations of Probability* (Chicago: University of Chicago Press, 1962); Carl Hempel, *Aspects of Scientific Explanation* (New York: Free Press, 1965); Ernest Nagel, *The Structure of Science* (New York: Harcourt Brace, 1961). For a useful guide to this and other topics of the present chapter see A. F. Chalmers, *What is this Thing called Science?*, 2nd edn. (Milton Keynes: Open University Press, 1983).

[2] R. E. Lipsey, *Introduction to Positive Economics*, many editions (first edn. London and New York: Harper and Row, 1963).

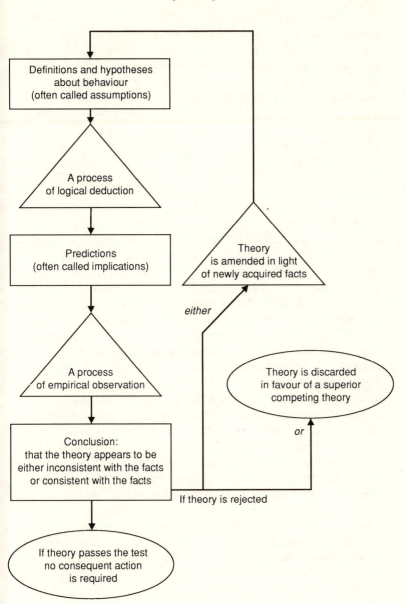

Fig 3.1

established to serve as a reliable source of explanations. The solid body constitutes a 'Positive' science, in contrast both to meta-physical speculations and to normative judgements. Lipsey lays this out in the Introduction to his *Introduction* and the rest of his book sets down the basis of a Positive economics.

Lipsey is not in fact relying *solely* on 'experience and observation'. The top left box of Figure 3.1 includes 'definitions' and mentions 'assumptions'. More is being covered by 'definitions' than the obvious point that hypotheses need to be clearly stated in words whose meaning has been defined. There is also a question of what words to use, what concepts to bring to bear. For instance, if the hypothesis were that nation states pursue their own self-interest, then one could ask not only what is to count as a nation state and as pursuit of self-interest but also why these particular concepts were the ones chosen. The answer might seem to be that experience tells us that nation states are a key fact of the current world and that they plainly do often behave in a self-interested way. But this misses the point. Sir Karl Popper, whose 'Conjectures and Refutations' is crucial for understanding the recent philosophy of science, points out that the mind can never be a passive register of experience.[3] He recalls once telling a group of students to clear their minds and observe what was going on in the room. As he expected, they found themselves quite unable to do as instructed. They could not 'observe' until they had been given an idea of what to look *at* and what to look *for*. It is simply not true that the mind is, as traditional empiricists used to suppose, a *tabula rasa* or blank tablet on which experience writes. Observation is an intelligent activity of bringing concepts to bear.

The point is potentially radical. But Popper limits its implications by distinguishing between the process of discovery and the logic of validation. The simplest form of empiricism is that there is a single method for both: observe, notice a pattern, generalize, test for new instances. This is a purely inductive method, tempting both for its simplicity and because it does without unobservables. Popper insists that neither facts nor hypotheses simply obtrude themselves. He adds, however, that to recognize the point is only

---

[3] K. Popper, 'Conjectures and Refutations', in his *Conjectures and Refutations* (London: Routledge and Kegan Paul, 1969). See also his *The Logic of Scientific Discovery* (London: Hutchinson, 1958) and *Objective Knowledge* (Oxford: Oxford University Press, 1972).

to recognize that testing is what matters. Let scientists get their ideas in the bath rather than in the laboratory, from imagination rather than statistics. All sources of conjecture are welcome, provided that science is then utterly strict about the logic of validation. Thus it is fine to think in terms of unobservable entities, provided that such theorizing results in statements capable of being tested.

On the logic of validation itself, Popper make the striking proposal that what counts is not confirmation but falsification. It is easy to suppose that it must be good news for a theory when experience confirms it. Not at all, says Popper in 'Conjectures and Refutations', citing the examples of Marx and Freud. A Marxist or Freudian theory is so constructed that experience is sure to confirm it. But this is no merit. Far from being models of scientific progress, such theories are not properly scientific at all. It is 'pseudo-science' to put forward a theory which runs no risk of refutation by experience. True scientists are always willing to state the conditions under which they would abandon their theories and to accept a refutation when the conditions turn out to hold.

Lipsey admires Popper and has embodied his message in the diagram. The 'assumptions' of the topmost box can include more than experience puts there, but whatever finds its way in has to be transformed by deduction into predictions which can be tested by observation. Yet, since confirmation is not what counts, the oval at the bottom, where theory passes the test, says austerely 'no consequent action' rather than 'rejoice!' Putting Lipsey and Popper together, we get a neat diagram of how to proceed, backed by a hugely influential rationale for it. The combination is sharp-edged. It removes a standard Behaviouralist reason for thinking that science should stick to observables and for presuming that observation can be pure. It issues a warning to systems theories so generously constructed that experience could never refute them.

But it leaves problems too. Figure 3.1 says that when prediction fails and the theory is 'apparently inconsistent with the facts', it is to be 'amended' or 'discarded'. But which? Suppose we are trying out a Rational Actor theory of the microeconomic sort applied to international relations and assuming that nation states pursue their self-interest. Contrary to prediction, we find Ruritania embarking on a hopeless war with a much stronger neighbour. Does this refute the assumption that nations pursue their self-interest?

There are many other options. For instance, if 'self-interest' means 'perceived self-interest' or 'self-interest as defined by a ruling elite', then a minor amendment will serve. If the exception is genuine but arises only because Ruritania is a small state whose affairs are heavily influenced by some powerful neighbour, then a larger amendment is called for. Meanwhile, Figure 3.1 says not 'Discard' but 'Discard in favour of a superior competing theory' and, since there are many shades and kinds of competition between rival theories, this leaves it unclear where amending stops and discarding begins. In other words, whereas Figure 3.1 presents the meeting of prediction with facts as a clear and decisive moment of truth, a little thought will show that there is always plenty of room for manœuvre.

This is not a point which arises because the diagram oversimplifies a complex process. It goes to the root of the Positivist idea that hypotheses can be tested one at a time by comparing their implications with objective, neutral facts of experience. The problem has been recognized in the International Relations literature, especially since the rise of Behaviouralism in the 1950s. Critics were quick to complain both that the available evidence supported conflicting theories equally well and, more radically, that the 'evidence' varied in interpretation between theories. Consider, for instance, the neutral-sounding question: 'Is there a link between levels of external and internal conflict?' Dozens of scholars have tackled it, without achieving much by way of agreement. That is partly, no doubt, because they use different sets of data and time-periods. But these differences reflect different ideas of what counts as relevant evidence; and much of the literature is a debate on evidence and the proper and improper uses of techniques for manipulating data.[4]

Graham Allison's study of the 1962 Cuban Missile Crisis provides an example in the realm of foreign policy decisions.[5] He shows how the same events can be given at least three explanations, each related to different facts, or to the same facts differently interpreted. The explanations are not flatly in conflict but neither

[4] For a discussion of this debate see M. Sullivan, *International Relations: Theories and Evidence* (Englewood Cliffs, NJ: Prentice-Hall, 1976), ch. 4; James Dougherty and Robert Pfaltzgraff, *Contending Theories of International Relations*, 2nd edn. (New York: Harper and Row, 1980), ch. 8.

[5] G. Allison, *Essence of Decision: Explaining the Cuban Missile Crisis* (Boston: Little, Brown, 1971).

are they compatible—a nuanced matter which suggests that facts and interpretations cannot be kept apart. At any rate, this has increasingly become the received wisdom in the philosophy of science, where the neutrality assumptions of Positive science have been under persistent attack. The major lines of objection have come from Quine's pragmatism and Kuhn's work on paradigms, and it is to these that we now turn.

PRAGMATISM

Quine's article 'Two Dogmas of Empiricism' remains the best short statement of three radically subversive reasons for despairing of a Positive science constructed in the manner of traditional empiricism.[6] The first is that the five senses do not and cannot give us 'unvarnished news'—information independent of the concepts used to classify it. A concept is not just a sticky label, so to speak, which we apply to objects as they present themselves to our senses. In applying a concept we pick out relevant and reliable features of what we perceive. We group features of one experience with those of other experiences (relevance) and presume that the grouping is significant for other cases too (reliability). There is no way of describing experience independently of its interpretation. There are no 'brute' facts—no facts prior to interpretation.

Secondly, therefore, the process of testing cannot be as described earlier. A test cannot be a moment of pure empirical truth where theory is judged against reality. Just as concepts are entwined with perception, so too theory is entwined with experiment. The question is never 'what do the facts show?' but 'which theory shall we prefer?' In that case, Lipsey's diagram includes a further moment of choice, in the box in Figure 3.1 where 'the theory appears to be either inconsistent with the facts or consistent with the facts'. Pragmatism would put the stress on 'appears'. Since theory is involved in deciding what the facts are, there is room for choice when deciding whether the theory at stake is consistent with them. To put it another way, a third option is always to save the theory by rejecting the facts! For instance, if the results of an experiment are too disconcerting, the scientist will

[6] W. v. O. Quine, 'Two Dogmas of Empiricism', in his *From a Logical Point of View* (New York: Harper and Row, 1961). For a basic guide to the spirit of Quine's pragmatism see Quine and J. S. Ullian, *The Web of Belief* (New York: Random House, 1978).

check to see whether the experiment was rightly conducted without breach of *ceteris paribus* ('other things being equal') conditions. Pragmatists maintain that such checks are not merely tricky but also always leave the same option of whether to accept their apparent results. Facts are always theory-dependent.

Thirdly, there is therefore never a single hypothesis at stake. Popper's case for the falsifiability of genuine hypotheses involved definite refutations by experience. Quine suggests very plausibly that, even if experience shows something to be wrong with a theory, it cannot point a finger at any particular hypothesis. The idea behind confirmation is that if hypothesis H implies prediction P, and if P succeeds, then H is confirmed. Popper objected that pseudo-scientific theories can be confirmed by this logic, and recommended the logic of refutation: if H implies P, and if P is falsified, then H is refuted. Now we find Quine saying that H is never a single hypothesis but a bundle of them. If H_1 and H_2 and H_3 . . . etc. imply P, and if P is refuted, then we must reject H_1 or H_2 or H_3 or . . . ; but there is no reason to think that the culprit is H_1 in particular.

We could continue in this vein, since pragmatism is a rich theory of knowledge and Quine an electrifying exponent of it. But that would take us deeper into philosophy than we have space to go. Here instead are two famous paragraphs from Quine's 'Two Dogmas of Empiricism', which sum up the spirit of this fashionable alternative to Positive science:

The totality of our so-called knowledge or beliefs, from the most casual matters of geography and history to the profoundest laws of atomic physics or even pure mathematics and logic, is a man-made fabric which impinges on experience only along the edges. Or to change the figure, total science is like a field of force whose boundary conditions are experience. A conflict with experience at the periphery occasions readjustments in the interior of the field. Truth values have to be redistributed over some of our statements. Re-evaluation of some statements entails re-evaluation of others, because of their logical inter-connections—the logical laws being in turn simply certain further statements of the system, certain further elements of the field. Having re-evaluated one statement we must re-evaluate some others, which may be statements logically connected with the first or may be the statements of logical connections themselves. But the total field is so underdetermined by its boundary conditions, experience, that there is much latitude of choice as to what statements to re-evaluate in the light of any single contrary experience. No particular experiences are linked with any particular statements in the interior of the field, except indirectly through considerations of equilibrium affecting the field as a whole.

If this view is right, it is misleading to speak of the empirical content of an individual statement—especially if it is a statement at all remote from the experiential periphery of the field. Furthermore it becomes folly to seek a boundary between synthetic statements, which hold contingently on experience, and analytic statements, which hold come what may. Any statement can be held true come what may, if we make drastic enough adjustments elsewhere in the system. Even a statement very close to the periphery can be held true in the face of recalcitrant experience by pleading hallucination or by amending certain statements of the kind called logical laws. Conversely, by the same token, no statement is immune to revision. Revision even of the logical law of the excluded middle has been proposed as a means of simplifying quantum mechanics; and what difference is there in principle between such a shift and the shift whereby Kepler superseded Ptolemy, or Einstein Newton, or Darwin Aristotle?[7]

PARADIGMS

Also crucial for the empiricist basis of Positive science is a distinction between 'analytic' and 'synthetic' statements. Analytic statements are those which relate concepts to concepts and are true (or false) solely in virtue of the meanings of their terms, for instance the statement that all bachelors are unmarried. Synthetic statements are those which make a claim about how the world is and are true (or false) accordingly, for instance that all bachelors are carefree. There is in fact no completely clear or uncontentious way to draw this distinction but the broad idea is enough for present purposes. The broad idea is that statements belong to languages and facts to the world. Sometimes we can judge the truth of a statement solely from its relation to other statements, as in mathematics. Such a statement is analytic, whereas the truth of synthetic statements can be judged only by reference to facts of the world.

By this test, a 'theory', as in Lipsey, is a mixture of hypotheses (synthetic general statements of regularities or laws of nature) and analytic statements, which define terms, introduce the logic and mathematics needed for deducing implications, and link the

[7] Quine, 'Two Dogmas', section 6.

hypotheses together. For International Relations, a good example
of theory so construed is James Rosenau's 'pre-theory'.[8] Because
facts do not speak for themselves, analysts need a 'pre-theory' or
conceptual apparatus to articulate their significance. Rosenau's
'pre-theory' consists of a set of definitions of the sources of foreign
policy, three measures of the type of state (size, economic development, and political system) and two analytical dimensions
(issue areas and permeability), which together define a matrix for
investigating foreign policy. The apparatus contributes no truth of
its own but, he claims, theory construction needs it because facts
become significant only through being lodged in a matrix defined
by analytic statements. The same line of thought has been
famously expounded for economics in Milton Friedman's essay on
'The Methodology of Positive Economics'.[9] The task of Positive
economics, Friedman says, 'is to provide a system of generalisations
that can be used to make correct predictions about the consequences
of any change in circumstances'. It is to be done by 'the
development of a "theory" or "hypothesis" that yields valid and
meaningful (i.e. not truistic) predictions about phenomena not yet
observed'. This theory is to be a blend of two elements, a
'language' and 'a body of substantive hypotheses'. In its former
role 'theory has no substantive content; it is a set of tautologies. Its
function is to act as a filing system . . .' In its latter role, 'theory is
to be judged by its predictive power for the class of phenomena
which it is intended to "explain" '. That is a memorably neat
summary of a Positive science approach.

The 'analytic/synthetic distinction' is crucial for Lipsey's diagram
(Figure 3.1), as for Positivism at large. It asserts that there is a
clear distinction between the two kinds of statement and that there
is no third kind.[10] That there are no hybrid statements which defy
classification is a crucial 'dogma'—one of the two radically

[8] J. Rosenau, 'Pre-Theories and Theories of Foreign Policy', in R. B. Farrell
(ed.), *Approaches to Comparative and International Politics* (Evanston, Ill.:
Northwestern University Press, 1966), pp. 27–92.

[9] M. Friedman, 'The Methodology of Positive Economics', in *Essays in Positive
Economics* (Chicago: University of Chicago Press, 1953). The quotations are from
the opening pages.

[10] The Logical Positivists were well aware that they set themselves problems by
making the analytic/synthetic distinction exclusive and exhaustive. In particular,
how should one classify 'bridging statements' which yielded criteria for applying
parts of a theory of the world? Nevertheless there *could* be no third kind, on pain of
undermining the whole approach. For discussion see the references to Carnap,
Hempel, and Nagel cited in footnote 1 above.

attacked in Quine's 'Two Dogmas of Empiricism'. That there is no third kind is crucial for the denial that Reason has the sort of task which Newton assigned it in detecting the underlying order of things. Disconcertingly, however, Thomas Kuhn's account of the development of science in *The Structure of Scientific Revolutions* makes a strong case for a third kind, even if not quite a kind which would suit Newton.[11]

Kuhn's study of the history of science led him to notice that there are sometimes abrupt conceptual revolutions in science and to ask why they occurred. To see the point of the question, generalize Lipsey's diagram and reflect that, since amendment and replacement are fluid alternatives, one would expect a process of gradual and continuous accumulation. Kuhn's answer is that the thinking of a scientific community takes place within a 'paradigm' which governs what scientists are to make of recalcitrant experience. Experience which conflicts with a so far accepted theory can be treated in two ways. It can be seen either as a counter-example, demanding that the theory be amended or discarded, or as an anomaly, in which case it is put in the pending tray or discarded. Which of these responses is made depends on how deeply the scientific community is committed to the theory.

Deep commitment takes the form of a 'paradigm', meaning both a set of very broad assumptions whose falsity is almost unthinkable and a set of institutional practices governing the current conduct of science. For instance, Newtonian assumptions that all events are causally determined by the operation of forces and causal laws acted as a paradigm in both senses. Apparent exceptions were put on one side to await later explanation within the Newtonian framework; and this was the proper attitude for anyone wanting public recognition as a good scientist. Thus routine science and routine scientific progress occur while, and only while, the governing paradigm copes successfully with apparent exceptions. But sometimes the pending tray becomes overloaded. So many and such large anomalies pile up that the paradigm suddenly collapses, as, for instance, when Einstein put the exceptions to the Newtonian paradigm together and proposed the theory of relativity. When this happens, there is a scientific revolution and the old paradigm is replaced with a new one.

---

[11] T. Kuhn, *The Structure of Scientific Revolutions*, 2nd edn., (Chicago: University of Chicago Press, 1970).

Kuhn stated the idea boldly, making paradigms very general and unitary and making their collapse very sudden and complete. Thus he considered the social sciences too messy to have a paradigm or even to be likely soon to acquire one. But the line of thought can readily be adapted to our previous reasons for questioning Lipsey's diagram. The diagram presumes that which theory it is rational to hold is (or can be) fully determined by the findings of experience. If, however, there are always general substantive assumptions being made, which are not at the mercy of experience, because they govern the interpretations of experience, then the diagram is not a complete model of scientific method. If theory is underdetermined by experience, which is itself permeated by theory, then the rational choice of theories is still mysterious.

This so exactly catches the current position in the social sciences that, with or without Kuhn's blessing, 'paradigm' has entered the language of social science. In International Relations specifically there is much talk of competing paradigms, meaning not just that there are conflicting unrefuted theories but that the conflict reflects starting points which can hardly even be compared. For instance, Realism and Idealism are not in direct competition, in so far as the former relies on a view of scientific method which the latter rejects. Each has systematic ways of dealing with apparently awkward cases and there is no hope of specifying neutral conditions for testing one against the other and thus deciding between them. Or, to take another example which will occupy us in later chapters, there is a similar snag to the dispute between Rational Actor and Bureaucratic Politics models of national decision-making. Each model can cope with all the evidence and the choice between them is thrown back on criteria like elegance, economy, fruitfulness, or perhaps, indeed, conformity with deep underlying presumptions about human nature.

The point is well illustrated by the current literature on international relations. In the last chapter we argued that there were three main current approaches, Realism, Pluralism, and Structuralism. Each of them has many adherents in the discipline, and at first sight it looks as if the approaches are in direct competition. Yet it is virtually impossible to think of a way in which they could be tested against one another. It is not simply that they have different views of the world, but that they each define what is the evidence in a different way. There is no body of evidence that we could use to compare their explanations. For example, those who adhere to Realism simply do not see the same world as those who adhere to Pluralism or Structuralism: they see different actors, different issues, and different pieces of evidence. Nor could we expect the adherents of each approach to treat *any* anomaly as a reason for rejecting it. Each of the three approaches operates as a kind of intellectual club: each has its own journals, meetings, and leaders. Each knows the weaknesses in its own and in the other approaches and therefore debates between them tend to result in predictable discussions within a well-trodden terrain. Inter-paradigm debate is very rare and indeed, if we follow Kuhn in casting doubt on the final scope of Popper's falsifiability criterion, impossible.

TRUTH, THEORY, AND EXPERIENCE

Quine and Kuhn give very solid reasons for agreeing that scientific theories contain more than experience can pronounce upon. This will not surprise anyone in the old tradition which opposes Reason to Experience and contends that the absolute knowledge which science seeks comes only when Reason certifies the findings of Experience. But this kind of rationalism largely yielded to empiricism with the rise of the Logical Positivists and it is therefore disconcerting to find that experience cannot do its job. The threat to truth as the goal of science is not just a threat to absolute certainty. If Quine and Kuhn are right, there is no longer a universal test of what is probable or what it is rational to believe on the basis of experience. Yet we must hold on to the basic idea that science discovers the truth of how the world works. In what follows we shall try to suggest a way of combining theory and experience, which draws on work by Imré Lakatos, Roy Bhaskar, and others but can be read as it stands.[12]

The tasks of a scientific theory are to *abstract*, to *generalize*, and to *connect*. Abstracting is a matter of grouping together events,

[12] I. Lakatos, 'Falsification and the Methodology of Scientific Research Programmes', in I. Lakatos and A. Musgrave (eds.), *Criticism and the Growth of Knowledge* (Cambridge: Cambridge University Press, 1970), the other articles in which are also very relevant. See also his *Proofs and Refutations* (Cambridge: Cambridge University Press, 1976) and *Collected Papers* (Cambridge: Cambridge University Press, 1980; and Roy Bhaskar, *A Realist Theory of Science* (Brighton: Harvester, 1978) and *Scientific Realism and Human Emancipation* (London: Verso, 1986).

situations, or objects which are not identical. For instance, all mice are different; yet all mice are mice. For some purposes it matters that mice are not cats, while for others what counts is that both are animals. The groupings vary with the concepts applied. It may (or may not) be useful to abstract from the behaviour of nations according to similarities of geography, size, weather, constitution, race, religion, economic organization, and so forth. Indeed, even 'nation' is an abstraction, grouping France and Fiji in distinction to General Motors or Hitachi, which sometimes behave more like France than Fiji does. To perform the abstraction one needs well defined concepts (for example, what exactly is meant by 'a democracy'?) and criteria for applying them (for example, is Indonesia one?).

Generalizing is a matter of saying what else things identified by the same concept have in common, not as a matter of logic but as a matter of fact. This distinction is clear-cut only at its extremes. Democracies have freely elected governments as a matter of definition and elect a minority of women as a matter of fact; but their possession of a rational–legal system is not so easily classified. Generalizations hold for the known cases which prompted them but are not scientifically interesting unless they also hold for others. For instance, Milton Friedman gives examples of economies where expansion of the money supply has been followed by inflation. Can this sequence also be found in other cases? That is the moment for 'empirical observation' in Lipsey's diagram (Figure 3.1). Even granting that theory is involved in applying concepts like 'money supply' and 'inflation', and that there is room for dispute about which is prior to which, there is no substitute for observation.

So far so good. The problems lie in the connections. John Stuart Mill remarks in *A System of Logic* (Book VI, Chapter 7): 'It is not the empirical generalisations that count but the causal laws which explain them.' He strikes us as right; but Lipsey's diagram bears no trace of this distinction between generalizations and causal laws. Perhaps one agrees that expansion of the money supply and inflation do often go together but refuses to accept it as significant unless told *why*. If the diagram were complete, it would have to include a call for further, perhaps broader, correlations, logically linked into a bundle but not different in kind. The diagram equates explanation with the success of prediction (and the failure of rival predictions). Are we just being unreasonable in asking *why* the predictions hold?

Well, what is being demanded? That brings us back to Condorcet's remark that the general laws dictating the phenomena of the universe are necessary and constant. The demand is for some kind of necessity, some sense in which an increase in the money supply *must* result in inflation. Current philosophy of science largely remains hostile to the idea that iron laws and irresistible forces are at work. The objections remain that we cannot know of them and do not need to postulate them. Yet the current view is also that explanation involves an appeal to causal laws and not solely to generalizations. A cause has a power to produce its effect. This way of putting it is meant to attribute causal properties to things (or to the structure of things), falling short of a grand determinist scheme but still thinking in terms of real productive powers. But, although making claims for Reason less ambitious than those of the seventeenth century, it still sets a problem of how causal powers can be known to exist.

The problem can perhaps be addressed from the standpoint of theory. Concepts, criteria, definitions, and their implications seem at first just verbal and so a matter of convention or even arbitrary. But this typically Logical Positivist view can be disputed. Take the rationality assumptions of microeconomics or of Morgenthau's Realism, for instance. Although they embody a real-world claim about how agents are motivated, they function more like a paradigm than a generalization. They regulate the interpretation of behaviour and hence make it at least very difficult for evidence to count against them. For example, Realism relies on the concept of national interest. Yet, if every state is following its national interest by maximizing power, how can Realists account for situations when states seem to behave in a way that undermines their power? Think of the Vietnam War or of the British policy of appeasement in the 1930s. The answer from Realists is that the leaders had either misperceived the situation or miscalculated what to do in it. Examples of power not being maximized can always be explained by redefining the actions as mistakes or miscalculations. In this way all actions can be made to fit within the framework.

Or consider the claim of the Bureaucratic Politics model that foreign policy is decided by the most powerful domestic bureaucracy (or coalition of bureaucracies) involved in the process. It is sometimes objected that this 'middle-range' theory is an over-bold generalization of the American scene. But its advocates can readily concede that the Russian or British equivalents of, say, the US State Department have less national influence without thereby conceding an inch on the general proposition about the power of bureaucracies. There are plenty of Russian or British bureaucracies to fill any gap and a fertile general theory of bureaucratic role-play to cement any cracks. *Of course* foreign policy decisions are made by persons who represent bureaucratic pressures on the outcome. This middle-range theory is wholly equipped to interpret any process of decision consistently with its assumptions.

In that case the necessities which account for what is constant in foreign policy are those of the conceptual logic of the explanatory theory. A theory is a model whose internal logic we understand together with a claim that reality conforms to the concepts and logic of the model. Mathematical models of, say, the behaviour of particles are a good example. The mathematics includes equations relating variables and allowing the values of some to be deduced, given the values of others. These internal connections are explanatory of the behaviour of particles in so far as the world conforms to the model.

This way of looking at causal laws is a delicate compromise. On the one hand, one is inclined to say that it gets the relation of theory to reality the wrong way round. Models are supposed to reproduce the causal features of the world and so the necessities must be those of the world, not those of the model's inner logic. If the USA and the USSR are locked into an arms race, this is a fact of *Realpolitik*, not of Game Theory. On the other hand, there is no alternative to understanding the world through interpretations and models and hence through what are, in the last analysis, intellectual fictions whose warrant is only that it is *as if* they were true. It is *as if* the USA and the USSR were caught in the logic of the Prisoner's Dilemma or the Chicken Game and the only sense in which this is not mere fiction is that it lets us predict successfully what will happen next.

These conflicting considerations are both to be taken seriously. One insists that science has at least something in common with map-making. The world is discovered, not invented, and, just as a map should record the presence of dragons only if there are dragons, so science should deal in forces and causal laws only if there are such things. The other insists that science has much in common with model-making, which differs from mapping in the modeller's licence to construct an artificial world and include in it all sorts of features beyond all possible observation. The test of whether there are unobservable electrons cannot be the test just given for the presence of dragons. Both points are presumably right but each sets a problem for the natural idea that explanation is the discovery of hidden order.

A compromise attempts to deal with both problems. The test of the 'fictions' in a model cannot merely be the success of prediction. For, as we have seen, interpretation is involved in the description of facts (including the results of tests) and hence the consistency of prediction with fact is partly a matter of how we choose to read it. Besides, theories can live with anomalies. So the success of prediction is neither necessary nor sufficient for explanation. Theory has more to it than experience can check and the further elements are not just fictions. The theoretical structure of the model represents the workings of the world modelled; or rather, this is the claim made when a model is offered as an explanatory device. But the empirical evidence for this claim is only that the facts can be read consistently with it.

This kind of compromise, we confess, raises as many questions as it answers. But it does at least help in seeing why debates among Realists, Pluralists, and Structuralists in International Relations are so hard to umpire. Theories of such general character all fail Popper's demand for clear conditions under which experience would be deemed to refute them. But this is bound to be so, granted Quine's case for the role of theory in interpreting experience. Each, in any event, offers explanations at a level deeper than prediction. The explanations, being of differing character, are not directly comparable. Consider their explanations of the US–Soviet arms race. Realists present it as the natural response to a bipolar international system. Pluralists make it the outcome of bureaucratic battles within each state. Structuralists trace it to the workings of a permanent arms economy, necessary both to capitalism and to state capitalism. Each explanation creates anomalies but, as noted, a theory can live with many anomalies before they need be deemed counter-examples. Meanwhile, each leads us to expect the arms race which experience confirms.

Why, then, is Realism dominant? Kuhn's paradigms are not only intellectual frameworks but also accompanying institutional practices. It is not hard to see how Realism has become so firmly established in research programmes supported by official funds and to construct a sociology of knowledge explanation of its dominance. But that is, finally, not where we want to leave the question of truth. In Lakatos's reply to Kuhn, all turns finally on a distinction between progressive and degenerating research programmes.[13] In that case, Realism is dominant because, despite anomalies, its selection of aspects of events and identification of trends is more enlightening and fertile than those of its rivals. If this is indeed so, then that is an intellectual answer to the question. But, we are bound to add, its intellectual superiority is by no means plain.

CONCLUSION

It would be immensely helpful to have a clear and simple account of explanation in the natural sciences as a guide to scientific method in the social sciences. When Realism first took the stage, there seemed to be one. A loose Positivism, in the broad spirit of Comte's Positive sociology and embracing all who thought of themselves as bringing the scientific revolution to the study of the social world, had been newly refined by the Logical Positivists. This powerful form of empiricism yielded a scientific method where the success or failure of predictions was the key to identifying causal laws, which were, at heart, simply correlations between variables. So Realists could suppose that hypotheses, derived from a theory got by generalizing from observation, could straightforwardly be tested against the observed facts of an independent world. The hypothesis that states pursue their national interest could be shown to be empirically superior to its rivals, thus grounding a Positive science of international relations.

Unfortunately, the facts of the independent world are more elusive. Even facts of observation need interpreting before they can be counted on, and any facts about underlying mechanisms or structures are 'visible' only through theoretical spectacles. The

[13] Lakatos, 'Falsification and the Methodology of Scientific Research Programmes'.

point serves as a corrective to behaviourist tendencies in general, and therefore to Behaviouralism in International Relations, since it undermines a main reason for holding that science must stick to observable behaviour. But it adds nuances to even the basic questions of objectivity and scientific method. So the Lipsey diagram (Figure 3.1) is as simple as we could plausibly manage, and it is not a definite guide. In particular, it fails to guide the choice between amending and discarding theories which are in trouble with the facts, and it fails to acknowledge that facts depend on theory to identify them. Meanwhile, it squarely embodies an assumption that causal laws are correlations, thus ruling out reference to structures and structural forces to explain the correlations. Realists in International Relations will not be content to abandon structural explanations.

We shall not offer a neat summary of the present position in the philosophy of science. There is no neat position to summarize. The note must be one of unfinished business. Theories must be allowed to contain more than experience can pronounce upon. This makes it always possible to rest competing theories on the same facts. Also, it is usually possible to dispute the facts themselves by challenging the theory involved in their identification. It is usually possible, too, to live with awkward facts as anomalies awaiting further explanation. All this does not mean that the natural sciences are in disarray. But it does mean that there is no definitive or agreed canon of scientific explanation on which theories of international relations can rely. If International Relations aspires to be a science, it must be open-minded about what that entails.

Finally, in transition to the next chapter, we close with an awkward point about truth. Nuclear fusion is in the news as we write. If this scientific breakthrough comes, nature will unmistakably have yielded up another of its secrets. Despite all the nuances we have introduced in the last few pages, there is no other way to put it. Whatever we may have said about theory permeating experience or paradigms governing science, truth will sometimes out, because nature is not a human creation. But can the same be said about the social world? From some points of view it is clearly a human creation. Perhaps nothing follows from that. But there are reasons to wonder, or even to suggest that the goal of International Relations should be understanding rather than explanation.

4

Understanding

When it rains, those who predicted otherwise are proved wrong and those who refuse to believe it is raining get as wet as anyone else. However subtle we are forced to make our idea of science, nature remains an independent realm awaiting discovery. It is indeed possible to say the same about the social world; but it is also possible to deny it. International affairs are at least less independent of what human beings believe about them than are the shifts in the weather. It may turn out that it is therefore a mistake to construe social science along the lines of natural science. But, whether it does or not, there are certainly differences between natural events and social actions which affect the kind of theories most promising for International Relations.

KINDS OF MEANING

Natural science is happy to take a spectator's view of the workings of nature, and any retreat, as in quantum theory in physics or for the philosophical reasons in the last chapter, is reluctant. But the most obvious fact about the social world is that what happens in it has meaning for the inhabitants. Here are four senses in which this is true and which do not apply to the atoms studied in physics or chemistry, even if biologists might want to use some concept of meaning when thinking about animals.

First, people find meaning in their experience. Here we should distinguish between signs and symbols. When we say that a ring round the moon means rain, we refer to a connection in nature. A ring round the moon is a natural sign of or evidence of rain to come, just as a paw print in the dust is a sign that an animal has passed by. When we say that a flag at half-mast means that someone has died, we refer to a social convention that death shall be marked in this way. Natural signs and social symbols might seem to form a continuum, marked by the presence of convention at the social end but always involving natural expression too. For instance, a flag at half-mast is a symbol of grief, whereas tears are a sign of grief. But the symbol is meaningless on occasions when no one in fact feels what it expresses. On the other hand, symbols can be manipulated, so as to convey false messages. When President Nixon put all US forces on a heightened state of alert during the Yom Kippur War of 1973, it 'meant' that he was worried and ready to intervene. Or did it? Perhaps he merely wanted the signal to be read in that way. Decision-makers in crises take trouble in analysing how their words and actions will be interpreted by others, sometimes so as to avoid misinterpretations, sometimes so as to create them. These possibilities exist because some of the meanings which human beings find in experience depend on symbols and can only be given symbolic expression. There is no parallel in the home life of the hydrogen atom or even in that of the rabbit.

Secondly, language being the usual vehicle of expression, linguistic meaning is a crucial component of social life. Luckily, theories of international relations need not grapple with the nature of language in any depth. But we should distinguish at least between the meaning of an utterance and what the utterer meant by it. Words have public meanings, governed by the rules for their use, whereas people who use words have intentions and motives in using them. To see the difference, think of the arcane debates about the 'real' meaning of the 1972 Anti-Ballistic Missile Treaty, given new life by the decision of the US administration in 1985 to shift to a 'broad' interpretation, allowing 'Star Wars' research to continue within the terms of the treaty. This led to complex debate between the USA and the Soviet Union about what the terms of the treaty really meant, and to acrimonious dispute between the US Congress and the President over the meaning of various key phrases. A treaty is an agreement to abide by whatever the words of the treaty mean. A dispute over what they do mean is, in principle, like a legal dispute over the meaning of a statute. What each side is up to in advancing its interpretation is a different kind of question. We shall say no more for the moment, but the difficult topic of meaning, intention, and motive will be central to Chapter 8. It is not a topic which concerns physicists.

Thirdly, there is a wider question about action and its context, which can be put as one about meaning. It starts with a distinction similar to the one in the last paragraph, between what an action meant and what the actor meant by it. Actions, like words, have a meaning governed by public rules—a deployment of missiles, for instance, may mean war. The actor need not have intended war to come about. But 'context' is a loose term, extending well beyond the moment of action. The Russian occupation of Berlin in 1945 did not 'mean' the start of the cold war at the time, although, with hindsight, it has come to mean this. One task of theory in International Relations is to find a meaning in actions and events, which may elude all the actors involved. It is not the same sort of task as that of the natural scientist in search of hidden causes, because the context of action cannot be divorced from the actors' understanding of the context.

That becomes clearer, if, fourthly, we notice that ideas have meaning for social actors. What people mean by their actions depends on what ideas inform their thinking. These include what they think valuable or worth striving for—'ideology', in brief. But they also have ideas about how the social world works and what makes its inhabitants tick. As we shall show later, what people mean by their actions depends on what *expectations* they have about the actions of others. Whether this matters for International Relations is disputed. Some theories, especially those pitched at the level of the international system, refuse to enquire what the human actors have in their heads. But other theories do enquire and thus have to take an interest in what actors think that other actors think. These are questions with no parallel in physics and very little in biology.

Since some of what is in people's heads is taken from social science, there is a complication worth mentioning at the start. Theories of international relations influence those who decide foreign policy. For example, many International Relations scholars are directly involved in the US foreign and defence policy community. They try to use their theories to improve policy-making and they search for theories which will be relevant and useful for this purpose. A very high proportion of work in the field has closing chapters on policy-making implications. Even if this degree of interpenetration is peculiar to the USA, policy-makers in other countries must allow for it in their dealings with US policy-makers. Hence the truth of International Relations theories has something to do with which theories are known and applied in the process which they purport to analyse. They are, so to speak, tied to their own tail—an intriguing thought if one grants that what happens in the social world depends on what people expect to happen.

Nothing follows at once from the presence of these various kinds of meaning in the facts of experience, language, action, and self-consciousness. But we can see already that disputes are looming. It may be that meaning is only a complication and that social science can allow for it by regarding human affairs as simply more complex than the other workings of nature. Alternatively, however, it may be that considerations of meaning take us beyond the scope of scientific method. In that case there are two broad options. One is to put meaning sternly aside and concentrate on behaviour, on the ground that science must stick to what can in principle be tested against experience and observation. This response leads to behaviourism, whose International Relations version is known as Behaviouralism. The other is to make meaning central and to construct a scientific method peculiar to the social world. This response leads to 'hermeneutics' or the interpretative tradition in social thought—*hermeneus* is the Greek for an interpreter—which we described briefly in the introductory chapter. We shall next explore some leading hermeneutic ideas, setting off from Max Weber.

A WEBERIAN APPROACH

'The science of society attempts the interpretative understanding of social action,' wrote Max Weber in the opening pages of *Economy and Society*.[1] Weber there distinguishes between *Erklären*, or the kind of causal *explanation* proper to natural science, and *Verstehen*, or the kind of *understanding* proper to social science. The social sciences study social action. In 'action' he includes 'all human action, when and in so far as the acting

---

[1] M. Weber, *Economy and Society* [1922] (New York: Bedminster Press, 1968). This famous essay has often been reprinted, a good version being G. Runciman (ed.), *Weber: Selections in Translation* (Cambridge: Cambridge University Press, 1978).

individual attaches subjective meaning to it'. The idea of 'subjective meaning' is a loose one, covering all ways in which someone may act deliberately or expressively and excluding only reflex actions. For example, compare winking with blinking. There is no obvious physical difference, but winking has 'subjective meaning' and blinking is merely reflex.

By 'social action' Weber refers to action 'which takes account of the behaviour of others and is thereby oriented in its course'. When it rains, people put up umbrellas. This is not social action. When riding bicycles, people watch for the signals of others and steer accordingly. This is social action. The distinction is not clean and complete, partly because the umbrella has some social significance and is not customary everywhere, partly because some behaviour, like avoiding other people when wanting to be alone, takes account of the behaviour of others without exactly being social. But the idea that social behaviour is oriented by and to the behaviour of others is one from which we can start.

To locate the idea in an interpretative or hermeneutic setting, we need to specify that there is meaning both in 'the behaviour of others' and in the 'account' which the acting individual takes of it. That leads directly to the central hermeneutic theme that *action must always be understood from within*. The theme has the two elements which we picked out earlier. One is that the investigator needs to know the rules, conventions, and context governing the action—the meaning of the action regarded as a move in a socially defined 'game'. The other is that the investigator needs to know what the agent intended by and in performing the action: why this agent played this move in the 'game'.

The rules of the social world are, from a hermeneutic point of view, importantly different from causal laws. In the first place, to group actions by reference to rules is unlike grouping objects by reference to their observable properties and to the causal laws which they obey. For instance, winking groups with other ways of warning or of doubting or of sharing complicity, depending on a context which is a matter not of physical description but of the form of social intercourse. Blinking groups with all unconscious rapid closing and opening of eyelids in humans and animals; it can be described physiologically and there are causal laws to account for its occurrence. Two people winking are not always doing the same thing. One might be doing what can also be done by whispering 'Do not believe what I said to George'; the other might have winked to say 'We are being watched'. Two people blinking are in the same physical state and that is all there is to it. To misuse or break the rules of winking is to produce misunderstanding, puzzlement, complaint, or some other social reaction. Every blink conforms to the causal laws of this physical movement. In short, although a wink is a movement of the eyelids, the movement is no help in understanding its meaning. The meaning is given by the relevant rules, of which there are several, each giving the wink a different significance.[2]

The last paragraph sums up a standard hermeneutic objection to behaviourism. A behaviourist is committed to finding differences in behaviour to accompany differences between winking and blinking and differences between one kind of wink and another. The task is either hopeless or depends on a very bold speculation about brain differences, if one focuses only on the wink itself. But since different kinds of wink cause other people to behave differently, there is no quick way to settle the dispute and we are not trying to say that behaviourism is plainly wrong. Equally, the contrast just made between rules as breakable conventions and laws as something 'necessary and constant' (to echo the previous chapter) would also be rejected by behaviourists. They would retort that, if rules are causally effective, it must be in the manner of other causal laws. Thus, for Behaviouralists, the task of explaining international relations is not made impossible by the existence of ideologies and religions, each with its own internal meanings. How deep the problem goes we shall see later in this chapter. For the moment we simply note that the hermeneutic objection to behaviourism (and hence to Behaviouralism) marks a basic crux for International Relations.

Part of understanding action from within, then, is understanding the rules which are operative. The neatest image is perhaps that of playing a game like chess. To know what is happening when a small bit of wood is shifted, one must grasp the rules of chess and so grasp what move has been made. It is possible to argue that there is, in principle, nothing more to understand, because the 'subjective meaning' of an action consists in conformity to the governing rules. For example, Peter Winch comes at least close to

---

[2] P. Winch, *The Idea of a Social Science* (London: Routledge and Kegan Paul, 1958).

maintaining not only that there can be no action outside some governing public rules but also that a full account of the rules obeyed also yields a full account of the action done.[3] But, as the image of chess suggests, one may want to ask why the agent played the move. Kasparov conforms to the rules when playing *P–K4*, but that is not why he picks *P–K4* from among his legal options. Nothing follows at once, because the formal rules of chess are not the only ones. There are also informal rules of good play (like 'castle early') and perhaps social rules governing the proper conduct of chess matches. So to ask why Kasparov played *P–K4* may be to look for further rules. All the same, however, it is at least tempting to think that 'why?' here demands a switch of attention from rules to the intentions and motives of the agent.

Weber makes the switch by applying a microeconomic model of rational action in order to understand action which is a calculated means to an end. Action occurs within a framework of shared meanings—rules and collective values—but is not dictated by that framework. In the style of economists, we are to reconstruct the agents' choices, given their preferences and information sets, assuming that they are rational agents. Unlike other sociologists, notably Emile Durkheim, whose basic emphasis is on social structure, Weber is firmly individualist in his insistence that individuals choose among alternatives according to their particular aims, interpretations, and calculations. Understanding proceeds by reconstruction at an individual level. This Weberian line has been much used in International Relations, especially in the sub-field known as Foreign Policy Analysis. Here the concern is to understand decisions from the standpoint of the decision-makers by reconstructing their reasons. The foreign policy behaviour of states depends on how individuals with power perceive and analyse situations. Collective action is a sum or combination of individual actions.

The last paragraph introduces a contrast within hermeneutics between understanding individual actions through social rules and collective meanings—what one might call 'top–down'—and understanding collective arrangements through their individual elements—'bottom–up'. This general contrast will engage us later. For the moment we shall focus on Weber's way of introducing the

---

[3] Winch, *The Idea of a Social Science.*

individual elements. One common source of distrust of hermeneutics in social science is that the idea of 'meaning' is so various
and elusive, as the first few pages of this chapter make all too
plain. Action can be said loosely to have all sorts of meanings.
When Weber remarked initially that he would consider 'all action
when and in so far as the acting individual attaches subjective
meaning to it', he invited the comment that there are all sorts of
subjective meanings. 'Meaning', in short, lacks that exciting
mixture of generality and precision which marks the explanatory
concepts of the 'hard' sciences like physics. *This* billiard ball
behaves precisely like *any* billiard ball in the same conditions, and
there are causal laws to explain why. Any attempt to nail down
individuals with the aid of rules and collective values seems
doomed to vague and complex generalities. Recourse to 'subjective
meanings' threatens to make each action unique, to say nothing of
the problems set by asking whether the actors need be conscious of
them. Meanwhile, if actors' perceptions and values are caused,
then we seem to be back with explanation again.

Weber's crucial suggestion is to take 'rationality' as the key
concept. Rational actors in the same situation make the same
choices, but only in so far as the situation is the same from within.
To make this precise, he takes a well-defined notion of instrumental
rationality (*Zweckrationalität*) from economics, as specified for an
ideal-type case where the agent is fully rational and the rational
choice fully calculable. In standard modern terms, the rational
agent has:

1. *fully ordered preferences* (for any pair of possible outcomes, the
agent prefers one to the other or ranks them equal; and the sum of these
pair-wise rankings is a *consistent* and *complete* ordering);

2. *perfect information* (the agent has true—or at least rational—
beliefs on all relevant matters; and, where an action may have several
possible consequences, can assign a subjective probability to each); and

3. *accurate information processing* (the agent makes all sound inferences,
inductive and deductive, from the information, as if equipped with an
efficient computer).

The rational agent can then calculate the *expected utility* of each
action by assigning a 'utility' (a quotient of happiness, so to speak)
to each consequence and discounting it for how likely or unlikely it
is to be the actual consequence. This may not always produce a
uniquely best action, because a higher probability of lesser utility

may equal a lower probability of greater utility. But, at least, the agent never makes an inferior choice, never choosing x when y has greater expected utility. The rational agent is a bargain-hunter.

This is a good moment to recall Morgenthau's Realism again. He proposed that decision-makers should be understood to act *as if* they were maximizing utility. Even if foreign policy was not so fully rational in practice, this was still the best starting assumption, with 'utility' being glossed as 'power'. Similar lines of thought, sometimes with nations as the rational maximizers, sometimes with individuals, have been common in International Relations. The international system is often conceived along the lines of a market system whose moving force is maximization. Yet it sounds an oddly unrealistic assumption, especially for a theory proudly named Realism!

The 'ideal-type' case is certainly very idealized. In practice agents do not, or even perhaps could not, have complete and consistent preferences, partly because what they want is often affected by what they believe, and they do not, or could not, have perfect information. In particular, probabilities often cannot be quantified (even if it is *likely* to rain there may be no percentage probability of rain) and so the image of the efficient internal computer is suspect. Here lies a hugely difficult and disputed area of doubt about the relation of the ideal-type model to the real world, and we shall need to air some of the disputes presently. But, for the moment, we should think of the ideally rational agent as a limiting case or abstraction from *homo sapiens* in social life. Economists sometimes liken the abstraction to the use of frictionless motion as an ideal model of a world where there is always some degree of friction.[4] It is important to know what the acceleration of a body down a surface would be without friction as a start to explaining its actual acceleration. In much the same way, Morgenthau wants to know what a fully rational decision-maker would do in order to start explaining foreign policy behaviour.

Irrationality is a departure from the ideal type through defective information, defective processing, or, up to a point, defective preferences. Thus, if one wants to get to London, it is irrational to take a train which one should have known not to be going to

---

[4] For example, M. Friedman, 'The Methodology of Positive Economics', in *Essays in Positive Economics* (Chicago: University of Chicago Press, 1953).

London or which one wrongly calculated to be quicker than the bus. That is straightforward (at least until questions about the marginal costs of information are raised). Defective preferences need more care. A desire to get to London can be irrational only in relation to other desires. If one wanted to meet someone in London who is in fact elsewhere and had to spend a morning travelling which one could pleasantly have spent in bed, then the desire to travel can be faulted. Immediate desires can be at odds with longer-term satisfactions. A set of desires can be inconsistent in the sense that they cannot all be satisfied. But there can be nothing irrational about preferences which are reflectively consistent, so that the agent who pursued all of them would have no regrets. In other words, instrumental rationality has nothing to say about either the source or the rationality of the agents' goals. It is all to do with the most effective means to ends, at least some of which must be given (and thus are perhaps open to structural explanations of how the agent came to have them).

Instrumental rationality is not the only kind recognized by Weber. There is also 'value-rational' (*wertrational*) action, where the goal is so dominant for the actor that it drives out all calculation or concern for consequences. Acts of self-sacrifice or heroism may be rational, and so understandable, in this sense. Pure cases are rare, not so much because humans are selfish as because action on principle or from duty often involves the weighing of consequences, especially in politics. But here too we are invited to start with a limiting or ideal-type case to serve as a reference point for mixed cases. Economists tend either to ignore *wertrational* action or to assimilate principles as 'ethical preferences' which, like others, are a source of utility. International Relations theorists too tend to treat states which seem not to be power-maximizers either as unimportant or as maximizing power in their own eyes and according to their own ideas. Scandinavian countries, for example, have been treated in these ways. But Weber gives *wertrational* action its own standing and importance and, when we come to think about expressive rationality later, we shall return to the topic.

To complicate things, Weber adds two further kinds of action: 'traditional' and 'affective'. Affective action is simple, unreflective action prompted by immediate desire, like drinking water when one is thirsty. This is commonplace enough but not theoretically interesting. Traditional action, however, may be very important. It is a typical form of action in 'traditional' societies which are governed by custom, in contrast to the rational–legal organization of modern ones. Weber's thoughts about rationality are directed to the modern world of industry and bureaucracy. So he is dismissive about traditional action, defining it as 'the expression of settled custom' and glossing it as 'simply a dull reaction to accustomed stimuli'. But the modern world is not neatly distinct from traditional society, even in its most Westernized corners, and it would be a mistake for International Relations to suppose otherwise. Think, for example, of the force of traditionalism represented by contemporary Islam. Also, even bureaucrats, those Weberian embodiments of modernity, do not behave in a purely rational–legal manner, we shall find. In short, we shall want to apply a notion of rationality to foreign policy decisions which is neither wholly calculative (*zweckrational*) nor mindless of consequences (*wertrational*) nor a mere mixture of the two.

These are the ingredients of Weber's notion of 'understanding'. The notion itself works like this. *Verstehen* has a first, primary sense of 'empathy' or 'direct understanding', which tells the inquirer what action is being performed. By 'empathy' one knows, for instance, that a man swinging an axe is cutting wood or that a man is aiming a rifle. Whereas natural science works with a basic or datum language of physical *behaviour*, which, if adopted for social science, would mean that action-descriptions were *inferred* from descriptions of behaviour, Weber offers the social sciences a datum language of *actions*. The 'subjective meaning' of what the woodsman or marksman is doing is built in to the basic description or interpretation of the facts. This fits neatly with his initial remark that the social sciences study social action and that action is connected with the subjective meaning which the acting individual attaches to it.

Secondly, there is 'explanatory understanding' (*erklärendes Verstehen*), by which we know that the woodsman is earning a living or the marksman engaged in a vendetta. The action of aiming a rifle can have many reasons and a vendetta is only one of many possibilities. Explanatory understanding is a matter of assigning the action to the right 'complex of meanings'. This can be done, Weber says, in three ways. One is 'historical', where we want to know what particular motive moved a particular actor on a particular occasion. For instance, the marksman is hunting his brother's murderer, not taking part in army manœuvres. Another is 'sociological', where we lodge the action in an institutional practice, like the vendetta, as 'intended by the average agent to some degree of approximation (as in sociological studies of large groups)'. In other words, we cite the rules governing the conduct of business in this arena of social life and show how the agent was acting in accordance with them. The third is 'ideal-typical', as when we invoke microeconomic theory in order to model the rational choice by the agent (in so far as the action was *zweckrational*).

Of these markedly different ways of understanding why someone does something, the 'ideal-typical' is the least clear. In economics, its use is a blend of two ideas, abstraction and pure problem-solving. As when working with a model of frictionless motion, it is useful to abstract from the real world with its impurities and interferences and to study an agent's alternatives in an idealized setting. As with model answers to mathematical problems, one can then see how close the agent came to finding the right alternative by the right route. That leaves obvious questions about why exactly this illuminates decisions by finite human agents in worlds full of 'friction', but we would rather leave them to Chapter 6, where Game Theory will be found illuminating for thinking about international relations in an ideal-typical way.

Meanwhile, to make it harder, Weber adds another kind of 'ideal type'. This is a more social one which works by analysing a concept, like 'feudal', 'patrimonial', 'bureaucratic', or 'charismatic', so as to be able to use it clearly as a theoretical term. For instance, his concept of bureaucracy defines a bureaucratic organization as one where rules and procedures are the source of actions and, since this is again a pure case, the only source of actions. The relations among the actors all relate to their positions in the bureaucratic organization and it is as if the bureaucracy were a self-contained world, except for the points of contact where commerce with the rest of the world enters and leaves. The ideal type codifies a scheme of reasons which would motivate someone who was wholly a bureaucrat, and understanding proceeds from what such purely rational–legal persons would think and do. But, witness this example, there is no single method for conceptualizing which would let one idealize bureaucrats and, say, charismatic leaders together. Let us just say that we are dealing with pure conceptual models of types of social action.

The two ideal types relate to reality in different ways. If economic agents do not arrive at the solutions indicated by the economic model (or if foreign policy decision-makers do not choose the strategies recommended by game theory), that is, one might say, so much the worse for the agents. But if bureaucrats turn out not to organize and act as in the model, then that is so much the worse for the model. The economics 'ideal type' idealizes a problem; the social or conceptual 'ideal type' idealizes an institution or practice. One sees the purpose of each and how each might help the inquirer understand what would be a rational course of action in the context. But they are none the less so different that many questions arise.

Perhaps the most urgent is that of how the elements in ideal-type models relate to actors' own beliefs about what they are up to. Are shoppers somehow at fault if they have no concept of liquidity preference? Conversely, is an ideal theory of bureaucracy somehow at fault, if bureaucrats do not think in its terms? Weber gives no general guidance. But he does introduce what he calls 'average types' of the kind needed for statistics. The 'average bureaucrat' might be average in two ways. One is, as in the last paragraph, by embodying the core of the theory. The other is by being representative of the majority of actual bureaucrats, rather as the average reader of a newspaper like, say, *The Times* is simply a profile assembled out of the actual features of actual readers. The point of introducing averages is to be able to show that the ideal type is relevant to the actual world. Do bureaucrats in fact behave as Weber's theory of bureaucracy says? To find out, we need empirical and statistical techniques for sampling what goes on in offices. Theory provides a possible account but does not guarantee its own scope and truth.

That might also seem to mark a difference between understanding and explaining, with the former for making possible sense and the latter for identifying actual causes. At any rate, Weber may have this in mind when he makes his famous distinction between 'adequacy on the level of meaning' and 'adequacy on the causal level', adding that both are required:

Without adequacy on the level of meaning, our generalisations remain mere statements of *statistical* probability, either not intelligible at all or only imperfectly intelligible . . . On the other hand, from the point of view of sociological knowledge, even the most certain adequacy on the level of meaning signifies an acceptable *causal* proposition only to the extent that evidence can be produced that there is a probability . . . that the action in question *really* takes the course held to be meaningfully adequate.

Certainly this captures a common view of how meaning relates to causation. Generalizations in social science are mere generalizations unless (a) they reflect internal connections in a system of rules for action and (b) there is hard evidence that actors are really moved by the causal elements identified.

For example, an account of group decision-making couched in a logical context of rational deliberation might seem pleasingly adequate at the level of meaning as a reconstruction of how groups decide. But it might then fail dismally to be causally adequate. For instance, Irving Janis has developed an account of foreign policy-making which he termed 'Groupthink'; according to this account, members of a decision-making group may fail to voice their reservations over proposed courses of action in order to remain on good terms with the rest of the group.[5] Critical thinking is replaced by a consensus that is illusory. If dissent is voiced, self-appointed mind-guards apply verbal and non-verbal pressure to isolate dissenters. The effect of this self-censorship of doubts and the application of sanctions to any dissenter results in policy fiascos. Janis argues that this applies to cases such as the Bay of Pigs invasion of 1961, the Vietnam War, and the Korean War. More recently, this phenomenon has been applied to the attempt to rescue the US hostages in Iran in April 1980.[6]

Philosophically, a further problem arises when we ask what notion of 'causation' to apply at the causal level. Weber himself seems to take a Humean or Positivist view of causation. Whether 'the action in question *really* takes the course held to be meaningfully adequate' depends on assigning a high probability, which in turn depends on appealing to a well-established generalization. But, as we saw in the last chapter, there may be reasons to reject this analysis of causation in favour of the one involving real connections or causal powers or both. In that case

[5] I. Janis, *Groupthink*, 2nd edn. (Boston: Houghton Mifflin, 1982).
[6] S. Smith, 'Groupthink and the Hostage Rescue Mission', *British Journal of Political Science*, 1985, 15(1), pp. 117–23.

we are still unclear how a 'meaning' account, in terms of actors' choices within a set of rules, relates to a claim to have identified what *'really'* moves them to particular actions. Is it merely that evidence of probability provides reassurance that the 'meaning' account is correct? Or does the causal level contain factors of another sort which do the *real* work? Is the meaning account merely preliminary to a real causal explanation? Or, conversely, do alleged causes finally need to make sense in a system of rules and rational choices? Although we shall postpone further discussion to later chapters, we want to put these questions firmly on the agenda. They are central both to the 'level-of-analysis' issue and to problems of how seriously to take the actors' own explanation of their actions.

Meanwhile, we must return to the point where we introduced rationality as a Weberian way of making precise the concept of meaning. That let us think of the understanding of action in individualist terms, typified by the rational choices of the individual microeconomic agent. This is indeed a possible approach and one very important in International Relations when, just as economists treat firms as rational individuals, International Relations theorists treat nations as rational individuals moved by national self-interest. But it is not the only approach. Had we emphasized not the choices made but the social rules followed by social actors, then a more collective account of social action would have emerged. Our passing reference to Peter Winch's *The Idea of a Social Science* can now be pursued.

PETER WINCH'S IDEA OF A SOCIAL SCIENCE

Winch, inspired by Wittgenstein, offers an analysis of social life in terms of the concept of a rule. He starts by remarking that scientists and (at that time; he was writing in the 1950s) philosophers usually take science as the understanding of an independent reality, with the presumptions that they know what it is for something to be 'real' and for someone to 'understand' it. The book boldly attacks both presumptions. First, to be real is to satisfy criteria for being real which belong to some social practice or institution. For instance, there are particles because physics has tests for the existence of particles and rules for referring to particles. Equally witches are real if and only if there are criteria for identifying witches. The parallel is disconcerting but deliberate. In some, but not all societies, it is therefore true to say that there are witches; the same goes for subatomic particles; there is no more ultimate sense in which things belong to reality. 'Our idea of what belongs to the realm of reality is given for us in the concepts which we use.'[7]

Secondly, to understand something about the world is to have mastered the use of the relevant concepts, which belong to some organized practice or institution, for example physics or religion. To learn about the world is to learn the rules of the institution, to come to know, in Wittgenstein's phrase, 'how to go on'. Think, for example, about Scottish dancing, which one comes to understand as one learns what the right steps are. Thus the Gay Gordons has some particular rules (like the rule telling the dancers when to form trios) within broader rules for the proper conduct of all Scottish reels. These rules, like those for, say, the conduct of prayer among Muslims, govern the meaning of behaviour and (as we said apropos of winking and blinking) so constitute actions. The same goes even for apparently outward-looking practices like experiments in physics. Muslims too claim to address themselves to an external reality and their claim is parallel to the physicists'. There are, of course, differences between science and religion but they are institutional differences in the kinds of rule which govern 'how to go on'. In the end there is nothing external to the broadest and most significant institutions. As Wittgenstein put it: 'What has to be accepted, the given, is—so one could say—*forms of life*.'[8]

'Social relations are expressions of ideas about reality,' Winch holds.[9] Social relations are the key to all ideas and hence to whatever reality a culture constructs. Even the criteria of logic 'are not a direct gift from God but arise out of and are intelligible only in the context of ways of living or modes of social life'.[10] Nor are subjective meanings or rational choices independent of public social rules for doing the right or rational thing. Hence to understand action we must begin by identifying the intention and motive involved in it. But intentions and motives are themselves a

---

[7] Winch, *The Idea of a Social Science*, p. 15.

[8] L. Wittgenstein, *Philosophical Investigations* (Oxford: Blackwell, 1953) section ii, p. 226.

[9] Winch, *The Idea of a Social Science*, p. 23.　　　　[10] Ibid. p. 100.

matter of rules of right and rational conduct in socially defined situations. Individuals' purposes do not determine their forms of life: their forms of life determine their purposes.

Winch's argument has notable relativistic implications for the study of international relations, where there are systematically different ideologies and world views. The international system not only has a major division between communist and capitalist states but also deeper cultural divisions between what are usually termed the First and Third worlds. Many commentators believe that the superpower divide has its source in ideology, thus making impossible any long-term co-operation or peace between the protagonists. This assumption has been behind much of the conservative reaction to the 'Gorbachev phenomenon'. The Soviet Union, so the story goes, is simply a different type of state, and we cannot expect it to live peacefully or comfortably with its main adversary. Indeed, the differences in ideology between the USA and the USSR are often said to result in the two sets of decision-makers seeing different worlds. Their ideologies create enclosed belief-systems that cannot be affected by evidence which contradicts them. Normative perceptions colour empirical perceptions. Their world views are so different that we cannot treat them as participants in the same world. They are, to use Wittgenstein's term, distinct 'forms of life'.

If this is true of differences between the two superpowers, then it is truer still of differences between the First and Third worlds. (The point is only strengthened by noting that the Third World itself spans several deeply discrepant ideologies.) For example, think of the depth of difference between Britain and Iran. The Rushdie affair, touched off by Muslim reactions to the publication of Salman Rushdie's *Satanic Verses* and reaching a crescendo in 1989 when Ayatollah Khomeini called for Rushdie's assassination, revealed irreconcilable views about the duties of government in the face of blasphemy. The publication of a book by a private citizen led to the breaking-off of diplomatic relations. A similar problem arose when the USA had to deal with Iran over the seizure of its Embassy staff in 1979–81. Notions of law and morality seemed to be so far apart that the two sides were talking different languages.

Such examples suggest a strong case for claiming that the existence of deeply different forms of life constitutes a formidable barrier to a theory of international relations. How can there be an underlying *Realpolitik* common to all states? How can Morgenthau's Realism explain the behaviour of states as different as the USA and Iran? What sense is there in seeing the international system as affecting all states in the same way, when these states practise such widely differing forms of life? Furthermore, differing moral codes give different guides for state action. How can we understand Iranian foreign policy without seeing it as reflecting Islamic notions of morality? On the surface these seem to be very serious objections to the whole enterprise of analysing international relations by means of a general theory.

These questions are so plainly hard to answer that it is worth pausing to consider why they have not had more effect on the development of International Relations theories. The broadest reason is the influence of systems theory, with its view that the foreign policy behaviour of states is determined above all by the location of the state in the international system. We shall consider systems theory in the next chapter. Meanwhile, there have been two basic responses to the kind of intellectual position implied by Winch.

The first is that forms of life themselves reflect material causes. Ideology is a result of a set of material factors, and so has no independent explanatory role. Ideology is an effect, not a cause. The second is that the pressures emanating from the international system override the specifics of forms of life or ideology. This is clear in Morgenthau's work, where he argues that the requirements of national interest drive out ideological considerations in the formulation of foreign policy. One great advantage which he claimed for Realism was that it allowed the analyst to dispense with the motives and intentions of the decision-makers. Morality could not take precedence in the determination of foreign policy because of structural differences between the setting for individual behaviour and the setting for international behaviour. International politics, he claimed, was the domain not of morality but of power politics.

For these reasons the moral dimension of world politics has not been deemed to constitute an overriding objection to the development of International Relations theory. Even states with very different forms of life and different moral world views do in fact behave in similar ways. During the Rushdie affair, the Iranian

Foreign Ministry was busy trying to prevent the breaking-off of diplomatic relations with Britain, and seemed willing to take a conciliatory role. Similarly, the Iran–Contra deal indicates not only the differences between US statements and actions over terrorism, but more revealingly the Iranian government's willingness to engage in *Realpolitik*. More generally, while there is no denying that leaders couch their statements in moral language, which seems to emphasize differences and minimize similarities, their actions often bear little resemblance to these moral pronouncements. Although President Nixon may have come to the White House committed to ending the war in Vietnam, it just so happened that his way of ending it was to escalate it.

The thesis that moral codes *function* similarly, despite differences in content, has been analysed within International Relations in the literature on belief-systems.[11] The analysis has been helped by assuming that its task is to *explain* how belief-systems operate, whereas Winch invites us to *understand* why they matter. From the point of view of *explanation*, moral and ideological features of social life can be treated as legitimizing devices which may facilitate but do not account for what is really going on. Here lies a central dispute throughout the social sciences, and it is one to which we will often revert.

To return to Winch's account of social life, readers may well have two other sorts of query. One is about the assimilation of natural science to religion (or, for that matter, to Scottish dancing). The other is about the absorption of individual action by the system of rules governing it. Both raise key issues for the social sciences, and, although Winch's text is the occasion of our raising them, we are not claiming to exhaust his subtle text, which well repays reading in full.

In likening natural science to religion, Winch is presenting both as ways of ordering experience by means of rules which tell us how to go on. They remain different ways, because the institutions of natural science involve the practice of giving causal explanations with the aid of models and statistics, whereas those of religion involve nothing of the sort. But both are self-warranting, in the sense that each declares what is real and rationally believed through its own internal practices. There is no neutral, objective,

[11] See R. Little and S. Smith (eds.), *Belief Systems and International Relations* (Oxford: Blackwell, 1988), especially chs. 1–3, for an overview of this approach.

external criterion for reality or rationality. Crucially, therefore, causal explanation is the proper procedure when we engage in natural science but not elsewhere. It is not the proper procedure for anyone trying to make sense of other areas of social life. The central theme of hermeneutics, that action is to be understood from within, suggests that causal explanation is of interest only where people (like physicists) use causal explanation and that this is a fact about them, not about nature.

The point brings to life the contrast between explaining and understanding. But it does so in a relativistic way which needs to be examined with care. It is one thing to say that the understanding of how people order their experience is in contrast to the explanation of how the world works. It is quite another to argue that there are as many worlds as there are ways of ordering experience. Hermeneutics is committed to the first and hence to giving some account of how internal orderings relate to reality. But the second is only one such account, and a more relativistic one than hermeneutics may care to adopt. At this stage we want only to make an initial contrast between explaining and understanding. To understand is to reproduce the order in the minds of actors; to explain is to find causes in the scientific manner.

The second query is prompted by Winch's idea that the order in the minds of the actors is to be traced by identifying the rules which guide their thoughts and actions. As a suggestion for a hermeneutic notion of social structure, it seems to us to have great merit. For instance, it would let International Relations theories refer to 'the international system' if and only if there is enough of a set of rules (explicit, tacit, or even perhaps latent) which international actors share and follow. This is in contrast to theories like Morgenthau's and Waltz's, which deliberately employ natural science notions of a system. It is in accord with Morton Kaplan's *System and Process in International Politics*, where different rules are formulated for various international systems.[12] Waltz's criticism of Kaplan to the effect that *rules* do not make a *system* invites a hermeneutic retort that nothing else possibly could in the social world.

But, if the idea is that, in understanding the rules governing action, we understand everything about the actors, then one may

[12] M. Kaplan, *Systems and Process in International Politics* (New York: Wiley, 1957).

wish to demur. Weber speaks for an individualism which starts out
from the 'subjective meanings' which individuals attach to their
actions and, when he moves to ideal types of rational action, his
focus remains on individual choices. An ambitious theory of
rational choice, coupled with Game Theory, can attempt to
account for rules, practices, and institutions, as we shall see in
Chapter 6. Meanwhile, hermeneutics is not committed in advance
either to understanding rules in terms of actions or to understanding
actions in terms of rules. Equally, there is a good case for holding
that understanding should proceed in both directions, although,
like all such compromises, that sets problems with the tension
involved in combining them. In other words, the 'level-of-analysis'
problem set in the last chapter also arises for Understanding. It
belongs to a large question about holism and individualism which
plagues every approach.

CONCLUSION

By combining this chapter with the last we can see why
International Relations is so unsettled and so ready to try very
varied approaches. The reason is not just that international affairs
are hard to reduce to intellectual order, perhaps because they are
changing character even as one tries. It is also because there are
radically competing ideas of intellectual order. Thus Realism was
able to make a quick conquest by importing a neat and powerful
idea of science and showing how an economics-style analysis of
nation states as pursuers of national interest scored high as
science. But it has since proved vulnerable both to changing ideas
of natural science, which have undercut Positivism, and to
hermeneutic ideas about how the social world should be understood.
In terms of Weber's call for adequacy both at the level of meaning
and at the causal level, there is argument at both levels, which, of
course, much complicates questions of how to relate them to each
other.

At the causal level, the main argument concerns theory and
experience. The starting point is the contention that experience is
not neutral, uninterpreted fact and cannot serve as an independent
umpire of what theories it is rational to accept. Hence there is
room for competing middle-range theories, and not merely

because not enough empirical testing has been done. That is good news for those which claim to identify hidden structures and forces, although this itself does nothing to tell us how to justify such a claim. Also, pragmatists draw the very different moral that the test of a theory is whether it organizes our beliefs into an elegant and suggestive web of belief. That moral is no help to claims on behalf of hidden forces and external structures.

The clearest way to focus the questions raised so far is by posing the level-of-analysis problem with more care. As Singer put it originally, it was a problem of deciding whether to explain the units of the international system in terms of the system or vice versa. This makes it a problem about explanation (not about understanding) posed with the tradition of natural science in mind. Its most striking answer in International Relations has been systems theory, which we shall examine in the next chapter. The most ambitious suggestion will be that the units behave in a way *functional* for the system, as demonstrated by showing why the system could not otherwise maintain its impetus. This is even stronger than saying that the dynamics of the system *determine* the behaviour of the units, as causes determine their effects, because 'functional' presumably implies something about the purpose of the states' behaviour in achieving equilibrium, thus going beyond mere causal determination. But even a softer claim that there is causality, with the system as the primary cause, will be hotly disputed by anyone opposed to holistic theories.

This classic dispute does not exhaust the level-of-analysis problem, which recurs as one about whether the foreign policy behaviour of states has international or domestic determinants. The latter answer is given, for instance, by those favouring a Bureaucratic Politics model, where policy emerges from the interplay of domestic bureaucracies, as we shall see in Chapter 7. Here the state is, so to speak, the system, the bureaucracies the units, and the question still one about explanation. Nor does this dispute exhaust the problem. One can also ask whether bureaucracies determine the behaviour of the men and women who take part in the process of decision or whether these human individuals determine, among other things, the behaviour of the bureaucracies to which they belong. In other words, the dispute between system and unit is a formal dispute which can be filled out according to what is claimed to be the relevant system and what the relevant unit. An individualist rational choice or Game Theory line can take states as units or take flesh-and-blood individuals as units; witness the way in which microeconomics often treats firms as individual units needing no further analysis.

The present chapter has given the level-of-analysis problem a new dimension. The chapter on Explaining made trouble for Positivist ideas of explanation but did not suggest that they might be beside the point. The present chapter has suggested precisely that. If Understanding proceeds by rational reconstruction of rules and reasons for action from within, then it seems radically different from the enterprises of natural science. How radical is radical? That depends crucially on how seriously we are to take the actors' own accounts of what they do. Every hermeneutic approach takes them as the alpha of understanding but not all make them also the omega. In the first place, actors never see all of the game and, even in the corner which they do see, they are not always transparent even to themselves. Secondly, actors inherit collective ways of seeing the world, languages for describing it, and institutions for organizing it. Their autobiographies owe more to this intimate social context than they recognize. Thirdly, particular actors are rarely, if ever, indispensable to the processes in which they take part. The more interchangeable they are, the more it matters to understand the process independently of the actors. As Marx remarked, even when we make our own history, we do not make it in conditions of our own choosing and much of it is made behind our backs. Although strenuous versions of individualism have answers to all three points, one sees their force.

Hence the level-of-analysis problem also troubles a hermeneutic approach. There are similar disputes, first, between a Grand Theory of history (system) and the claim that states (units) make whatever international society there is; secondly, between analyses that make the national state internally sovereign in its policy and decisions (system) and those which fragment it into its bureaucracies (units); thirdly, between bureaucracy (system) and the human individuals who play the internal roles (units). The chapter has introduced these disputes without trying to settle them.

Nor have we tried to decide whether rules and reasons can *only* be considered in a hermeneutic framework incompatible with causal explanation. Although Winch contends that there cannot be causes for the rules followed or for the intentions and motives of the actors who follow them, other philosophers disagree. There are plenty who hold that beliefs and (especially) desires can be causes of action.[13] This argument will be taken up later. For the moment, we mention it to point out that the relationship between Explaining and Understanding is not yet clear. Since there is an interesting case for each, it certainly seems that there may be a compelling case for combining them. That is what Weber bids us do, when declaring that the final account must be adequate both at the level of meaning and at the causal level. This would be easy in principle if the world-from-within were somehow lodged in an external world, which held the causal key to it. Then Understanding would be the alpha and Explanation the omega. But the hermeneutic tradition prevents such final accounts at least from being easy and perhaps from being possible. So we shall draw no conclusions yet. Instead, we shall next deploy a grand systems theory, conceived in the scientific manner and presenting the units of the system as if they were 'black boxes' whose inner workings need not be examined. When it turns out that we do need to 'open the box', we shall be readier to ask whether the workings are to be explained, understood, or both.

---

[13] J. S. Mill, *A System of Logic* [1843] (London: Duckworth, 1988). Book vi, especially chs. 1, 2, remains classic. A strong recent case is made by Bernard Williams, 'Internal and External Reasons', in *Moral Luck* (Cambridge: Cambridge University Press, 1981). Central to recent discussion, but not ultimately coming down clearly on one side, are Donald Davidson's essays on the subject, especially chs. 11–14 in *Essays on Actions and Events* (Oxford: Oxford University Press, 1984). L. Doyal and R. Harris, *Empiricism, Explanation and Rationality* (London: Routledge and Kegan Paul, 1986), ch. 3 is a relevant and useful guide.

5

The International System

Our survey of the main theories of international relations in Chapter 2 revealed a strong tendency to construct theories by reference to 'the international system'. Realism especially saw theoretical virtue in thinking of nation states as constituents of an international system which determined their behaviour. Parallel tendencies in other social sciences at the time also led to structural and functional theories, where the demands of some system were paramount and where the units were so subordinate that there was no need to ask what went on inside them. This was the heyday of structural–functional sociology, which aspired to be as systematic about the social world as Newton had been about the world of nature. The aim was explanation on a grand scale which made human individuals of secondary importance and understanding how things seemed from the inside of no interest. Although that heyday is over, the attempt has left an enduring mark and the reasons for it still represent a pull to the systemic which every social theorist feels.

In International Relations there has been the same urge but neither quite the same timing nor the same fascination with functional explanation. When Idealists spoke of the international system, they had something less impersonal and determining in mind—an international *society*, fragile and in process of construction, rather than a *system* of forces. When Realism was first propounded, it included assumptions about human nature. Only recently have thorough attempts been made at a fully systemic theory, where human individuals and human nature have no place. Hence systems theory has been waxing in International Relations while it has waned in other social sciences. It is a live option at present and one which will remain of methodological interest, whatever its fortune in debate.

For the purposes of this book, it represents the purest claim that International Relations theory should proceed 'top–down' with the aim of Explaining, rather than Understanding. We shall present it as a Realist position, which has emerged first by driving out Idealism and then by refusing to compromise with theories which assign explanatory work to the units of the international system. It is thus a theory which denies all need to 'open the box'. That may make it seem as if any rival theory which works 'bottom–up' by analysing the behaviour of the units must insist on 'opening the box'. It will save confusion if we say now that this is not so. Chapter 6 will examine the scope of Game Theory as an alternative to systems theory. Game Theory is an example of a theory which treats the units as rational actors and argues that the behaviour of the system is the (often unintended) sum of the choices made by the units. But its assumptions are designed to avoid having to ask how exactly the units are internally organized. It is enough to know that they behave *as if* they always arrived at rational solutions to problems of maximizing the value of the relevant variables. The box will remain closed until Chapter 7, in which we move to the next layer of the level-of-analysis problem, where bureaucracies enter the picture. In the present chapter and the next the main dispute is being conducted strictly on the topmost layer, where the state is the smallest unit and neither domestic politics nor human individuals are allowed to matter.

FROM INTERNATIONAL SOCIETY TO INTERNATIONAL SYSTEM

Realism has always inclined towards structural explanation, but has not always embraced it with the thoroughgoing fervour of Neo-Realists like Kenneth Waltz.[1] We shall start by tracing the development of Realist ideas of structure and then refine the case for a purely structural theory like Waltz's.

The international system seems a clear example of the sort of social order long of interest to political theorists, namely, an anarchical grouping of self-interested units who co-operate only in so far as it suits them. As such, it stands in marked contrast to the structure found in domestic society, where the constituent units have a body above them to act as law-giver and law-enforcer. The

[1] K. Waltz, *Theory of International Politics* (Reading, Mass.: Addison-Wesley, 1979).

anarchic international system contrasts with the *hierarchical* domestic system. At first sight this should mean a weak set of structural international determinants, as opposed to the more obviously coercive hierarchical domestic system. After all, the international system seems only the sum of interactions among the constituent units. It has no separate organizations or bodies outranking state sovereignty.

Accordingly, much early work in International Relations used the concept of society rather than that of system. International relations seemed well suited to the theory of the social contract in one or other of its main traditional forms. One form comes down to us from Thomas Hobbes's *Leviathan*, published in 1651 in the wake of the English Civil War, and embodies a 'conflict' model of society. The other, inspired by John Locke's *Second Treatise on Civil Government* (1690), offers a 'consensus' model. Both models have their attractions.[2]

Hobbes thought that human beings were competitive by nature and that their natural state—the 'state of nature'—was one marked by a war of all against all, with 'the life of man solitary, poor, nasty, brutish and short'. The basic problem, therefore, is how a commonwealth can arise and flourish. Hobbes's answer was that even ruthlessly self-interested individuals will make a social contract, provided that it creates a 'power to keep all in awe'. This power would need to be a limited central government with a complete but narrow monopoly of coercive authority—'Covenants without the sword are but vain breath.' Then each citizen would obey, because the government could guarantee that others would obey also, and all could enjoy 'commodious living'. This model appeals to Realists in International Relations because its Rational Actor assumptions include the self-interested motivation which Realists ascribe to nation states.

Locke took a less harsh view of human nature and so thought co-operation more natural and less fragile. Indeed, civil society so plainly offered benefits to all that the reader sometimes wonders why government is necessary. Locke's answer is the one enshrined in the American constitution, which was drawn up by people influenced by his writings. It allows for a more tolerant and

---

[2] T. Hobbes, *Leviathan* [1651] (Glasgow: Fontana, 1983); see especially ch. 13. J. Locke, *Two Treatises of Government* [1690] (Cambridge: Cambridge University Press, 1967).

pluralistic style of government than does Hobbes, and, in International Relations, appealed especially to Idealists. If peace, rather then war, is the natural state, then harmonious international relations should not need a world government armed with the sword.

Both versions of social contract theory work 'bottom–up', thinking of society as a group of individuals, and of its institutions, its rules and norms, as having emerged by mutual consent from anarchy. One standard objection to such an account of domestic politics is that the 'state of nature' envisaged as a starting point is surely a historical fiction and, moreover, one which could inspire a social contract only among individuals who *already* had the practice of making contracts. This objection does not apply to an International Relations version where the individuals are nation states, which do indeed already understand contracts and where an international 'civil society' is apparently in the process of emerging before our very eyes. Accordingly, there has been a powerful group of scholars who think in social contract terms and define international society not as a determining structure or system but as a network of norms and rules governing a society of states.[3]

One might object that what has been emerging before our very eyes, especially since 1945, is as likely to be several societies as just one. The objection would be that the 'society' of the Western states does not extend across the entire system. The Third World is essentially omitted from the practices and understandings of the developed world. There is no single international society, if by society one means an integrated grouping with a common identity and a common way of seeing the world. But it is more to our purpose to note the existence of 'bottom–up' theories in order to contrast them with the theories of the international system which work 'top–down' by maintaining that state behaviour is caused by structural factors. This contrast has interesting parallels in other social sciences. In economics there is an argument between those who think of market forces as a system, which dictates the behaviour of firms, and their opponents who insist that the internal organization of firms affects what happens in the market.

---

[3] See, for example, H. Butterfield and M. Wight (eds.), *Diplomatic Investigations* (London: Allen and Unwin, 1966); M. Donelan (ed.), *The Reason of States* (London: Allen and Unwin, 1978); J. Mayall (ed.), *The Community of States* (London: Allen and Unwin, 1982).

In sociology, social structures are seen by some as determinants of social life and by others as groups of institutions thrown up by social interaction. In general, a 'top–down' approach has the attraction that, if it works, the social scientist need not worry about what goes on inside the units of the system because they are bound to conform to the demands of the system. This attraction has been strong in International Relations too.

How, then, has the international system been treated in the main theories of international relations? As we have seen, both Idealism and Realism had a place for the system, even though the two theories actually relied much more on other factors to explain international behaviour. For the Idealists, the system obtrudes in so far as war is blamed on misunderstanding and misperception. Improving the system was a necessary condition for eliminating war. This view resulted in a very specific role for the League of Nations and for 'men of peace'. The very subject of International Relations had to be reoriented so as to assist the better working of the international system. However, beneath the surface in Idealist thought was a liberal view of human nature, which, by assuming rationality, downplayed the role of the international system. Conflict was avoidable, and its causes could be found in the domestic settings of states. The international system was involved in the causes of conflict only in exacerbating misunderstanding. There was nothing intrinsically conflict-inducing in the international system. International society was, therefore, not something that needed structural reform if war were to be avoided. War had other sources, and the international system needed attention only to ensure that it allowed the process of mediation to function smoothly. This reflects a very specific view of human nature, and implies a very limited role for systemic causes in international relations.

But, of course, the events of the late 1930s were a powerful reminder that war is not only the result of misunderstanding. That called for a less complacent view of the international system. At the very least, it implied that the system had to be so arranged as to allow for collective security. The system looked as if it might encourage war by its structure, if not cause it. This seemed to be a central message of Realism, with its stress on the need for means to ensure national security. Yet, in the early versions of the Realist case, attention was concentrated on the nature of human beings as the source of conflict in the world. This was certainly the lesson that Morgenthau drew from the events of the 1930s. For Realists, the international system was important because its anarchical structure required that, to avoid war, the mechanisms of diplomacy, international law, and the balance of power operated effectively. It was therefore imperative that states' leaders understood the power-maximizing tendencies of individuals. This not only required a conception of morality between states different from that which applied within societies (since different structures were operating), but also implied that the system somehow operated by the ebbs and flows of the power of states. For Morgenthau, it was the centrality of power that allowed scientific precision to be used in explaining international relations. The theory was a *power-politics* model, and the anarchical structure of the international system was central in explaining how power politics operated.

The nature of the international system determined the basic foreign policy orientations of any particular state, and, Morgenthau held, whether a state followed a policy of *status quo*, *imperialism*, or *prestige* depended on its location in the international power structure. This, as we saw in Chapter 2, allowed Morgenthau to claim that the personal motives and values of decision-makers were irrelevant to any explanation of the policies of their states. From this angle, Realism looks very deterministic, leaving little room for the individual decision-makers to act. Yet this is only part of the Realist picture, since, as with Idealism, the central theoretical mechanism at work was again human nature. For Morgenthau, it was the nature of individuals that was the final source of explanations of international relations. The international system was not important as a *cause* of state behaviour; at most it provided conditions in which human nature could cause war. But this was not how critics saw Realism at the time, and many of the early critiques condemned its failure to deal with the particular motives and values of the individual decision-makers. The Behaviouralism of the 1950s explicitly rejected the determinism of Realism and tried to move away from a 'billiard ball' conception of international relations in which power was the only motive force.

Yet the Behaviouralist critique in fact sharpened the issue of the importance of the systems level, precisely because it sought to be explicit about how theories of behaviour were to be built. Two examples are especially interesting. One is the work of Kenneth

Waltz on the causes of war.[4] In his widely cited 1959 monograph, *Man, the State and War*, he outlines three levels at which we might explain the occurrence of war. The first is that of the nature of individuals, and essentially assumes that human nature is fixed, and is either evil or at any rate selfish. The second traces war to the character of some kinds of states, and postulates that there would be no war in an international system composed only of a pacific type of state. The third sees war as the result of the structure of the international system, with the central cause being the anarchical structure of the system.

All three levels have received attention in the literature of International Relations over the years, and Waltz's concern is partly to identify the arguments applying on each level. But his aim is also to offer a view as to why war in general (as distinct from specific wars) occurs. He therefore introduces the system itself as a causal factor in a very explicit way: 'Wars occur because there is nothing to prevent them,' he writes.[5] The point is to show that, although the first two levels may explain the reasons for any specific war, without the third level there can be no general understanding of why war happens. In Waltz, the framework within which other causes operate is the *structure* of the international system. Given the sovereignty of the constituent units of international society (states), and the consequent absence of any authority above the separate states, states are their own umpires. The anarchical structure of the system imposes on all states a security dilemma, whereby they have to ensure their own security without increasing the fears of other states in the system. These factors, claims Waltz, are systemic, and are not reducible to the motives, beliefs, values, or capabilities of the units that comprise the system. To explain international relations, then, we must theorize at the level of the international system.

Waltz was the first to discuss openly the notion that there were a number of levels at which international relations could be explained, but his was very much the voice of a theorist. The notion really took hold in earnest with our second example. This is the work of one of the leading Behaviouralist scholars, Morton Kaplan, who, in his 1957 book, *System and Process in International*

---

[4] K. Waltz, *Man, the State and War* (New York: Columbia University Press, 1959).   [5] Ibid. p. 232.

Politics,[6] proposed that the new science of international relations be built on a systems approach. This would proceed by constructing deductive models of the international system, and then examining history for examples of them. Systems would obey two sets of rules: a set of characteristic behavioural rules that were necessary for the system to stay in equilibrium; and a set of transformation rules, dealing with how a system might change to another type of system. Kaplan outlined six of these systems, and insisted that there was no need to identify the nation states involved, since what happened in the system determined the rules of the system and hence the behaviour of the units. It is easy to imagine how this type of thinking fitted well with the quantitative approach to the subject. For several years systems theory was all the rage in the discipline.

These two statements of the need to adopt a systems approach were accompanied by many other attempts to explain the nature of international relations by referring to factors outside the individual nation state. Haas, for example, looked at the impact of international integration on the policies of states.[7] Herz wrote of the effects of the development of nuclear weapons on the freedom of action of the superpowers.[8] Rosecrance was concerned to show how international and domestic factors could combine to explain different periods of world history.[9] Masters claimed to discern a powerful analogy between the nature of international and primitive political systems.[10]

THE 'LEVEL-OF-ANALYSIS' PROBLEM

This is the moment to say more about the 'level-of-analysis' problem, which we presented in the introductory chapter as a useful way to organize the themes of the book. In his celebrated

[6] M. Kaplan, *System and Process in International Politics* (New York: Wiley, 1957).
[7] See E. Haas, *The Uniting of Europe* (Stanford: Stanford University Press, 1958).
[8] J. Herz, *International Politics in the Atomic Age* (New York: Columbia University Press, 1959).
[9] R. Rosecrance, *Action and Reaction in World Politics* (Boston: Little, Brown, 1963).
[10] R. Masters, 'World Politics as a Primitive Political System', *World Politics*, 1964, 16, pp. 595–619.

1961 article, David Singer contended that throughout the social sciences analysis proceeds on two levels, that of the unit and that of the system.[11] He argued that International Relations had, with the exception of the work of Waltz and Kaplan, largely failed to take the systems level seriously. The bulk of his article dealt with the advantages and disadvantages of each level for purposes of description, explanation, and prediction.

Two central conclusions emerged. First, each level introduces bias into the explanations it provides. The unit or state level exaggerates the differences among states, and underestimates the impact of the system on the actions of states; the systems level assumes that states are more homogeneous than they are and overestimates the impact of the system on the behaviour of the units. Secondly, and more radically, the two levels cannot be combined to arrive at one overall explanation of international relations. This was, said Singer, for the same reason that the two most popular map projections, the Mercator and the Polar Gnomonic, could not be combined to give one accurate map of the world. The reason was that each overemphasized some parts of the world and under-represented others, because it is impossible to represent accurately a three-dimensional globe on a two-dimensional surface. For a Positivist like Singer this was especially problematic, since he hoped that a progressive theory of international relations would emerge from the cumulative growth of data. He was concerned that unless the level of analysis were recognized, researchers would not realize that data generated at one level could not simply be combined with data from another level. The biases involved at the two levels would, like the two map projections, make it impossible to construct an accurate overall picture of international relations. More problematic still was the tendency for researchers to shift unawares between levels of analysis in the middle of a study.

For Singer, then, there could be no overarching theory which explained how system-level and unit-level factors interacted to produce state behaviour. He also declared that the state level, so popular among historians concerned with the specifics, could offer explanations only as long as it made crucial assumptions. The most

[11] J. D. Singer, 'The Level-of-Analysis Problem in International Relations', in K. Knorr and S. Verba (eds.), *The International System: Theoretical Essays* (Princeton: Princeton University Press, 1961), pp. 77–92.

important of these was that state behaviour could be explained by reference to individual decisions without worrying about the source of the perceptions which informed the decisions. This assumption needed correcting, since the perceptions of decision-makers were themselves caused, and the international system was an influential source of these perceptions.

Singer's article located the issue of the impact of systemic factors within the Behaviouralist mainstream. The system could explain aspects of state behaviour (with the actor always assumed to be the state) which could not be explained at the state level. Taken together, the work of Waltz, Kaplan, and Singer firmly established the notion that the international system was a distinct level of analysis, over and above the sum of intended and unintended consequences of state activity.

MULTIPOLARITY AND BIPOLARITY

But this was still far from developing a theory of the impact of the system on the behaviour of its constituent units, despite lengthy debates about the effects of different polar configurations of the system. By the mid-1960s the key topic was not the importance of anarchy, but whether the post-war stability in superpower relations was due to the fact that the international system was bipolar in character. This had been a theme in the work of both Morgenthau (who had argued for the stabilizing qualities of multipolarity) and Kaplan (who had also argued that multipolarity was more stable), but this conventional wisdom was being challenged. Once again, this view became associated with the writings of Waltz, who argued that the bipolar structure of the international system was the reason for the absence of great power conflict since 1945.[12]

The debate about the rival merits of multipolarity and bipolarity involved alternative accounts of systemic influences and how they work. There emerged from it a much more thorough and powerful analysis of what is involved in systemic theorizing. The point of departure is to see the international system as so strongly determining the behaviour of states that there is no need to consider what goes on within them. The motives and beliefs of

[12] K. Waltz, 'The Stability of a Bipolar World', *Daedalus*, 1964, 93, pp. 881–909.

individual decision-makers drop out of account, as do the ideologies and political processes within the states, to be replaced by the workings of the international political system with its power structure or hierarchy. Power is still the crucial variable, the attempt to maximize it being what drives actions and its distribution being what determines the interactions of states.

Treating the internal setting of states as exogenous to explanation means casting aside much of what seems to divide states from one another. Was not the cold war about ideology? Does it not matter what Gorbachev thinks? Are not the British Labour Party's views on defence important? The critical implication of the systemic account is that these factors cannot be understood except within a context that is external to all states, namely, the international system. There are two main aspects of the system that we need to discuss in order to indicate what a systems account looks like. These are anarchy and polarity.

The concept of international anarchy most commonly used in international relations is a Hobbesian one. It refers to the fact that there is no body above the state; states are the only bodies in international society with sovereignty. States are judges in their own causes, with their location within a situation of anarchy imposing a security dilemma on them. This means no prospect of completely enforceable international law, or of a universal moral code to guide the actions of leaders. Might may not always be right, but unless it is met with equal might it may well prevail. There is no escape from this anarchical setting, and the attempts that states make to get out of some of its worst consequences account for the patterns of arms racing and alliances. Anarchy can only be mitigated, not transcended. As long as the structure of the system remains anarchical, states must continue to ensure their own defences, and force, or the threat of it, will continue to be a possible outcome of any international interactions.

The second key systemic characteristic is the polar structure of the system. By polar structure we mean the number of independent great powers and their interrelationships. The most common subdivision is into multipolar and bipolar systems, with the former having at least five roughly equal great powers, and the latter having only two. The number of great powers is usually measured by seeing where a natural gap occurs in a hierarchy calculated from military and, to a lesser extent, economic indicators. There has been much debate as to whether multipolarity or bipolarity is the more stable, in terms of how each maintains equilibrium in the system. The critical question is why the post-war system has stayed stable, and, in particular, whether and how nuclear weapons have helped the maintenance of peace between the great powers.

An answer pitched at the state level, and one favoured by most historians, would address itself to the internal workings of the two superpowers and the history of their changing relationship since 1945. A systemic account, by contrast, points to the fact of bipolarity and to how bipolarity stays stable. A simple contrast between bipolarity and multipolarity on this score might be that, whereas multipolarity stays multipolar by the workings of the balance-of-power mechanism, bipolar stability works through a balance of terror. Similarly, the role of alliances is very different in the two systems. In multipolarity, alliances are flexible and are made between approximate equals with no country able to dominate the alliance. In bipolarity, alliances seem to be held together by an ideological glue, and are hierarchical, with each dominated by one superpower. The resulting pattern of international relations in each of the two systems is also distinctive. In multipolarity, alliances are constantly shifting, with ideology playing no role in determining membership; wars are fought when the balance-of-power mechanism breaks down, with the aim of re-establishing that balance after the war. By contrast, in bipolar systems alliances do not shift and ideological differences seem to be at the very root of the division of the world. Yet wars are not fought between the superpowers, or between their main allies. As John Herz has remarked, 'absolute power equals absolute impotence',[13] since, in a bipolar system marked by constant pressure and crisis, any war would be an all-out affair of complete mutual destruction.

This sketch serves to show how systemic accounts can talk of the nature of international relations without having to identify the states involved. How very unlike the attitude of the national leaders—and, indeed, the media! So, let us be absolutely explicit: it does not matter who the two superpowers have been since 1945. Even two powers with similar ideologies would have been antagonists. Had they been the United Kingdom and the United States, or China and the Soviet Union, the systems perspective

[13] Herz, *International Politics in the Atomic Age*, p. 22.

argues that the basic nature of international relations would have been the same. The systems perspective also implies that the invention of nuclear weapons has only strengthened the bipolar nature of the post-war order, and not created it. A bipolar world without nuclear weapons would be much the same as one with nuclear weapons. Similar reasoning causes systems theorists to worry about a multipolar world with nuclear weapons, since the logic of multipolarity suggests that short wars will be fought to redress the balance of power, even if they are short *nuclear* wars.

NEO-REALISM AND KENNETH WALTZ

So far we have established that International Relations has fastened on two main aspects of a systemic account: the anarchical and polar structures of the system. These operate regardless of the internal workings of the states involved and do not require us to enquire into the motives of those making the decisions on behalf of the states. The claim for their validity is a bold one and needs to be made precise and embedded in a rigorous theory. Since such a theory is still in the process of formulation, there has, unsurprisingly, been little general acceptance of the claim so far within an academic community increasingly concerned with explaining the policy choices of particular nation states. Nor has a systems approach been very popular with historians. Nor has it found its way into the public domain, where the nature of the political process ensures that foreign and defence policy continue to be seen as areas of choice which are affected by values. International Relations has remained very firmly fixed on a state level of analysis.

Yet since the late 1970s and through the 1980s this position has begun to change, partly for the reasons already outlined in Chapter 2 (mainly the switch towards an economic conception of international relations), and partly as the school of thought known as Neo-Realism has developed. The main point to note from our summary in Chapter 2 is that Neo-Realists used the notion of an international system to explain the economic and political scene of the late 1970s. In doing so they have refined the Realist notion of a system and extended it to include economic issues. The leading author in this development has been Kenneth Waltz in his celebrated 1979 study, *Theory of International Politics*.[14] We shall next outline what Waltz has to say about the international system, making it clear that Waltz's system has much in common with the work found on systems in many of the other social sciences. The general comments made in the previous two chapters about the ways in which social action can be explained or understood apply to this developed form of a systems account. We need to warn readers, though, that Waltz has, in our view, modified his position on the nature of the international system. In his *Theory of International Politics*, we see him adopting a strict structural account of international relations, which commits him to seeing structures as real. In his more recent work we see him shifting to a softer notion of structure, one which gives more room for the internal make-up of the units to matter. This ambivalence leads to a serious question as to what Waltz takes as real and primary, structures or units. We shall need to be clear which has priority, ontologically speaking (to use the philosophical term for matters of what exists, from the Greek word for 'being'). Given his persistent objections to 'reductionist' theories which make units primary and structures their (often unintended) product, he seems committed to taking structures as basic, and perhaps the only basic, elements. At any rate his hard-edged notion of structure seems to us the one from which to start.

Waltz begins with the by now familiar point that theories of international relations can be divided into two groups, those that see causes operating at the level of the individual states, and those that see causes operating at the systemic level. The former he terms 'reductionist', the latter 'systemic'.[15] Reductionist theories explain the whole by analysing the attributes and interactions of the parts. Waltz cites as examples the work of Hobson and Lenin on imperialism, in which the international political behaviour of states was explained by a set of domestic economic forces. He goes on to argue that much of the recent literature on the international economic structure is, in fact, reductionist. Reductionist theories, he contends, miss out a set of causes that operate at the systemic level and which cannot be unearthed by looking at the attributes and interactions of the parts. This point recalls his comment about

[14] Waltz, *Theory of International Politics*.
[15] This discussion of reductionism is based on Waltz, *Theory of International Politics*, ch. 2.

the causes of war, since reductionist theories imply that removing the causes that operate at the unit level will, in some way, remove the effects. Put simply, Waltz believes that this is treating the symptoms, not the cause.

Waltz complains that reductionist theories fail to notice the difference between the intentions of actors and the results of their interaction. As he puts it, there is a difference between the two statements 'He is a troublemaker' and 'He makes trouble':

The second statement does not follow from the first one if the attributes of actors do not uniquely determine outcomes. Just as peacemakers may fail to make peace, so troublemakers may fail to make trouble. From attributes one cannot predict outcomes, if outcomes depend on the situations of the actors as well as on their attributes.[16]

The central message is that there is a set of factors belonging to the system, and not to the units, and that these factors determine the outcomes of interactions between states. In order to take reductionist theories seriously, Waltz states, 'we would have to believe that no important causes intervene between the aims and actions of states and the results their actions produce. In the history of international relations, however, results achieved seldom correspond to the intentions of actors.'[17]

What is it about the system that comes between the intentions of actors and the results of their interactions? In Waltz's view,

the apparent answer is that causes not found in their *individual* characters and motives do operate among the actors collectively. Each state arrives at policies and decides on actions according to its own internal processes, but its decisions are shaped by the very presence of other states as well as by interactions with them. When and how internal forces find expression, if they do, cannot be explained in terms of the interacting parties if the situation in which they act and interact constrains them from some actions, disposes them towards others, and affects the outcomes of their interactions.[18]

This set of causes gives rise to the patterns and regularities in international relations, despite massive changes in the internal organization of states, technology, and the whole nature of political and economic life. It is, for Waltz, highly significant that these patterns have remained relatively constant for millennia. As he puts it,

[16] Waltz, *Theory of International Politics*, pp. 60–1.
[17] Ibid. p. 65.   [18] Ibid.

The texture of international politics remains highly constant, patterns recur, and events repeat themselves endlessly. The relations that prevail internationally seldom shift rapidly in type or in quality. They are marked instead by dismaying persistence, a persistence that one must expect so long as none of the competing units is able to convert the anarchic international realm into a hierarchic one.[19]

This is all well and good, but surely there have long been systemic theories in international relations? Here Waltz makes one of his most important and controversial claims: none of the existing systems theories is, in fact, a systems theory; they have all been reductionist. He argues at length that this is the case for writers such as Morgenthau, Kaplan, and Rosecrance.[20] He even comments that Singer has not understood what a systems level is really about, since Singer seems to think that there is only one system, the world, and that the two levels are merely different ways of seeing the same processes at work.[21] What Singer fails to realize, says Waltz, is the fundamental difference between politics within a state and politics in an anarchic system. Nor do the other writers mentioned have a clear notion of what a system is, and so they end up with their system being merely the interactions of their units. For all their concern with being systemic, they are finally reductionist, in that their causal processes all operate at the unit level. Waltz criticizes Kaplan for stating that his systems are 'sub-system-dominant'. As Waltz comments: 'A subsystem-dominant system is no system at all.'[22] Notwithstanding all the attention paid in the literature to systemic causes of international relations, Waltz firmly believes that no one has yet managed to develop a system in anything other than name.

So precisely what constitutes, for Waltz, a systemic explanation of international relations? He defines a system as comprising two elements: a structure and a set of interacting units. The difficulty, he admits, is to define a structure in a way that does not reduce it to the attributes of, and interactions between, interacting units. Failing to distinguish between the structure and its units would mean confusing the variables of the units with the variables of the structure. Yet he is clear that both the unit and the structure are conceptual, not real: they are theoretical concepts. He quotes the

[19] Ibid. p. 66.
[20] Ibid. chs. 3 and 4.
[21] Ibid. pp. 61–2.
[22] Ibid. p. 58.

anthropologist Meyer Fortes: 'When we describe structure, we are in the realm of grammar and syntax, not of the spoken word. We discern structure in the "concrete reality" of social events only by virtue of having first established structure by abstraction from "concrete reality".'[23] It is the arrangement of the parts within a system and the principle of the arrangement that define a structure. The same move is made, he says, in anthropology and in economics, where, in each case, enquiry does not take the form of asking about the motives, views, and personalities of the persons involved. In each case, the motives of the individuals and the interactions among them are omitted from analysis when it comes to explaining the effect of the situation on the behaviour of the actors in it. Economists are concerned not with the personalities of managers but rather with the nature of the market in which the firm has to operate; anthropologists are interested not so much in the values of the members of a tribe as in the effect of the tribe's structure on the behaviour of its members. This distinction between unit-level and system-level properties applies across the social and natural sciences, he believes.

According to Waltz, we can explain international relations only if we are able to distinguish between these unit- and system-level factors. Since he has defined the system as comprising interacting units plus a structure, it is clear that he has to define the structure very carefully if he is to avoid his own reductionist trap. He says that there are three defining characteristics of a system's structure. They are: first, the principles by which the parts are arranged; secondly, the characteristics of the units; and thirdly, the distribution of capabilities across the units.

The first refers to the way in which the units comprising the system are ordered. Here he draws a contrast between the ordering principles that apply in political systems and those which apply in the international system. This is a contrast between hierarchy and anarchy, a distinction between a political system in which the units stand in a relationship to one another that is constitutionally and legally organized in terms of a hierarchy of power, and a system in which there are none of the same formal power relations at work. A state of anarchy is one in which the system is essentially a self-help one. The contrast between the

---

[23] Quoted in Waltz, *Theory of International Politics*, p. 80.

structures found in a political system and those in the international system is, for Waltz, the basic difference between domestic and international politics, and it cannot be grasped by observing the attributes of the units that make up the system.

The second characteristic simply refers to the functions that are performed by the units in the system. Whereas domestic systems are marked by subordinate and superordinate relations between the parts, international systems do not involve units that perform different functions. The units in the international system are states, and all states have to carry out the same functions. This is in clear contrast to the differentiation of functions that occurs in domestic politics. Waltz says explicitly that states are not, and have never been, the only actors. They have, however, been the most important ones. Crucially, all states possess the attribute that is axiomatically linked to the anarchical structure of the system, namely, sovereignty.

The third characteristic of structures is the distribution of capabilities among the units that comprise the system. For Waltz this is the critical characteristic, because *all* international systems are anarchical, and in *all* international systems the units are functionally undifferentiated. International systems differ only in the way in which capabilities are distributed among the units. As the distribution of capabilities changes, so, argues Waltz, does the structure of the system. Is this not committing the sin of reductionism that he is so quick to point out in the work of others? His answer is simple: 'Although capabilities are attributes of units, the distribution of capabilities across units is not. The distribution of capabilities is not a unit attribute, but rather a system-wide concept.'[24] What emerges from this is a positional picture of how states stand in relation to one another, with 'positional' simply referring to the power of each state *relative* to other states, not to the absolute capabilities of each state. This positional picture does not require us to inquire into the ideologies or beliefs of leaders, nor into the alliances and interactions among the units only into their relative power situation. As has already been outlined above, a change in the distribution of capabilities results in a changing polar configuration. Thus, Waltz sees the only variable which can shift within the international system as being that of its polar structure.

[24] Ibid. p. 98.

Waltz's analysis can, therefore, be summarized by saying that the international system acts to determine the behaviour of its units by virtue of its anarchical structure and its polar structure. Together these operate to set the situation within which all units must exist. If the structure changes, then the range of possible outcomes to unit interactions also changes. In a bipolar structure there are certain norms or regularities in the ways in which the units interact; in a multipolar system these norms and regularities are different. Structures work, then, by setting the range of expectations within which the units can operate.

There is little doubt that Waltz's analysis is powerful, if one grants that the analysis of unit attributes and the intentions of their leaders cannot explain the setting within which each unit operates. This setting is not simply the result of the interactions between the units, nor can examining the attributes of any one unit tell us anything about how that unit stands in relation to other units. It is also clear that the characteristic behavioural patterns observed in multipolar systems differ from those observed in bipolar systems: witness the different role of ideology in the two types of system, or the nature of alliances and wars. Think also of the processes by which the peace is kept.

PROBLEMS FOR A SYSTEMIC THEORY

However, Waltz has proved contentious, as witness a collection of critical essays edited by Robert Keohane.[25] In what follows we pick out three lines which seem to us most clearly to sum up the problems of a systemic theory of international relations. They address respectively the notions of power, structure and function, and explanation involved in a theory pitched as far as possible wholly at the systemic level, and will lead us to conclude that there is a need to 'open the box' after all.

First, Waltz needs a well-defined notion of power to account for motion and change in what would otherwise be a system in static equilibrium. Power is a notoriously difficult topic as soon as it is conceived in terms of human agency, with the key factor being the ability of agents to impose their will on other agents. (For a very

[25] See R. Keohane (ed.), *Neorealism and its Critics* (New York: Columbia University Press, 1986).

helpful analysis see Lukes's *Power: A Radical View*.[26]) But this need not be a problem for Waltz, if he can, in effect, define power in terms of force, by analogy with the interaction of forces in a physical system like the solar system. After all, physicists or astronomers do not worry about power as agency because they do not deal in agents. There remains, though, an obvious question of how power in the international system is to be measured. In Newtonian mechanics, for instance, forces are related to mass and there is a definite state to which the system tends. Within Newtonian assumptions, forces can be measured with instruments and the effects of a shock to the system predicted. International forces are, to put it mildly, more various. Military power can perhaps be measured in tanks and warheads (if one assumes that factors like training and morale are a function of quantities of hardware) but economic power has many more facets. Also, since economic and military power do not always go together, there are questions about the unitary measure needed for the idea of a hierarchy of powers (meaning, this time, nation states). These seem to us difficult problems not resolvable without lengthy discussion. So, for the sake of argument, suppose them to be technical problems not drastic enough to undermine a claim to know that the USA is more powerful than France, or that France has more power in the Middle East than Spain does.

The second set of critical questions is concerned with the notions of structure and function and whether there is an analogy between the international system and a natural system, one strong enough to keep the notion of agency at bay. It would suit Waltz best if the analogy were with a system which can be explained without reference to the properties of the units. Failing that, he would still be in business if the relevant properties of nation states did not involve treating them or their leaders or their other members as conscious agents. Otherwise, the problems of measuring power will not just be technical but will reveal a huge flaw in the model.

In one sense it is plainly impossible to explain a system without reference to the properties of its units. The planetary system would not behave as it does, if the planets were made of gingerbread. But in another sense the idea is not absurd. An electronic system, for example, can be conceived in terms of its

[26] S. Lukes, *Power: A Radical View* (London: Macmillan, 1974).

logic, without saying more about its physical components than that they embody the properties of the logic. Flaws in the components might then account for failures of the system but, granted that the system is working logically, there is no need to worry about how the components function physically. It is enough to know that they are delivering what the system demands of them. The behaviour of the parts can then be explained by their functions as defined by the ordering principles of the system. Parts made of different materials are functionally interchangeable if and only if they do the same job.

This is the systemic view at its grandest. It sets up a model of a fully functioning system and then claims it as an idealization of what we observe actually at work in the universe. It is an explanatory, not a descriptive, device. Unsurprisingly, one can object both to the vision in general and to the claim that international relations are a case where it applies. In general, what does 'fully functioning' mean? The answer has to be in terms of purpose—a goal-state to which the system tends, both as it evolves and if it is disturbed. This is because 'functional' implies more than 'causal'. Whether a causal process is functional depends on what it is functional *for*. For instance, the evolution of poison-resistant rats is functional for the survival of the rat species, dysfunctional for the health of human beings, and imponderable for the global ecosystem. Even if rats adapt and evolve in ways which allow them to survive, it is not thereby obvious that their evolution is 'functional' for the species in a sense which *explains* the evolution. It is simply not obvious that *any* events or trends in nature are purposive. This is not a remark which depends on thinking in terms of divine or, somehow, moral purpose. It holds equally for purpose defined in terms of any equilibrium or goal-state to which a process is claimed to tend. It is simply not obvious that there is anything more to the changing physiology of rats than a series of causes and effects.

What more might there be? A functional explanation implies not only that the causal series lets rats survive but also that it takes the form it does *because* it lets them survive. Here the example of an electronic system is misleading. Human beings design electronic systems. So of course their causal workings have a further explanation in terms of how they serve the purposes of the human beings who designed the system. Consequently, a visiting Martian who stumbled on the parts of an electronic system would be right to infer that the parts belonged to a system. But Waltz is not suggesting that anyone designed the international system. His claim that nations behave as the system demands must do without analogies with human intentions.

There are examples of systems theory being a powerful explanatory device. For instance, a termite colony functions in a very intriguing way. It depends for its survival on keeping a balance between the numbers of worker-termites, who see to its food supply, and soldier-termites, who deal with its predators. If there are too few workers, the colony starves; and, if there are too few soldiers, it is wiped out. The balance is struck far below ground, where the solitary queen spends her life laying the eggs which hatch as workers or soldiers in proportions varying with events on the distant surface. How does the queen manage to get the proportions right? The functional explanation is that the queen is responding to the demands of the system. But this by itself, one might say, is mere mysticism. *How* does the queen manage it? The answer is not at all mystical. Her food reaches her down a chain of termites, some of them workers and some of them soldiers. As it passes from jaw to jaw, it picks up traces of secretions. The juices secreted by workers are chemically different from the juices secreted by soldiers. So, when the food arrives, it contains a stimulus to change the proportions of eggs. Given this feedback mechanism, we can plausibly speak of the termite colony as a system whose parts adjust and adapt so as to perpetuate the colony. But notice that we mean only that the colony would not otherwise survive.

A different kind of example, very popular with systems theorists, is the working of markets in economics. According to the Chicago school of economists, one can understand the behaviour of firms without having to ask what goes on inside them. This is because market forces drive out firms which do not respond to the market environment by finding ways to maximize profit. So, given the ordering principles of the market (the laws of supply and demand), one can be sure that successful firms are behaving in ways functional for the working of the market or, to be precise, its tendency to equilibrium. Firms survive only if they consciously aim to maximize profit or, more subtly, happen to imitate the routines of profit-maximizing firms (a case of functional equivalence). Otherwise they go bust or are taken over.

This example is so appealing that International Relations systems theorists are tempted to borrow it uncritically. So it is worth pointing out that it is utterly contentious. We know of no evidence that markets tend to equilibrium, that successful firms maximize profits on purpose (or even by accident), or that 'market forces' are more than generalizations about rational activity by individual firms. Still less is there any reason to think of markets in the deterministic manner which seems suitable enough for termite colonies. Since this is not the place to plunge into economic theory, we shall put the point as a challenge. Although one can postulate a system of determining market forces which tend to equilibrium, is there any fact about markets which cannot equally be explained as the intended and unintended consequences of decisions made by firms?[27]

Waltz's notion of a system is, therefore, imprecise. As John Ruggie has pointed out, Waltz has a 'generative' conception of structure, in that his three characteristics operate at different depths.[28] Waltz, of course, argues that there are only two structural characteristics at the international level (the functional differentiation of units dropping out). Of these, Ruggie argues that one, ordering principles, is a deep structural characteristic, while the other, the distribution of capabilities, is a more empirical characteristic. Ruggie contends that Waltz is mistaken in dropping the second structural characteristic. He contends that the transformation of the medieval into the modern international system can be analysed only by realizing that the units involved altered in the functions they performed. This was a transformation of one kind of unit into another.

A further problem with Waltz's notion of structure, for Ruggie, is that the deepest characteristic of structure, namely, ordering principles, is not observable. All that is visible are the hypothesized effects of the ordering principles at work. The problem here is that Waltz surely cannot mean that the choices of firms or states are completely determined, as if the market or international system worked like a clockwork model. If not a strict determinist, Waltz

[27] For further discussion see J. Elster, *Explaining Technical Change* (Cambridge: Cambridge University Press, 1983), chs. 1–3; Martin Hollis, *The Cunning of Reason* (Cambridge: Cambridge University Press, 1988), ch. 9; and Alan Ryan, *The Philosophy of the Social Sciences* (London: Macmillan, 1970), ch. 8.

[28] John Ruggie, 'Continuity and Transformation in the World Polity: Towards a Neorealist Synthesis', in Keohane (ed.), *Neorealism and its Critics*, pp. 131–57.

might accept that he was a situational determinist; but this opens up a final problem with his notion of structure, which is that it has to be real if it is to act as the cause of the behaviour of the units. Can he be sure that the causes of unit behaviour are systemic and are not the intended or unintended consequences of unit behaviour? This, of course, gets us into the difficult area of reductionism, since Waltz has to show that the structure of the system is a separate causal mechanism to that of the units that comprise the system, if he is not to fall into the same trap as he criticizes all other international systems theorists for falling into. In short, his system has to be a real system, rather than the results of unit-level actions and interactions. The system, and not the units, must do the work.

This leads us directly into the third area of criticism, which is that Waltz's system is not actually capable of explaining much. Ruggie argues that what does most of the explaining is actions of the units and not anything at all that happens at the systems level. Specifically, he notes that Waltz's system can do nothing about explaining change. Waltz has two conceptions of change. The first is that an international system could change by becoming a hierarchical system. This would alter the ordering principle of the system. The second is that the structure of an international system may change as a result of a change in the distribution of capabilities among the units. The problem, as Ruggie sees it, is that, according to Waltz, only structural change can produce systemic change. Yet this cannot be right, since it must be the case that structural change has some cause. For Ruggie,

the problem with Waltz's posture is that, in any social system, structural change itself ultimately has no source *other than* unit-level processes. By banishing these from the domain of systemic theory. Waltz also exo-genises the ultimate source of systemic change.[29]

Waltz ignores unit-level causes. As Ruggie puts it:

Waltz reacts strongly against what he calls the reductionist tendencies in international relations theory. In the conventional usage . . . he finds that the system is all product and is not at all productive. He takes pains to rectify this imbalance. He goes too far, however. In his conception of systemic theory, *unit-level processes* become all product and are not at all productive.[30]

[29] Ibid. p. 152.   [30] Ibid. p. 151.

At any rate, as with the termite colony, it is clear that any systems explanation needs a mechanism through which feedback operates. For the international system the only candidate is, we suggest, the internal workings of the units of the system. This threatens to make the properties of the units more significant than Waltz might want, because it means invoking a mechanism which involves the beliefs and desires of the men and women who play roles within their states. Even if one tries to insist that the roles are covertly governed by the demands of the international system, this still requires a notion of power *within* the units, which relates power to agency after all. That damages the purity of the systems approach and reopens the prospect of treating change in the macro system as a sum of events at the micro level.

On further reflection, indeed, Waltz might welcome an internal source of change since, as we have noted above, change within the system must come from events within the units. Whatever the type of change, domestic factors will surely matter. It is, in short, hard to see how change can possibly be traced to its causes unless those causes lie in decisions taken within units, which, therefore, had better be included as contributing elements of the international system. But then we need to know what goes on inside the units.

Waltz has responded to such criticisms by granting that a systems approach cannot explain everything.[31] This is his softer notion of structure which we mentioned earlier. The task for a systems approach is now, more modestly, stated as being to provide the setting within which states have to operate. The setting cannot be understood by analysing the aims and values of decision-makers, because these aims and values are a poor guide to the results of national decisions. Hence there are two sorts of causes at work. The problem, obviously, is how to combine these two sets of causes. Waltz conceives of international structure as a matrix:

Structural thought conceives of actions simultaneously taking place within a matrix. Change the matrix—the structure of the system—and expected actions and outcomes are altered . . . A structure sets the range of expectations. A structural theory of international politics can fix the ranges of outcomes and identify general tendencies, which may be persistent and strong ones but will not be reflected in all particular outcomes.[32]

[31] K. Waltz, 'Reflections on *Theory of International Politics*: A Response to my Critics', in Keohane (ed.), *Neorealism and its Critics*, pp. 322–45.
[32] Ibid. p. 344.

Thus, even for as strict a systems theorist as Waltz, the structure of the international system cannot explain everything. It is important to note that he ends up by placing a lot of explanatory weight on what happens within the units. He summarizes his revised position in the following way:

Structures condition behaviors and outcomes, yet explanations of behaviors and outcomes are indeterminate because both unit-level and structural causes are in play . . . Structures shape and shove. They do not determine behaviors and outcomes, not only because unit-level and structural causes interact, but also because the shaping and shoving of structures may be successfully resisted . . . With skill and determination structural constraints can sometimes be countered. Virtuosos transcend the limits of their instruments and break the constraints of systems that bind lesser performers.[33]

This is a very important admission by Waltz, since it indicates not only that we need both unit-level and structural causes to understand international relations, but also because he thinks that structural causes can be overcome. If so, they are *not* determining. Now, while this does not completely undermine any notion of structural causes, it does indicate that these are not causes in the fullest sense: they are influences; but influences on what? If international anarchy and the polar structure of the system are two structural causes of unit behaviour, how do these causes work? What is the mechanism by which they are translated into the behaviour of states? There are two answers that we might consider. First, they influence the perceptions of those who take decisions on behalf of the state, giving them an agenda to respond to and a set of constraints on their freedom of manœuvre. Secondly, they influence the way in which the decision-making processes operate within the state. In effect, the structural influence will give more power in debate to some bureaucracies or interest groups than to others. Either way, we have to go 'inside the box' and look at the ways in which policies are made within the state.

CONCLUSION

Waltz's notable admission marks an important stage in our argument. Even the most rigorous and forceful attempt at a wholly

---

[33] Ibid. pp. 343–4.

systemic account of international relations cannot dispense with all unit-level causes. We have found three broad reasons why the units must be credited with contributing to the behaviour of the system. The first—inconclusive but suggestive—is that international power cannot easily be conceived by analogy with natural force, as if the military and economic power of the USA were like the mass of a large planet. This point is inconclusive because power is both a resource to be used by agents, which means that they have to know how to use it, and a structural feature, the importance of which does not depend on its being used or even being directly perceived by the actors. Secondly, a wholly systemic account would need very strong notions of function and structure. But, since the structure shows itself only in the behaviour of the units, and since functional explanations must involve purposive behaviour by the units, there is no way of inferring that the units are merely dependent. Thirdly, changes within and between the units are the only plausible explanations of change in the system. Even if unit changes are influenced in their turn, they must still be allowed to matter. The case rests with Waltz's remark, cited above, that 'the shaping and shoving of structures may be successfully resisted'.

This case, however, does not undermine the very idea of structural causation. Waltz can still maintain that structural theories, whatever their descriptive difficulties, have explanatory power. To grant that structures cannot explain every aspect of international relations is not to grant that they explain nothing. But the case does mean that we need to consider the units as well as the system and to see what happens if we approach the system 'bottom–up'. To repeat a point made at the start of this chapter, however, it does not yet mean taking an interest in the internal workings of the units. Only if the level-of-analysis problem cannot be settled by showing that system behaviour is the sum of unit behaviour or some compromise between structural forces and unit outputs will we need to 'open the box'. We shall indeed do so, but not until Chapter 7. In Chapter 6 the individualist retort to holism, as represented by systems theory, is like that of an economist whose micro theory contains nothing smaller than firms which behave like 'individuals' in the Theory of Games without reference to the internal organization of the firms or to the human characters of the people who work for them.

6

The Games Nations Play (1)

It is no problem for science, conceived as a search for general laws, that water boils at a higher temperature in Denver than in New York. The general law is not that it always boils at 100°C but that it does so at sea level—a formula connecting variations in the local values of variables. Denver is some 1,500 m higher than New York. The formula gives constant results for constant initial conditions and variations are systematic. It is not absurd to tackle the writing of history in the same spirit but the idea is notably less persuasive. To understand Napoleon's invasion of Russia do we really need to suppose that there is a constant formula at work, with Napoleon the local value of some variable in it? Have we the slightest idea what variables the formula would connect? Do we not already know more about France after the French Revolution than a formula could illuminate? Although some philosophers have argued that history is implicitly as much a general science as physics or biology, there do seem to be stubbornly particular elements which we manage to understand without generalizing.

This pull to the particular is awkward for hopes of modelling social sciences on the generalizing character of the natural sciences. One attraction of a systems theory in International Relations is that it firmly avoids the pull by making the behaviour of the units depend on the system. But we concluded that it matters how nations decide and so, one might suppose, how persons who represent nations think. How can we avoid adding that they think in ways too particular to generalize about? A promising answer, borrowed from economics and embodied in Rational Actor models, is that 'units' think and act *rationally*, each taking account of the behaviour of others. In this chapter we shall fill in the general idea of rational action, defined for individual actors and then extended with the help of the Theory of Games. Then we shall apply this impressive body of work to international relations as a counter to systems theory. The suggestion to be explored is that 'the international system' is the context and outcome of the games nations play.

RATIONAL CHOICE AND GAME THEORY

Microeconomic theory is perhaps the most impressive, elegant, and compelling theory in the social sciences. It is also implicitly very general, as becomes clear when it is allied to Game Theory. It is clearly an 'individualist' theory, being entirely concerned with what it is rational for individuals to do in order to maximize the value of some variable, given their preferences and the constraints which they must accept. This may give the impression that the theory operates at a genuinely 'individual' level, in the sense that it deals with human flesh and blood. Were this the case, any attempt to borrow it for International Relations purposes would mean working with units much smaller than the nation state, namely, individual citizens in positions of power. But this is not the case. Economic 'individuals' are units which satisfy the economist's definition of a rational agent. Rational agents need not be flesh and blood. In a sense, indeed, they never are, since a 'rational agent' is too much of an abstraction from human life to have any historical or social location. Consequently this will, for the most part, be a chapter about rational units, with nation states as the units in mind, and human beings merely an example of the wider abstraction. Despite occasional hints that flesh and blood come into international relations, we do not intend yet to 'open the box'.

With this warning, let us begin where economists begin, with a single rational and seemingly human actor in a natural environment—Robinson Crusoe alone on his desert island. Crusoe is a perfectly rational agent. He has fully ordered preferences ranging over the consequences of his feasible actions and perfect information about those consequences. He always chooses the course of action which maximizes his utility by best satisfying his preferences. This is the standard definition of instrumental rationality, as introduced in Chapter 4, for the ideal-type case where the agent is certain about all relevant matters and calculates with complete accuracy. For instance, Crusoe can catch two fish today and two tomorrow, using his hands, or, by spending half a day making a net, can catch one today and four tomorrow. If he prefers five to four (which is not obvious, as it means a day with only one fish), he will rationally choose to make the net. Granted that his preferences are consistent (so that he does not prefer fish to figs, figs to yams, and yams to fish) and complete (so that they include every alternative ranged on a single scale of utilities), he acts rationally by serving them with maximum efficiency.

Even for a natural environment, perfect information is only a limiting case. But it extends to probabilities easily enough. Each action need not have a unique consequence, provided that the actor has what economists call a 'subjective probability distribution' for the possibilities. If the net gives him a 20 per cent chance of three fish, a 50 per cent chance of four, and a 30 per cent chance of five (the maximum feasible), he can calculate an *expected utility* for the action of making a net. An expected utility is a measure of how much utility he would get from an outcome, discounted for the chances of not getting it. The idea is clearest where it makes sense to assign numbers to the chances, but it also works in a weaker form where chances can be given only in ordinal, more-or-less terms.

How does Crusoe know what the chances are, even ordinally? We equip him with a learning procedure. The standard one is 'Bayesian'. He starts with a random prior probability for an event and then corrects it by adjusting it in the light of what he finds by experience. The learning process continues until any errors in his expectations are *randomly* over and under the observed trend. Thus, if he is regularly expecting to catch more fish than he in fact does catch, he adjusts the probability downwards. Systematic error can be systematically eliminated. In this way the limiting case of perfect information can extend to cover the demand that a rational agent shall hold rational beliefs in a world of risk or uncertainty.

Armed with this notion of rational action, we can next think about a world containing several rational agents. Man Friday arrives. Social action, as Max Weber said neatly, is action 'which takes account of the behaviour of others and is thereby oriented in its course'. So let Crusoe's preferences now range over the consequences not only of his own actions but also of Friday's. Expected utilities are now directed to *outcomes* and the utility of each action can depend on what someone else does. This is the basic idea behind the Theory of Games, where an outcome is the sum of the 'strategies' chosen by each agent. Crusoe and Friday come to interact in ways which this theory analyses most instructively.

The simplest game is one where each agent has a choice between two strategies and there are thus 2 × 2 possible outcomes. Each agent derives utility from each of the four outcomes and may not rank the outcomes in the same order. Each outcome gives a (perhaps different) *pay-off* to each and we assume that these pay-offs are known to both. For instance, Crusoe and Friday have built a coracle which goes nicely if both paddle fast, tolerably if both paddle slowly, and round in circles if they paddle at different speeds. If fast paddling costs more effort (which each man dislikes), the situation can be depicted as in Figure 6.1 (the pay-offs are written in the form x, y, where x is Crusoe's and y Friday's; and the mathematical sign >, 'greater than', is here used to mean 'preferable to'). What happens? In the absence of any prior conventions, it depends on how they start. If both begin by paddling fast, they will continue. Neither has any reason to change to slow. If both begin by paddling slowly, this outcome is also stable, in that neither prefers that he paddles fast while the other paddles slowly. But one notices that *both* prefer fast–fast and it may be possible to build on this thought later. If they begin fast–slow or slow–fast, then either the fast one decides to save the effort, thus producing slow–slow, or the slow one reflects that an extra effort by him will produce his best outcome of fast–fast; or both switch, with equally unsatisfactory results. In the language of Game Theory, there are two equilibria, one inferior for both paddlers, and two other possible outcomes where rational choices are so far indeterminate.

The example could be either a 'one-shot' game, which is played just once, or one play of a 'reiterated' game, which is repeated,

	Friday	
	Fast	Slow
Fast	$a, \quad a$	$d, \quad c$
Slow	$c, \quad d$	$b, \quad b$

Crusoe (row player) $a > b > c > d$

FIG. 6.1.

perhaps with changing outcomes as the players respond to play in previous rounds. So think of it as a reiterated game in which each stroke of the paddle is one round. Then Crusoe and Friday have a mutual interest in establishing a convention which will stop the coracle going round in circles.

If each were indifferent between fast–fast and slow–slow, it would not matter to them which convention emerged. This would make the game a *co-ordination game*, to be solved by the emergence of a 'salient'. Since there would be no reason why one of the two salients would be indicated and since they as yet have no language for proposing conventions, it is not clear quite how salients emerge. But perhaps they paddle away until they fall into rhythm—a hope encouraged by the fact that each is looking for a salient to serve their mutual interests. At any rate, co-ordination games rationally should result in stable equilibria or, let us say, *consensual norms*, from which no one has any reason to depart.

In the actual example, one equilibrium was better for both players than the other but involved the extra effort of faster paddling. Let us suppose the extra effort is worth it to each, but only if he expects the other to make it too and to keep making it. Formally, the name of a game with this feature is an *assurance game*. There is a mutual interest in subscribing to a norm which embodies the best outcome for both players, but only for as long as each has the assurance that the other will subscribe. Although this sounds like the previous consensual norm again, the difference becomes clear with more players. For instance, to switch abruptly to real life, it might be in the interests of all nations to have no biological weapons. But it might also be the case that assurances could not be trusted, either because some nations saw advantage in giving the assurance while secretly stocking the weapons, or, more subtly, because some nations feared that others could not be trusted. Then the assurance norm would be vulnerable, unlike a consensual norm, from which no one has any reason to renege. Thus, an assurance game falls between a co-ordination game and some other type of game yet to be mentioned.

Having switched to real life, let us stay there. Replace Crusoe and Friday with the USA and the USSR and replace the coracle with nuclear weapons. Figure 6.2 is a possible diagram of the situation facing disarmament negotiators. Here Disarm–Disarm is better for both than Arm–Arm and, one might think, will

		USSR Arm	USSR Disarm
USA	Arm	c, c	a, d
USA	Disarm	d, a	b, b

$a > b > c > d$

FIG 6.2

therefore emerge with mutual assurance. But, at least if the game is one-shot, the theory says not. The USA, being a rational agent, reasons, 'If USSR arms, then the USA does better to arm ($c > d$); if USSR disarms, then the USA does better to arm ($a > b$); so USA does better armed *whatever the USSR does*'. Meanwhile, by parallel reasoning, the USSR also decides to be armed, whatever the USA does. The outcome is therefore third best for both, even though *both* would have done better with Disarm–Disarm.

This game, with its dominant logic leading to a mutually inferior outcome, is crucial for Game Theory. It is named the *Prisoner's Dilemma*, because of the story originally used to illustrate it.[1] In the original tale, the police have arrested Alf and Bert, both of whom they can prove to have committed a robbery and, although they cannot prove it without a confession, rightly suspect of committing a murder. Alf and Bert are put in separate cells and each made a tempting offer. The police tell Alf that a conviction for robbery is certain and will carry a sentence of two years. But if he confesses to murder and Bert does not, then he will be charged with neither robbery nor murder, although Bert will then get a life sentence for murder. If both confess, however, both will be charged with murder and, since they have helpfully confessed, will both get a reduced sentence of ten years. Bert is made an analogous offer. What will each rationally do? The dominant logic is as just stated. Alf reasons, 'If Bert confesses, I do better to confess; if Bert does not, I also do better to confess; so I do better to confess, *whatever Bert does*.' Bert reasons similarly. Both confess. Each gets ten years, when each could have got away with two.

As with arms control, it will seem that those caught in the logic

[1] The story is attributed to A. W. Tucker by R. Luce and H. Raiffa in *Games and Decisions* (New York: Wiley, 1957), p. 94.

could escape by making a contract. If the police gave Alf and Bert a moment together, they could agree not to confess. But, alone again in his cell, each wonders whether to keep the contract. Alf reasons, 'If Bert keeps it, I do better to break it; if Bert does not keep it, I do better to break it; so I do better to break it, *whatever Bert does.*' Bert reasons similarly and their agreement fails, even though both are then worse off. Equally, with an unverifiable procedure rather like a return to separate cells, an arms control agreement is then defeated by the dominant logic which made it necessary. Writing 'Break' and 'Keep' for 'Arm' and 'Disarm' in Figure 6.2 leaves the game unchanged.

How seriously should we take this as a representation of human affairs? The question goes very deep, as we shall show in a moment. But first let us explore the logic of the game a little further. The two-person, one-shot Prisoner's Dilemma is an exact and limited case, with precise real-life examples hard to find. It is not plain that arms control illustrates it precisely, although there is an interesting resemblance.

Even in a bipolar world, is disarmament a two-person game? The USA and USSR are not the only nations whose interests and likely behaviour are at stake; bilateral negotiations are rarely simply bilateral. So, a more complex framework seems to be needed. The best reply is, we think, to grant the risk of oversimplification but then to point out how two-person games can be extended to *n* persons, often with a gain in power. The Prisoner's Dilemma, for example, extended to several players, is revealing about the 'free rider' problem. With only two players, any norm which emerges to prevent defection collapses at once, if either defect. With several players the norm can survive a few defections. So each player can seriously contemplate a free rider's delight, where other players continue to supply benefits for which the free rider need not pay. Whaling makes the point very clearly: a small catcher of whales may be tempted to break a general convention limiting the catch because still able to count on the convention to ensure that there are whales to catch. Meanwhile *each* of the many players of this *n*-person game can reason, 'It pays me to catch more whales, if others behave moderately; it pays me also, if others are immoderate; so it pays me to break the convention, *whatever others do.*' Once again the rational choices sum to leave everyone worse off.

Relatedly, are international games really one-shot? This year's disarmament negotiations belong to a series, with everyone aware what happened last time and looking ahead to next time. In a *supergame* (the Game Theory term for a series) players may act differently from how they would act in a one-shot game. If today's free riders are going to be judged in tomorrow's game, they may decide not to ride free today. The thought offers a plausible counter to the dominant logic of the Prisoner's Dilemma. But it needs to be treated with care for two reasons, one narrow and one broad.

The narrow reason is that the *final* game in a finite series of Prisoner's Dilemma games is, in effect, one-shot. There will be no further occasion when it will prove costly not to have acted co-operatively. So the dominant logic applies to the last game. All players, being rational agents, realize this in the last-but-one game, which therefore becomes, in effect, one-shot too, because no penalty will be effective in the final game. But this makes the last-but-two game, in effect, one-shot also; and so on. The 'supergame' decomposes into a mere series of one-shot games, and the original problem is reinstated. Although Game Theorists hesitate over what to make of this paradoxical result, it does at least give one pause. On the other hand, it may not apply where the series is indefinitely long (meaning not that it is infinitely long but that it does not have a limit known in advance), thus leaving a probability that defections will not be free. The theoretical ground is tricky.

The broad reason is that it is not plain how to introduce 'supergame' considerations into each occasion of play. Given the definition of a rational agent and the assumption that a rational agent maximizes expected utility, they presumably operate either on the utilities or on the expectations of getting them. Either way, however, that seems to change the pay-off and hence the game being played on each occasion. For instance, fear of future reprisal might change the pay-offs as shown in Figure 6.3; this would be a co-ordination game again, if *a*, *a* was equally as good as *b*, *b*, and is, in fact, the assurance game already mentioned. Alternatively, the new table might be as shown in Figure 6.4. This is a new game, whose name is *Chicken*. (Texas teenagers in the 1950s, it is said, used to borrow the family cars and drive down the centre of a long road towards one another. Whoever swerved was 'chicken' and

	USSR Keep	USSR Break
USA Keep	a, a	d, c
USA Break	c, d	b, b

$a > b > c > d$

FIG. 6.3

the other won. If both swerved dishonour was equal. If neither swerved, there was a disaster for both. Put 'Swerve' for 'Keep', and 'Don't Swerve' for 'Break'.) The Chicken Game is a possible way of representing the arms race and a very frightening one, if one party believes that it has the stronger nerve. Meanwhile, the game also introduces a new category of games without predictable solutions, at least with the apparatus given so far.

Here we find ourselves embarking on technicalities of Game Theory, which are beyond this book. With the suggestion that choice of strategy may depend on what one rationally believes about the other player's strength of nerve comes the thought that it may be worth investing resources, at some short-term cost, in acquiring a reputation for bravado. Here lies the fertile but hugely complex theory of bargaining, where manœuvres depend on usefully imperfect information. This too is beyond our scope. So we shall make just one general point and leave the reader to pursue the theory of games and bargaining elsewhere, with a promise that the effort will be found worthwhile, for example, in considering the options for first-strike and second-strike missile systems.[2] The general point is that the effect of embedding a

	USSR Keep	USSR Break
USA Keep	b, b	c, a
USA Break	a, c	d, d

$a > b > c > d$

FIG. 6.4

[2] Among the many books on the Theory of Games, A. Rapoport, *Two-Person Game Theory: The Essential Ideas* (Ann Arbor: University of Michigan Press, 1966) and Luce and Raiffa, *Games and Decisions*, remain very useful. N. Frohlich and J. Oppenheimer, *Modern Political Economy* (Englewood Cliffs, NJ: Prentice-Hall, 1978) extends the basic ideas to economics and politics.

one-shot game in a supergame depends on the context and the particular character of the agents. In the basic and pure Theory of Games, agents are simply 'rational agents' and context consists simply of specified constraints within which rational choices can be calculated. Bargaining theory allows some stylized variety in the types of agents and some uncertainty in their view of one another. But departures from basic and pure abstraction cannot be very great if stylized calculation of probabilistic strategies is to be possible. So there is always going to be a crucial question about the relevance of these abstractions.

THE RELEVANCE OF CONTRACTARIAN THINKING

The question is not about abstraction as such, since every science needs to abstract from the variety of the real world in order to theorize. The crux is whether the variety of international dealings can be instructively simplified with the aid of an ideal type taken from the Theory of Games. The best reason for believing that it can lies in the anarchic character of international society, as we suggested earlier. Game Theory is a splendid tool of contractarian thinking—the rational individualism which has inspired most versions of the social contract. If one regards society, or at any rate its practices and institutions, as a construct by individuals with aims which cannot be pursued in a 'state of nature', then the idea of contract is compelling and Game Theory its neat embodiment. Individuals co-operate to erect a framework within which they can make lesser contracts for particular purposes. Rational agents do not enter contracts unless it suits them, and interaction in a world of rational agents can be analysed as the outcome of individually rational choices of strategy.

Contractarian thinking draws, as noted earlier, on two main theories of the social contract. Locke's *Second Treatise of Civil Government* presumes that even in a state of nature we are naturally inclined to fellowship and communion. Government emerges so that we can reap mutual benefits (provided that it is good government). In this amiable version, there is no puzzle about co-operation, a point captured earlier in the chapter by starting with co-ordination games and showing how they might lead on to assurance games. Although Locke sets out to account for the emergence of government as a source of necessary assurances, it is clear that his state of nature is already in some sense an orderly society, where some co-operation occurs. So international society can be analysed in this contractarian way, even though no world government has yet emerged.

On the other hand, Hobbes's theory of the social contract is more of a challenge. As we noted in a previous chapter, the state of nature here is one of 'war of all against all' and the only exit is by creating an absolute power to keep all in awe. That makes the Prisoner's Dilemma the basic game, since it illustrates so revealingly how rational individuals can make rational choices which sum to defeat their aims. The Prisoner's Dilemma game is bound to end in tears, unless any contract agreed to is enforced by the sword, since 'covenants without the sword are but vain breath'. Only after Leviathan has been created can milder games, like assurance games, be played with happy endings. The challenge in general is that, because the state of nature is itself a Prisoner's Dilemma, it is hard to see how Leviathan can emerge from it, since there is as yet no government with a sword. The challenge for international relations is that, without a world government, all agreements should be dangerously fragile and prone to free riding. In a world of nuclear weapons, Hobbes might say, covenants not backed by a central authority which wields them are but vain breath, and there is going to be a war of all against all, which will leave us all dead.

The broad merits of contractarian thinking are a matter of dispute. An obvious doubt is the appeal to a state of nature as the historical state from which institutions and governments emerge by rational contract. But modern contractarians reply that the theory should be treated as analysis rather than history. As in Game Theory, we are being offered a timeless account of what rational individuals can be expected to do in certain conditions. If a historical note is wanted, then look forwards rather than backwards and ask what would happen if national or international order were to break down. Threats to the stability of the modern world are revealed by the Theory of Games, contractarians maintain. That strikes us as a good reply, if one grants the underlying individualism its account of human nature and is content to construe interaction as a 'game' in the sense defined by contractarian thinking. For the moment we shall, with a promise to resume the topic in Chapters 8 and 9. Meanwhile, it is worth exploring the application of Game Theory to International Relations in rather more detail.

As suggested by the earlier examples, the games that International Relations has tended to use are Chicken and the Prisoner's Dilemma. Most of the textbooks show how arms races can be analysed by using the Prisoner's Dilemma, and how the Chicken Game is appropriate to international crises.

The major initial contributions have come from Herman Kahn, Thomas Schelling, and Anatol Rapoport, all writing in the late 1950s and early 1960s.[3] These three writers extended the existing work on Game Theory into international relations, and ushered in a new way of thinking about strategic issues. Nuclear strategy became a subject dominated by rational choice models, and mathematical models were used to demonstrate various deterrent strategies. For Kahn especially, deterrence was very much akin to the Chicken Game, and the language of that game accordingly entered nuclear strategy: deterrence was all about commitment, communication, and credibility. The task became how to manage the strategy of the plays of the game. US–Soviet relations were likened to several plays of a game of Chicken, and nuclear forces were to be used to manipulate the actions of the other side.

The central concept in nuclear strategy, that of deterrence, itself reflected the basic message of Game Theory in taking the outcome to be dependent on the behaviour of both sides. Nuclear strategy was to do with influencing the other side to act in a specified way. For Kahn, signalling commitment meant managing the process of escalation in a crisis, and he proposed that the best way to think about crises was to imagine an escalation ladder.[4] Leaders, he argued, had to realize that international relations were like the

[3] See H. Kahn, *On Thermonuclear War* (Princeton, NJ: Princeton University Press, 1960), *Thinking About the Unthinkable* (New York: Horizon Press, 1962), and *On Escalation* (New York: Praeger, 1965); T. Schelling, *The Strategy of Conflict* (Cambridge, Mass.: Harvard University Press, 1960) and *Arms and Influence* (New Haven: Yale University Press, 1966); A. Rapoport, *Fights, Games, and Debates* (Ann Arbor: University of Michigan Press, 1960) and *Strategy of Conscience* (New York: Harper and Row, 1964).

[4] See Kahn, *Thinking About the Unthinkable*, ch. 6; *On Escalation*, ch. 2.

Chicken Game, with leaders on a ladder of escalation and each knowing that other leaders were thinking in the same way. The nature of crises could be understood best by seeing both sides as trying to manipulate, or dominate, the ladder of escalation. Kahn's ladder had forty-four rungs, ranging from the ostensible crisis through conventional war, local nuclear war, counter-force war, and counter-city war, to 'spasm' war.[5] In managing this process, the key concept was 'escalation dominance', by which Kahn meant being able to control the crisis at any given rung on the ladder. Examples of escalation dominance would include the dominant side having sufficient force advantage at a given rung to mean that it would lose least from any movement further up the ladder. Kahn's work acquired great influence in US defence circles. Indeed, much of his research was sponsored by the Pentagon. But it also provoked an enormous attack on this application of Game Theory, voiced notably by Philip Green and Anatol Rapoport.[6]

This attack will be discussed when we reach the critiques of the application of Game Theory in International Relations; its central point was that the scientific methods of Game Theory (allied with scientific approaches such as systems theory) gave strategy a spurious authority. Moreover, the use of these methods ignored the centrality of moral judgements in politics. Policy problems could not be neatly divided into analytic and moral dimensions. Since Game Theory deals only with the analytic, it is a misleading and incomplete account of national strategy.[7]

Rapoport had already taken the field in 1960 with *Fights, Games, and Debates*, which explicitly applied Game Theory to international relations.[8] He illustrated 'Fights' by using mathematical models of the arms race, took 'Games' in the Game Theory sense, and examined 'Debates' with the aid of work on the nature of images and belief-systems. Also in 1960, Thomas Schelling published his influential *The Strategy of Conflict*.[9] In this collection of essays, he used Game Theory to build up an account of international conflict. He dealt with a much wider area of concern than did Herman

[5] Kahn, *On Escalation*, p. 39.
[6] See P. Green, *Deadly Logic* (Columbus, OH: Ohio State University Press, 1966); Rapoport, *Strategy of Conscience*.
[7] See Green, *Deadly Logic*, pp. 259–60.
[8] See Rapoport, *Fights, Games, and Debates*.
[9] Schelling, *The Strategy of Conflict*.

Kahn, and the central focus of the essays is on the emergence of tacit communication. For Schelling, formal Game Theory cannot predict outcomes which involve what he terms the emergence of focal points, or situations of prominence. These emerge through tacit understandings, and not through the rules of the various games. He cites examples from game-playing experiments and introduces the notion of tacit communication into the subject of international relations. In a large and celebrated section of the book he takes up the issue of how to signal and manipulate events in a crisis so as to achieve tacit agreement and co-operation. In so doing, he introduced a set of phrases now central to the analysis of international relations, terms such as 'brinkmanship', 'the threat that leaves something to chance', and 'the reciprocal fear of surprise attack'. The book extends Game Theory from an account of choices within rules to a wider explanation of the way in which co-operation and agreement can be arrived at outside the formal game framework, thus achieving a major increase in its scope.

More recently, there has been a renewed interest in Game Theory following the work of Robert Axelrod and Steven Brams. In *The Evolution of Cooperation*, Axelrod uses the Prisoner's Dilemma to develop an account of how selfish individuals can learn to co-operate.[10] Many of the empirical examples he cites are from international relations, notably the US–Soviet relationship. The book starts by asking how co-operation can emerge in a world of egoists without central authority. He immediately gives Hobbes's answer. Without government, life in the state of nature would be 'solitary, poor, nasty, brutish and short'.

Axelrod invited Game Theorists to take part in a computer tournament involving a supergame consisting of several plays of the game. Each was asked to write a strategy for playing the game several times against the same player. The winning strategy was Tit-for-Tat (sent in by Anatol Rapoport). This strategy proposed co-operating on the first move then doing exactly what the other player had done at the previous move. Axelrod tried to explain why this co-operative strategy won, and what it meant for the wider question of how co-operation could emerge without a central authority. The result is surprising in an approach which credits Hobbes with the primary insight. His explanation was that co-operation can emerge if 'individuals have a sufficiently large

[10] R. Axelrod, *The Evolution of Cooperation* (New York: Basic Books, 1984).

chance to meet again, so that they have a stake in their future interaction'.[11] He gives as an example the live-and-let-live system which emerged in trench warfare during the First World War. Here, despite orders to the contrary, soldiers in the front line refrained from shooting soldiers on the other side, provided that the other side exercised similar restraint. This was possible because the same units tended to face one another for long periods. They had, in Axelrod's terms, a stake in their future interactions. Note that this co-operation emerged in the absence of friendship and despite very limited communication. There was certainly no central authority to enforce co-operation.[12]

In the rest of the book, Axelrod develops an account of the conditions for such co-operation. It involves ensuring that individuals will have a stake in their future interactions, and he discusses this in connection with superpower relations. By showing how co-operation can emerge as the best strategy even in the Prisoner's Dilemma, Axelrod hopes to show that friendship and trust are not required for the two superpowers to co-operate. The book soon became a focal point for much research in the US academic community, and in 1985, the journal *World Politics* published a symposium entitled *Cooperation Under Anarchy*, for which Axelrod (with Robert Keohane) wrote the concluding essay.[13] The result of the *World Politics* collection and Axelrod's book is that Game Theory is currently a major theoretical tool for developing theories of the behaviour of states in the international system. Since it is now generally accepted that international relations theory must deal with issues of international political economy as well as with military issues, Game Theory has the advantage over the old Realist model that it can deal with mixtures, of conflict and co-operation of the kind required.

Another recent major development is Steven Brams's *Superpower Games*.[14] Brams aims 'to show how game theory can help elucidate the rational basis of different aspects of [superpower] conflict'.[15] Most of the book uses the Chicken, Prisoner's

[11] Ibid. p. 20.
[12] The story is told in detail in T. Ashworth, *Trench Warfare, 1914–1918: The Live and Let Live System* (New York: Holmes and Meier, 1980).
[13] K. Oye (ed.), *Cooperation under Anarchy*, Special issue of *World Politics*, 1985, 38(1).
[14] S. Brams, *Superpower Games: Applying Game Theory to Superpower Conflict* (New Haven: Yale University Press, 1985).   [15] Ibid. p. xi.

Dilemma, and Truth games to explain three areas of superpower relations: deterrence, arms races, and verification. These games, not being 'zero-sum' (in the sense that whatever one player gains another must lose), allow scope for co-operation. In applying them as an accurate representation of current superpower relations, Brams can therefore strike a note of modest optimism.

The Chicken Game has no stable co-operative equilibrium because the best strategy against a 'chicken' is to play for victory and the best general strategy is to issue threats so unswerving that the other will play 'chicken'. Yet, since the other will not rationally believe that anyone would carry out a threat of annihilation for *both* sides regardless, the threats will be ignored with mutually disastrous results. Brams therefore suggests that probabilistic threats should be introduced. If a Prisoner's Dilemma, whose dominant logic says 'defect', is applied to the arms race, the players will go on arming, even if they promise otherwise. So Brams considers ways of weakening the dominance of this destructive logic by means of shared intelligence data and policies of conditional co-operation. He sees this as changing the rules of the Prisoner's Dilemma—a move that we dispute, since changing the rules makes it a different type of game, and no longer a Prisoner's Dilemma. Relatedly, he uses the Truth Game to study verification procedures for arms control treaties. This game, which is a game of imperfect information, gives one side of the options of lying or telling the truth and the other side the options of believing or disbelieving. Brams suggests how compliance with arms control agreements might improve if there were more sophisticated inducements to reward and encourage policies of honesty.

Axelrod and Brams prove the relevance of Game Theory to the study of international relations. Bilateral interactions without central authority are nicely mirrored by the structure of the Prisoner's Dilemma and the Chicken Game, especially when one considers deterrence and the arms race. Furthermore, Game Theory has entered the thinking of the US government about its foreign and defence policy and particularly affected the nuclear strategy debates of the 1950s and 1960s. The paradox is that this most 'academic' and mathematical of international relations theories has become much more part of governmental thinking and planning than have virtually all of the more 'commonsense' theories and models. Recall the image of the mad nuclear strategist, Dr Strangelove, in the 1964 film of the same name and reflect how deadly an exponent of Game Theory he would be.

FOR AND AGAINST THE USE OF GAME THEORY

It is clear by now that Game Theory is a powerful but ambiguous tool whose use poses many unresolved questions. We shall list here the main points commonly made for and against, both as an aid to judging between them and as a way of resuming the philosophical theme about explaining and understanding. To give warning, each point listed has been disputed in itself, and none could be decisive in any case while it remains unclear whether the merit of a social science theory depends on how exactly the actors understand their world.

There are eight main advantages claimed for the use of Game Theory in International Relations.

First, it focuses attention on how people behave, rather than on how they should behave. This contrasts with the common accounts which stress the ethics of action, whether from the Idealist perspective of achieving progress or from an insider perspective which takes actors to be moved by moral considerations. Game Theory takes a cool and, one might suggest, Realist standpoint. This does not mean that the morality of the actors has no place in the study of the subject, nor that policy should not be evaluated according to moral standards. But it does suggest that the Theory of Games is helpful in allowing us to understand the behaviour of the actors without worrying about their ideologies, or about the state of their friendships.

Secondly, because Game Theory deals with outcomes, it addresses us to the counter-intuitive reflection that the best outcome can elude the best individual choices. The Prisoner's Dilemma offers an explanation of why it is that both parties act rationally in confessing, and yet produce an outcome that is worse for each of them. This captures neatly one problem of the anarchical structure of international relations, and seems particularly useful in explaining arms races.

Thirdly, the Chicken Game is particularly well suited to the analysis of deterrence. This game offers a very useful way of thinking about crisis behaviour (whatever the ideologies of the participants), and, because of its concern with the use of signals and threats to force the other driver to swerve, it offers powerful insights into the ways in which commitment and pre-commitment might be signalled. Schelling's terms of 'brinkmanship' and 'the threat that leaves something to chance', both derived from the Theory of Games, have been particularly influential in the study of deterrence and crisis behaviour.

Fourthly, Game Theory has been much concerned with the concept of tacit bargaining, and this has been influential in analysing US–Soviet arms control behaviour. In the middle of the 1980s, there was a strong move in US defence circles towards a policy of arms control by reciprocal reprisals. This became characterized as 'arm and let arm', but the aim was to achieve restraint in the absence of formal agreements or communications. Moreover, this notion of tacit bargaining has a wider significance in explaining the role of force and the threat of the use of force. Think of the US intervention in Grenada, the US use of force in the Gulf, Gorbachev's unilateral conventional force reduction proposals in late 1988, or the reduction of British force levels in Gibraltar. In each case the aim has been to achieve goals without formally entering into agreement with the other party. In the area of arms control the notion of tacit bargaining has received even more attention, where Downs and Rocke see it as having significant advantages over traditional formal negotiations and treaties.[16]

The fifth advantage is the massive interest that it has stimulated in the area of the evolution of co-operation. This is currently one of the most fertile research areas and it is certainly one where theorists are most active; witness the work of Axelrod. There is intense interest in supergame strategies which offer co-operative escapes from the Prisoner's Dilemma. Because international relations look like a pure case of co-operation under anarchy, it is not surprising that developments in Game Theory are of great interest to the subject. This suggests a main avenue for the development of Realist theory in the future.

Sixthly, Game Theory upholds the claim of governmental decision-making to be rational. Even if not all policy is rational, Game Theory shows both how individual rationality can be

[16] G. Downs and D. Rocke, 'Tacit Bargaining and Arms Control', *World Politics*, 1987, 39(3), pp. 297–325.

understood within the structure of the game, and how best outcomes for all need not result if each acts rationally. Further, by focusing on rationality it gives a renewed sense to the treatment of states as individuals, since each may be conceived as a player in specific games.

The seventh point is that Game Theory provides an answer to the objection that states are not the only units (there are multinational companies, for example) and that states are not monoliths (because policy is the result of bargaining games within the decision-making group). In terms of their structural setting, states are units within an international system and their behaviour can be analysed by treating them as such. The anarchical structure of the international system results in states being in the kind of situations that the Theory of Games can model.

Finally, Game Theory, being general in its logic, permits striking analogies. By classifying state behaviour in specific circumstances along with that of other types of actors in similar circumstances, Game Theory links international relations to a much wider range of social behaviour. States in crises are like companies in a price war. Arms races are like pollution control. The key games, Chicken and Prisoner's Dilemma, apply to a very wide range of human behaviour, and to the extent that the structure of international relations resembles the structure of these games, they help us identify similarities in social behaviour.

To round off this list of advantages, we shall also note how the very fact that Game Theory has become fashionable adds to its relevance. If policy-makers are applying Game Theory, then we need Game Theory in order to understand what they are up to! This intriguing thought cannot simply be recorded as a ninth advantage, especially not if one is impressed by the claim of some Game Theorists that the theory lets us bypass what is going on in the actors' heads by concentrating on behaviour in relation to outcome. Some theorists argue that we need not worry at all about whether or not actors are acting rationally, only that they respond to the pay-offs presented to them by the game's matrix. But this is a point to which we shall return in Chapter 8.

Despite these advantages, there is a set of problems which limit the utility of the approach within International Relations. Again, we can summarize them in eight points.

First, the scope of a rational analysis is problematic, since there is much evidence that foreign policy decisions are not made rationally. This is not simply to say that they are often short-sighted or ill co-ordinated, but that they emerge from a decision-making process where decisions are often the unintended consequences of group interactions whose conduct is not suited to Game Theory. Decisions can result from group pressures or bureaucratic politics. Individuals may have restricted world views and not be susceptible to incoming information. The species of rationality displayed in experimental games designed by Games Theorists may be too far removed from the actual processes leading to decisions on major issues of defence or foreign policy. For example, the Falklands conflict involved very powerful forces of nationalism, which limited the amount of rational analysis possible. Think of rationality in connection with nuclear war. Surely, in crises leaders would be likely to act in ways that reflected stress and tension, rather than with the cool logic of a rational calculator. Also, the values in the pay-off matrix might change during the course of a crisis, particularly if that crisis involved nuclear weapons. Besides, Game Theory raises a serious problem by its very focus on decision-making. Since much foreign policy behaviour is the result of the processes by which it is *implemented*, a focus on the decision stage is unlikely to be able to explain it fully. To explain the decision or choice is not to explain the behaviour, and there seems no way that Game Theory can deal with implementation issues. This all makes signalling or tacit bargaining much more opaque in international relations than in two-person games.

A second problem concerns the view of the state as a unit, as a player in a game. There is really no such thing as 'Britain' acting in international relations, only a more or less co-ordinated set of agencies and ministries. It is not uncommon to find two government departments doing completely contradictory things. Similarly, bureaucratic politics implies that the game that is being played at any time may not be only the external one, since domestic manœuvring could also be crucial. Also, much political activity is confined to the realm of rhetoric. How can Game Theory cope with such different aspects of behaviour, especially when they may well be unco-ordinated, if not actually contradictory? The Foreign Office may have a foreign policy; so may the Defence Ministry, and the Trade Ministry, with the declaratory and operational policies of the political leadership acting as a further input rather than as a co-ordinator. Hence 'Britain' itself may not have a policy at all.

Thirdly, Game Theory makes assumptions that seem inappropriate to international relations. The most problematic are that the players understand the rules, can communicate (or at least have their strategies understood by the other player), and assign the same values to pay-offs. Yet, clearly, different societies evaluate the pay-offs differently, and the rules themselves are often perceived differently in different cultures. For example, US–Iranian relations in the early 1980s were marked by very different views of the world as epitomized in Iranian statements that the US could destroy Iranian oilfields, since Iran wanted to reverse the modernization process anyway. Similarly, the US had severe difficulties when it attempted to fight the Vietnam War as if it were an exercise in Game Theory. The Vietnamese constantly refused to rank the pay-offs in the same order as the US. Relatedly, it may be very problematic to assume that governments can assign interval utility scales to pay-offs, and they may not have consistent preferences. All these factors make the translation of Game Theory into international relations much less straightforward than it might appear at first sight.

Fourthly, a generic criticism of Game Theory is that it cannot deal well with the fact that the strategies individuals will follow will depend on their propensity to take risks. This is important for International Relations because of the very different cultures and sets of values involved. The main games depend on a similar attitude to risk. Put nuclear weapons into the picture and it becomes clear that the outcomes and strategies will depend on attitudes towards taking risks in a nuclear world. Would Chicken apply to a nuclear-armed Gadaffi–US crisis? Does 'the threat that leaves something to chance' require a similar regard for risk on both sides? It can be argued that whether an actor is governed by the Minimax or the Maximin principle (which refer, respectively, to the strategy of minimizing the maximum loss and maximizing the minimum gain) depends on an attitude to risk-taking or risk-avoidance that is cultural.

Fifthly, there is the question of whether incidents are to be thought of as one game or as repeated plays of the same game. Is each superpower crisis or arms control agreement a distinct game or are they all plays of the same game? This is in part a problem for the analyst but is also one for the players themselves. For instance, the USA might treat a crisis as a one-shot affair while the USSR treated it as one play in a series or supergame. The complexities of allowing for this in the analysis are a threat to the whole approach, especially if we add that the two sides may even differ about whether the game is, say, Chicken or the Prisoner's Dilemma.

Sixthly, the very fact that Game Theory has become so widely accepted makes it a dangerous tool of analysis in a world where policy-makers and planners try to apply it to what they too have come to see as a game. They will think of a crisis as an example of Chicken and try to design a dominant strategy. This has cumulative effects, especially if the other side comes to think of itself as a player too. As former US Secretary of State, Dean Rusk, has stated, there are real dangers for world peace if leaders treat crises as games of Chicken.

The seventh problem arises, relatedly, from the moral critique of Game Theory mentioned above. Because Game Theory claims to deal only in how people behave, and not with how they ought to behave, there is a danger that its values and assumptions will prevent consideration of moral questions. Political decisions always have a moral dimension. Yet Game Theory, by stressing rational choice and analytic logic, ignores morality in favour of technical expertise. By encouraging conceptions of brinkmanship and escalation dominance, it makes crisis management appear merely an exercise of scientific or technical knowledge. It encourages a notion of science and logic as being above political perspectives, and it gives considerable power to social scientists in white coats. Yet moral and ethical questions are at the centre of political debate and lie at the heart of policy-making. They cannot be avoided by claiming that what should be done is simply a matter of correctly understanding the pay-off matrix of the Chicken Game or the Prisoner's Dilemma.

Finally, Game Theory cannot be regarded as a scientific tool while there remain two radically different ways of conceiving its role. Is it, on the one hand, an observer's device for predicting and explaining what happens in situations with an objective structure idealized by the theory? Or is it, on the other, effective as a reading of the situation only if the players are themselves using it to read the situation, and, in that case, as an element in generating the outcomes? Here our distinction between Explaining and Understanding comes to life again, with the alternative pulling in radically different directions.

CONCLUSION

There is no simple summing up to be done. Game Theory certainly scores some successes, notably in analysing deterrence, crisis behaviour, and arms races in a way that other approaches cannot. As with the Prisoner's Dilemma, it shows why some outcomes occur regularly, despite the preferences and intentions of the players. It offers food for thought to any player or observer in search of escape from these mutually inferior outcomes. On the other hand, its abstractions and simplifications are so drastic that it becomes a suspect tool when it is pressed into service by policy-planners themselves. The actors need to be very sure that the situation confronting them is truly a Chicken situation before they make the choices which would be rational in the Chicken Game. They must also be sure that the choice that will emerge from the process of implementation will be their game choice and not something different, either in reality or in the eyes of the other players.

The crucial ambiguity remains the one just listed as the final disadvantage. Is it a theory about how actors think or about how the logic of their situation makes them behave? If it is the former, do its relevance and accuracy depend on whether the actors themselves are (or are advised by) Game Theorists? That these are far-reaching questions becomes clear as soon as we take a serious interest in the internal workings of states and organizations. That is the purpose of the next chapter and, when we return in Chapter 8 to the idea that international affairs are games which nations play, we shall find that we need a new notion of 'game' which is not the one proposed by the Theory of Games.

The eight doubts and queries about Game Theory are not conclusive but they do justify curiosity about the inner workings of the state. They at least postpone any conclusion that what systems theory cannot achieve by working 'top–down', Game Theory can complete by working 'bottom–up' with sealed units. It may be, of course, that no more than a detour is involved. It may turn out that, although the immediate causes of state behaviour need to be sought in domestic politics, the manœuvres of bureaucratic agencies, or the activities of particular human beings (as flesh-and-blood individuals), these factors have causes in their turn; which brings us back up to the topics of the last two chapters. But it may also be that the new account of the games nations play is one which calls for actors who are not throughputs in a larger calculation, and for understanding, rather than explanation. At any rate, the box is now open and the components most obviously visible to the inquisitive eye are the bureaucracies and other agencies of state.

7

Roles and Reasons

The last two chapters might have succeeded in settling the level-of-analysis problem without having to 'open the box'. This would have happened if a full-blown systemic determinism had carried all before it in Chapter 5. But even Waltz conceded that structures merely 'shape and shove', thus leaving room for some contribution to outcomes by the units of the system. Even so, we would still have settled the problem without opening the box if the hopes of Game Theory had succeeded in full in Chapter 6. In that case, states would have been suitable 'individuals' for purposes of an analysis where action was as construed by a theory of rational choice and interaction was as construed by Game Theory. Then whatever such an analysis failed to account for could have been attributed to shoving and shaping by the system, thus yielding an attractive compromise.

But we did not draw this conclusion. Chapter 5 left more room for questions about the decision-making process than Chapter 6 managed to fill. Game Theory relies on astringent assumptions about the rationality of actors, taken from microeconomic theories of individually rational choice. We found at least two kinds of element excluded by these assumptions and not attributable to the international system. One is the psychology of the individual human decision-makers and how it functions in small decision-making groups. The other is the bureaucratic organization of the domestic process of making policy and translating it into decision and implementation. The present chapter will explore these elements.

Opening the box does not settle the level-of-analysis problem. Indeed, it poses it afresh, this time as one about organizational structure and individual action. To bring this out, we shall put the emphasis on a 'Bureaucratic Politics' model which tries to analyse decisions by reference to the bureaucratic positions of those who make them. This will be opposed by the Rational Actor model as already introduced but now pitched at a more literally individual level instead of with states as 'individuals'. We shall not explore the psychology of the Rational Actor model in depth, however, nor argue out a parallel dispute between those who analyse individual psychology in terms of group psychology and those who analyse the group in terms of the individual. This dispute is, of course, interesting and important for the social sciences but it has not loomed large in International Relations and the theme of the book is better served by thinking deeply about the Bureaucratic Politics model.

Different ideas of Bureaucratic Politics give different scope for psychology, as will become clear. Our theme, however, is to do with Explaining and Understanding, rather than directly with the psychology of organizations. We shall begin with challenges to the Rational Actor assumptions of Game Theory which propose other ways of *explaining* the behaviour of states and then show how to recast the challenges, if the aim is *understanding*. It might sound as if the pivotal question is whether human actors have free will. But this is not the message. The Rational Actor model need not assume that choices are 'free', nor need the Bureaucratic Politics model deny it. Understanding need not assume the existence of a 'will', nor need Explanation deny it. The scope for free will is not irrelevant but does not directly favour taking particular sides or particular approaches.

More simply, International Relations has developed in ways which do not make free will the crux. The case for opening the box has arisen because Realism cannot keep it closed either in a full-blown systems version or in a version where the state is made a unitary rational actor by ascribing to it unitary self-interested motivation for Game Theoretic purposes. The case is therefore one about the inner workings of the process of decision. Historically it begins with two challenges which one might classify as psychological. We shall describe these briefly and then move on to the Bureaucratic Politics model.

THE PSYCHOLOGY OF 'RATIONAL' ACTORS

The first challenge stressed the need to identify the perceptions of those who took the decisions, and to recreate their 'definition of the situation'. This was seen by its proponents, notably Snyder, Bruck, and Sapin, who published their new framework in 1954,[1] as a massive attack on Realism, since it directly attacked the notion that states had interests and that the iron law of international relations was that states acted to maximize their power. Snyder replaced states with human individuals, and stressed not immutable laws of power maximization, but rather the importance of how the decision-maker defined the situation. This one publication was largely responsible for the development of the sub-field which came to be called 'foreign policy analysis'.

Of the many criticisms made of the Rational Actor framework, one is particularly relevant for our purposes. This was that the framework relied on a misleading notion of perception. Snyder was concerned with the reasons that actors give for their decisions, what may be termed 'in order to' motives. Critics retorted that the more useful kind of motives to concentrate on were what could be termed 'because of' motives. The difference is critical for how one attempts to open the box. The former type of motive concerns the *conscious reasons* actors give for their choices, whereas the latter involves the *conditioning* of the actors' choices. Why do actors see the world in certain ways? It is not explanatory just to say that this is how they see the world, if there are good grounds for thinking that their perceptions are caused by societal, cultural, historical, or economic factors. This has remained a strand in the discussions on the causes of foreign policy behaviour. It connects directly with the discussion in Chapter 5, in that the structure of the international system might be one major cause of decision-makers' perceptions of which issues are most important and which choices are most appropriate.

The second strand comes from the work done at the intersection of international relations and psychology.[2] Psychological attempts to explain the perceptions of decision-makers have become one of the most important areas of empirical analysis in International Relations in the last two decades. There are two main aspects. One is concerned with explaining how decision-makers misperceive

---

[1] R. C. Snyder, H. W. Bruck, and B. Sapin, *Decision-Making as an Approach to the Study of International Politics* (Princeton: Foreign Policy Analysis Series, no. 3, June 1954).

[2] The literature on belief-systems is summarized in S. Smith, 'Belief Systems and the Study of International Relations', in R. Little and S. Smith (eds.), *Belief Systems and International Relations* (Oxford: Blackwell, 1988), pp. 11–36.

and make errors of judgement in assessing information.[3] The other focuses on the generic concept of 'belief-system', and stresses the fact that perceptions of reality have to be, so to speak, filtered in order to simplify reality to manageable proportions. The filters work in a way fundamentally affected by the values of the decision-makers. Therefore, the box does not contain the pure rational choosers postulated by microeconomic theory. The information used in making choices, according to the belief-systems literature, is always shaped by wants and needs already programmed in the individual. If preferences affect information and its processing, we can no longer suppose that agents are rational maximizers or even rational satisficers.

For these reasons, it will not be easy to explain international relations without resort to notions of structure. At first sight, it seemed that once Waltz admitted that unit-level causes are important then we moved away from determining structures, and back to the familiar world of choice. However, when we move down from the systemic level to the unit level and then open the box, we find that the same set of issues re-emerges. Our actors may, at first sight, be rational human individuals, and this certainly seems far less remote and conjectural than notions of systemic causation. However, the battle between structures and choices is not the one involved in the first opening of the box. We will return to it in the following chapter when we look at the role of expectations and intentions in international relations. The point thus far is simply that opening the box does *not* move our explanations from the realm of cause to the realm of autonomous choice. Systems are not all-determining, but units (even human individuals) do not choose in a vacuum.

THE BUREAUCRATIC POLITICS MODEL

The units may themselves have structures that constrain and condition. They too, in Waltz's words, 'shape and shove'. Of many structures to which the student of politics could point, the most arresting is the bureaucratic structure of the state. It is hard to resist the thought that there is no such thing as a unified state, as

---

[3] R. Jervis, *Perception and Misperception in International Politics* (Princeton: Princeton University Press, 1976).

Realists and other systems theorists assume. Rather, the state is a set of bureaucracies, so related that decision-making within the state is not the action of a single unit.

The case has been most influentially put by Graham Allison in *Essence of Decision*.[4] The commonest way of explaining the foreign policy behaviour of states, he says, and the one used both by Realists and by those who reject the Realist account, is to treat the decision-making process within the state as a rational one. Allison's thesis can be summarized by listing his three main propositions:

1. Professional analysts of foreign affairs (as well as ordinary laymen) think about problems of foreign and military policy in terms of largely implicit conceptual models that have significant consequences for the content of their thought.

2. Most analysts explain (and predict) the behaviour of national governments in terms of one basic conceptual model, here entitled the Rational Actor or 'Classical' Model (Model I).

3. Two alternative conceptual models, here labelled an Organizational Process Model (Model II) and a Governmental (Bureaucratic) Politics Model (Model III), provide a base for improved explanations and predictions.[5]

The crux of his argument is that the dominance of the Rational Actor model results in a distorted account of foreign policy behaviour. It does so both when applied to states as units at the systems level and when applied to the decision-making process within the state. For instance, states are seen as personified by their leaders, who take decisions in order to achieve certain goals. Explanation consists in showing how the action was rational given the goals of the leaders. Rational Actor models explain foreign policy by seeing it as goal-directed, resulting from conscious choices made by leaders or groups with clear goals.

The problem with this account, says Allison, is that the state is not a monolith with interests. It is a collection of separate *organizations*, each with its own view of the world. Furthermore, decisions are not taken in accordance with some notion of a national interest, but result from pulling and hauling between bureaucracies.

[4] G. Allison, *Essence of Decision: Explaining the Cuban Missile Crisis* (Boston: Little, Brown, 1971). [5] Ibid. pp. 3–5.

In place of the Rational Actor account, Allison suggests two alternative models. The first is the *Organizational Process* model. Whereas the Rational Actor account characterizes decisions as the conscious choices of decision-makers, this model sees them as the outputs of large organizations, functioning according to standard operating procedures. This model is especially instructive for understanding the process of implementing a decision, which so often defeats the declared intention. But it invites the view that decision-making is itself an organizational process; and, of course, it is the behaviour as implemented that the decision-makers of other states have to respond to in terms of imputing intentions to that behaviour. This is a theme that will be taken up in the next chapter.

The second alternative account is more the concern of this chapter, with its basic argument that foreign policy is less the result of decision-making than of bargaining among the groups within the state's decision-making machinery. Foreign policy therefore is less the rational choice of *the* state than the end product of a process of bargaining between groups within the state, each of which has its own view of the interests of the state. Moreover, Allison goes on to say that these different views of the interests of the state are determined by the positions that the individuals concerned occupy within the decision-making apparatus. The golden rule is: 'where you stand depends on where you sit.'[6] Accordingly, the *Bureaucratic Politics* account offers a fresh view of decision-making. It also brings structure back in, since the choices made by decision-makers are determined by their bureaucratic positions. Their personalities and personal preferences are much less important in determining their stance on a policy issue than are the positions they occupy in the bureaucratic structure.

In *Essence of Decision* Allison tested the three models by their ability to answer the three central questions of the Cuban Missile Crisis. (Why did the Soviet Union put the missiles on Cuba? Why did the United States respond with a blockade? Why did the Soviet Union withdraw the missiles?) Since then his work has come in for much criticism,[7] but although this criticism may have shown that

---

[6] Allison, *Essence of Decision*, p. 176.
[7] These are discussed in S. Smith, 'Allison and the Cuban Missile Crisis: A Review of the Bureaucratic Politics Model of Foreign Policy Decision-Making', *Millennium*, 1980, 9(1), pp. 21–40.

Allison's account of the crisis is misleading, and has identified several problems with his alternative models of decision-making, the Bureaucratic Politics model remains the major alternative to the Rational Actor account of decision-making. Also, by replicating the system-level conflict between internal and external sources of behaviour, it forces us to consider whether opening the box does really invite a psychological concession to those who favour accounts stressing choice and calculation by those who prefer accounts phrased in terms of causes and structures.

THE IRANIAN HOSTAGE CRISIS

To examine the utility of the Bureaucratic Politics model we shall take a more recent case study which offers scope both to Allison's thesis and to its critics. In April 1980, the United States attempted to rescue fifty-three American hostages held in Iran.[8] The process by which this decision was reached illuminates three debates within the area of international relations: first, the relative impact of internal and external causes on foreign policy-making; second, the manner and degree of influence which a system has on its constituent units; and third, the importance of the reasons that individuals give for their policy preferences.

The decision of the US government to attempt to rescue the hostages in Iran in April 1980 offers a very good example of the conflict between Rational Actor and Bureaucratic Politics models of individual behaviour. Following the seizure of the hostages in November 1979 the US government undertook various measures to try to obtain their freedom.[9] Of these, the military route was the

[8] The detail of the case study is dealt with in a number of sources. Particularly useful are W. Christopher (ed.), *American Hostages in Iran* (New Haven: Yale University Press, 1985) and R. McFadden, J. Treaster, and M. Carroll (eds.), *No Hiding Place* (New York: New York Times Books, 1981). The outline used in this chapter is based on S. Smith, 'The Hostage Rescue Mission', in S. Smith and M. Clarke (eds.), *Foreign Policy Implementation* (London: Allen and Unwin, 1985), pp. 11–32.

[9] From the seizure of the hostages, the US government followed a number of paths in parallel to attempt to secure the hostages' release. They embarked on a series of economic measures (in the form of sanctions), used the offices of third parties (such as the United Nations Secretary General), built a coalition of political support for their case (for example by getting their allies to put pressure on the Iranians), and studied a range of military options. These are discussed at length in Christopher, *American Hostages in Iran* and McFadden *et al.*, *No Hiding Place*.

most controversial within the decision-making group and it was only when the prospects for successful negotiation seemed to be very low, in late March/early April 1980, that President Carter began to move towards a rescue mission. Among his advisers there was a fundamental division over the acceptability of using military force: on the one hand, there was a group of four who had advocated a rescue mission ever since the seizure of the hostages (National Security Adviser Zbigniew Brzezinski, Secretary of Defense Harold Brown, Chairman of the Joint Chiefs of Staff David Jones, and Head of the CIA Stansfield Turner); on the other, there was one individual who had consistently counselled against the use of force (Secretary of State Cyrus Vance). In between was a set of presidential advisers (Vice-President Walter Mondale, Press Secretary Jody Powell, and Political Adviser Hamilton Jordan) concerned above all with getting Carter re-elected. At three key meetings on 22 March, 11 April, and 15 April 1980 a plan to rescue the hostages was mooted, discussed, and then agreed. This plan was implemented on 24 April. It failed. The rescue force never got beyond its initial staging post in Iran, owing to the break-down of three of the eight helicopters that were to transport the force to the outskirts of Tehran.

How shall we try to explain the decisions taken, given the interplay of international and domestic factors, of differing bureaucracies, and of individual psychologies? Disciples of Allison will be quick to point out that throughout the crisis the policy advice offered consistently went with the bureaucratic position of the adviser. The mounting of the rescue mission is ready grist to the Bureaucratic Politics mill. At the same time, however, there is much that could be said about the psychology of the principal actors. They had their own perceptions, motives and beliefs. Hawks like Brzezinski gave hawkish advice; doves like Cyrus Vance counselled diplomacy. Autobiographies, here as always in foreign affairs, testify to the importance which the actors themselves attach to their personal judgements. Yet the Rational Actor and Bureaucratic Politics models make scant allowances for personalities. We shall next make it clear why this is so. Then we shall complain that both take the actors too lightly. But we do not thereby intend a plea for an independent psychology. The moral will be that the Rational Actor model needs an improved notion of a reason for action and that the Bureaucratic Politics model needs an improved concept of role. Once these amendments are made, it will turn out that the actors matter more than before; but not because personality is a key independent variable.

The Rational Actor model, as presented in earlier chapters, relies on an instrumental notion of rationality, where preferences (or goals or ends) are given and choices are confined to means. It does not care where preferences come from nor does it insist that they be aimed at profit, power, status, or any particular 'good'. It has nothing to say about the rationality of an actor's goals, except that they must be internally consistent. When it is applied to economics, it is thus a further step to claim that firms, rather than individuals within them, can be usefully treated as individuals and that profit, rather than anything else, is their goal. Similarly, a Rational Actor model in international relations is more basic than a theory about states pursuing national interests. Consequently, the model is not finished if advocates of Bureaucratic Politics can prove that analysis needs a smaller unit than the nation state or a motivating factor other than national interest. But that says nothing about personalities, and powerful generalizing models have a stake in doing without them.

Bureaucracies are party to foreign policy-making to a systematic and theoretically tempting degree. It is at least often plausible to think of 'the national interest' as a policy defined through a power struggle among competing bureaucracies and termed 'the national interest' as a mark of the winner's success in the competition. A stark version of the idea makes the actors wholly institutional. Men and women take the stage solely as mouthpieces or puppets of the bureaucracies which send them into the fray. These bureaucracies form structures whose effects make them seem as if they had a life and power of their own. They select, promote, and train the sort of people who will perceive situations and act in them as suits their bureaucratic position. This version, we hasten to add, is more starkly structural–functionalist than Allison and others would wish to propose, but it provides a limiting case to compare with an equally pure Rational Actor model.[10]

[10] Allison's account of the Bureaucratic Politics model does include a discussion of how preferences are formed (Allison, *Essence of Decision*, pp. 166–8), but, despite his claims as to the importance of perceptions and the influence of personality, his model works by the implication that position determines preferences. Because of this, our characterization of the mechanism of the model is

With the models idealized so starkly, neither looks appealing on its own. On the one hand, it seems plainly perverse for the Rational Actor model to try ignoring the bureaucratic input to the decisions of nation states. On the other, it seems just as plain that bureaucrats calculate means to ends and hence are in some limited sense rational actors. Hence it is tempting to demand a concession from both sides. It now matters that the nation state need not be the fundamental unit of the theory of rational choice, applied to foreign policy. The concession from the Rational Actor side is to be willing to switch from nation states to individuals when the occasion demands. Sometimes at least Jimmy Carter is to be thought of as Jimmy Carter maximizing his expected utility rather than as the embodiment of the US pursuing American interests. Provided that Jimmy Carter is not, so to speak, a law unto himself but is a predictable individual, that keeps the rational-economic-man core of the model while increasing its flexibility. The concession from the Bureaucratic Politics side is to grant that bureaucrats think for themselves in the service of their bureau-cracies. Then, apparently, the two models can be neatly combined, so as to make foreign policy the province of economically rational bureaucrats. This would leave a demarcation problem. Where you stand would depend both on where you sit and how you think, with the proportions requiring further examination. But the central theoretical dispute would have yielded to negotiated settlement with neither side needing to introduce 'personalities'.[11]

Our philosophical objection will be that *both* models have a wrong view of the nature of action. Crudely, both are too mechanical. If a pure bureaucrat would be merely a puppet and a pure *homo economicus* merely a set of preferences coupled to a computer, then a mixture would not be magically less pre-programmed than either. But the point needs making by means of discussing the philosophy of action in relation to the theory of roles, and that will come better if the case for it emerges from an

a stark one, but one that relates to the actual use Allison makes of the model in explaining the positions adopted in the Cuban Missile Crisis, since, despite Allison's claims to the contrary, the model is essentially a deterministic one with bureaucratic position dominating other sources of preferences.

[11] Allison goes so far as to suggest just this combination when he writes, in a footnote: 'How each [bureaucratic] player ranks his interests . . . is a subtle, complex problem. In one sense, players seem to have gone through a Model I [Rational Actor] analysis' (*Essence of Decision*, p. 171).

example. Let us pause to consider the hostage crisis as a test of the prospects for a compromise between the models.

As already noted, by late March 1980 it no longer seemed to President Carter and his principal advisers that there was serious prospect of releasing the hostages by negotiation. The case for a rescue mission was building up, but there was a fundamental split on the acceptability of military force. There was the group of four who had advocated a rescue from the start; at the other pole, Secretary of State Cyrus Vance had counselled against the use of force throughout. At the meeting on 22 March it was decided that a reconnaissance flight to verify the first desert staging post could take place. The decision to mount a rescue mission was taken on 11 April. Vance's rearguard objections were overruled at the 15 April meeting. While the two main factions (the four 'hawks' and the 'dove') stuck to their positions, the key determinant was a change on the part of President Carter himself and the group of 'presidential supporters'. This group owed its presence and immediate loyalty to the President and his office. With the US Presidential election in the offing and, they reckoned, little prospect of negotiations for another five or six months, they represented a pressure on the President to 'do something'. Action was needed to counter Republican charges of indecisiveness and a dramatic slide in the President's public opinion rating. By early April only Cyrus Vance was left resisting a strong consensus that Carter had to try a rescue mission.

The key meeting on 11 April was notable for the absence of Vance. He had left for Florida the day before to take a 'much-needed' vacation. Since he had voiced his opposition even to a reconnaissance, when that had been decided upon on 22 March, the others could not have doubted his opposition to a rescue mission and indeed were finding him a source of annoyance and frustration. So the fact that he was not informed that a rescue mission would be proposed on 11 April makes it most likely that his exclusion was deliberate.[12] At the meeting he was represented

---

[12] The memoirs of the participants claim that Vance 'just happened' to be away; Vance himself claims that his exclusion was deliberate. The press reports of the time indicate that he was indeed deliberately excluded. Given his well-known opposition to a rescue mission and the extent of agreement among the other members of the decision-making group it seems most probable that the meeting was arranged for a time when it was known that he would be away.

by his deputy, Warren Christopher, who, on hearing the proposal, spoke strongly against it. At this point he was erroneously informed by President Carter that Cyrus Vance had said that, if there was to be military action, he would prefer a rescue mission. Christopher had not discussed the proposal with Vance (whom he wrongly presumed to know of it) beforehand and, on finding himself a lone voice, did not register his opposition formally. When Vance learnt what had happened from Christopher on his return, he went to see the President and lodged a long list of objections. These he then presented to a reconvened meeting on 15 April, where they met with a 'deafening silence'. The decision was confirmed and on 21 April he tendered his resignation, with the understanding that its announcement would be delayed until the rescue mission had taken place with whatever result. The resignation was announced on 28 April.

At first glance this chronicle strongly favours the Bureaucratic Politics model.[13] The participants adopted policy preferences consistent with their various offices. Cyrus Vance (and Warren Christopher) had a State Department eye to wider implications in the Middle East, especially those concerned with the influence of the Soviet Union. It is also relevant that the hostages were State Department employees. As evidence that Bureaucratic Politics matters significantly, notice that Vance and Christopher spoke with one mind on a proposal which they had not discussed. Those concerned with national security addressed the crisis from the angle of national security. The 'presidential supporters' were nervous of the effect of a protracted stalemate on the end of the President's first term and his re-election chances. These allegiances are so striking that one might even surmise that, had the participants switched positions, they would also have switched preferences.

But the very thought of Brzezinski cooing like a dove is enough to suggest caution. Before even mooting this ornithological wonder, we need a clear theoretical account of the relationship between the positions which actors occupy and the choices which they make. We shall next do our best to offer one under the headings of 'roles' and 'reasons'.

---

[13] This is the argument put forward in S. Smith, 'Policy Preferences and Bureaucratic Position: The Case of the American Hostage Rescue Mission', *International Affairs*, 1985, 61(1), pp. 9–25.

REWORKING THE MODELS: ROLES AND REASONS

Even with options simplified and hesitations suppressed, the
hostage crisis decisions do not endorse the idea that positions
completely *dictate* actions. To define 'role' as 'the dynamic
aspect of a social position' (as beginners in sociology are often
invited to do) is only a start. How do the dynamics work? The key,
in our view, is that the imperatives of a role both constrain and
enable actors in their dealings with others. The constraining
element is easier to grasp. Think of the Bureaucratic Politics
model as involving:

1. a set of recognized *positions*, each with its own power;
2. normative expectations, constituting the *role* of each in-
   cumbent of a position;
3. obedient *actors*.

The constraint on the obedient actors lies in the normative
expectations upon them, reinforced by sanctions. 'Normative'
refers not to what is normal or usual but to what is required, in the
sense that failure to perform the role is open to criticism, censure,
and penalty. The expectations are partly those which go with the
positions and partly those of other actors in other positions, who
are role-partners (or opponents) in various settings. From this
standpoint roles do also enable, since the position which is the
source of the requirements is also a source of the power to carry
them out. But the requirements sound principally like commands
which take away discretion.

It soon emerges, however, that this apparatus sits rather loosely
on the actors. No role could possibly be specified in enough detail
to make all decisions automatic. There is no handbook, even a
mental one, in which Vance could look up 'Crisis, hostage,
Iranian, response to, (i) in a Presidential election year . . .'. There
are some specific duties of a role, some dos and don'ts which set
limits to what may be attempted. But there is also an area of
indeterminacy, governed only by a broad duty to act so as to be
able to justify oneself afterwards and to keep both one's job and
one's credibility. For instance, the fact that the hostages were
State Department employees made Vance particularly responsible
for their safety but did not oblige him to oppose a rescue. It did
make it harder for him to support one, but it still left it open to him

to argue that the bold course would be safer in the end or that other cares of state justified the risk. To be brief, 'normative expectations' are never fully specific and can be made formally complete only by including a general requirement to do one's best for one's bureaucracy.

A role is also prone to be inconsistent, at least in particular situations. It may well be, for example, that the President had no course of action open to him which would satisfy all the claims upon him. 'No win' situations are common enough. A subtler source of inconsistency is that roles are often defined in the course of internal manœuvres within a bureaucracy and carry traces of this internal conflict. The State Department, for instance, has a shifting and disunited view of the Secretary of State's job, which is hardly surprising when one notes that the State Department is itself a plurality of persons with different roles, as is any bureaucracy. Even where rules of priority are included in a role, they are bound to be rough and to leave the actor with some warrant for either of two incompatible choices.

Furthermore, role-players each have several roles. All those present at the key meetings had a duty towards the hostages. Although this duty could be said to be part of each role represented (National Security Adviser as well as Secretary of State), it is clearer to say that Brzezinski was not involved *solely* as National Security Adviser. Besides he was also, possibly, a churchgoer and a morally concerned human being. At some point one may wish to maintain that moral concern is not a role-expectation, because it is a personal matter (although this may also be a matter of cause not choice). But, leaving questions of this boundary aside for the moment, there is no denying that conflict between roles is as common as conflict within them. When it occurs the actor has to decide which role shall prevail. This decision cannot, in the nature of the case, be mechanical.

Even with an institutional idea of what constitutes 'position' and 'role', therefore, an obedient actor is not always a mechanical actor. The point becomes plainer still in another standard analysis of role-playing, where concepts are borrowed from the theatre. Social roles can be thought of by analogy with character parts, with episodes in social life conceived as if they had been loosely scripted for a given set of *dramatis personae*. There are two ways of reading this dramaturgical analogy, instructively different but neither making the actors mechanical, because both involve a notion of role-distance. The simpler thinks of play-acting as the donning and doffing of masks by actors who are pretending to be the characters in the play. By this account 'National Security Adviser' is a role to be played for Brzezinski's private purposes, which may or may not have much to do with the requirements of office. He must still be able to legitimate his actions by reference to national security, since he is there to represent national security. But the true motives for his actions need not be those which he professes. Whatever the merits of this account of theatre, its view of actors is markedly unmechanical.

We hasten to add that the analogy need not be read like this. On a different account of theatre actors do not merely pretend to be characters in the play but personify them. Think, for instance, of Gielgud or Olivier as King Lear. In this case, differences in how the part is played are a matter not of differing private aims but of differing interpretations of what the play means. In other words, role-distance can be thought of not as standing outside the play but as detached judgement within it. It will be plain by the end of the chapter that this is how we recommend taking the analogy ourselves. For the moment, we insist only that on both accounts of the theatrical analogy the notion of 'obedience' which role theory involves is a flexible one, reinforcing the crucial theme that roles enable as well as constrain. But, of course, the script is still the same, and so is the outcome of the play! We carefully leave open the question of how they constrain and how much they enable.

Roles enable, we suggest, in the sense that they assign particular, underdefined responsibilities to particular people together with (often inadequate) resources to help discharge them. On this view there is finally no substitute for the actor's own judgement. The area of judgement need not be conceived of as, somehow, internally generated and outside the role. When actors are called to account afterwards, the issue is their conduct of the office and not, or not always, their private integrity. Thus Vance's responsibility was to speak for the State Department, which had a special concern for the safety of its employees. It was his decision what to say and how to play the role. He was accountable for his stewardship of an office, whose power was probably not large enough for his voice to prevail alone, however he used it.

That seems to us a more promising version of the Bureaucratic

Politics model than one which gives all the work (or as much as possible) to the actor's position and fails to notice that positions enable as well as constrain. It does nothing to show why some positions have more *power* than others and it raises a suspicion that *personality* may, after all, count for more in the exercise of power, especially in élite decision-making groups, than seems to suit any version of the model. These matters will be taken up presently. First, however, we shall rework the Rational Actor model, so that it too is less mechanical.

Standard versions of the model, like the one which we gave earlier, seem not to involve any presumption about how the mind works. A rational agent is simply one who maximizes expected utility subject to constraints—a criterion which can be applied to units like firms or nation states as readily as to human individuals. But there is a standard philosophical presumption here. It is that action results from a combination of belief and desire, with desire supplying the impulse or, so to speak, motor. The source of it is David Hume's *A Treatise of Human Nature* (1739), which we mentioned before for its splendid attempt to say how a science of mind could be established. Central to it is a claim about the relation of 'Reason' to 'Passion' (or, in modern terms, information and its processing to preferences). Hume holds that 'Reason alone can never be a motive to any action of the will'; 'Reason is and ought only to be the slave of the passions, and can never pretend to any other office than to serve and obey them.'[14] The science of mind studies how passions are translated into action and how reason can be made to serve them more effectively.

It is worth pausing to notice what this does and does not imply about rational action. It implies that Reason, being only a slave of the passions, has no comment to make on the agent's preferences, provided that they are consistent. This is the source of the idea that motivation resides in given preferences, with no scope for questioning the rationality of ends. It does *not* imply, however, that rational action must always be self-interested, in the sense of 'selfish'. Agents cannot be motivated by belief alone (and so not by a pure belief that a course of action is morally right) but their motivating desires can include sympathy or affection for others. In

---

[14] D. Hume, *A Treatise of Human Nature* [1739], ed. L. A. Selby-Bigge (Oxford: Oxford University Press, 1978), book ii, part 3, section 3. For a helpful commentary see B. Stroud, *Hume* (London: Routledge and Kegan Paul, 1977).

other words, their passions must be their own but need not be egoistic in any narrower sense. It is an empirical question, not a matter of definition, whether human beings are 'self-interested' in the narrower sense so often assumed by economists and others impressed by economics.

We are not saying that Hume is right. There are eminent sources of a contrary view, notably Thomas Hobbes in *Leviathan*. But we do wish to point out that a Rational Actor model should not build in a narrow idea of self-interest without explicitly arguing the case for it. Similarly, neither are we claiming that Hume is right to hold that 'Reason alone can never be a motive to any action of the will'. Eminent sources of a contrary view here include Immanuel Kant, whose ethics of duty depend on proving that a rational agent can be moved to action just by recognizing that a course of action is the right one. A Rational Actor model, therefore, should not assume without argument even that preferences must be given. In theory, at least, it could include provision for rational actors to form their own preferences. Hume's philosophy of mind is squarely behind Max Weber's ideal type of instrumentally rational action. But it is contestable, either by confining the passions to narrowly egoistic 'self-interest' or by extending the scope of Reason.

Hence, if the standard Rational Actor model embodies too mechanical a view of the mind in action, it can be made more flexible. In particular, one need not treat Reason as a mere processing device for producing behaviour which maximizes the satisfaction of given preferences in response to changes in the agent's situation. It should be possible to allow the agent more scope for judgement and thus allow room for the sort of points just made about bureaucratic role-play. But we need to distinguish two ways of trying to combine the models. One works by injecting preferences originating in the agent's bureaucratic position into the preference schedule of the information-processing agent. This remains a mechanical account of action, since adding a bureaucratic mechanism to a computing mechanism does not produce something less mechanical than either. The other works by changing the theoretical character of the agent who plays the roles and judges the shrewdest course of action. But too much flexibility may threaten Hume's aim of founding a *science*.[15]

[15] For further discussion see M. Hollis, *The Cunning of Reason* (Cambridge: Cambridge University Press, 1988), chs. 5 and 6.

PERSONALITY AND POWER

We have shown how both models—Rational Actor and Bureau-cratic Politics—can be reworked so as to take account of enable-ments as well as of constraints. To make it plainer what this comes to, we can now pursue the question about personality and its bearing on the exercise of power. We might hope that a more flexible Rational Actor model would have scope for personality. But, as just noted, that depends on how the flexibility is achieved. If it is done merely by enriching the agent's preferences, then the model will still work by ironing out individual differences. It will still consist of a universal computing unit programmed for whatever preferences agents may have. If the preferences are simply generated by the demands of bureaucratic position, we are no further forward.

So let us try a large change in the character of rational agents, by emphasizing the fluidity of role-play and enlarging the scope for Reason. Consider, for instance, the factor of 'hawkishness'. The standard Bureaucratic Politics move is to say that some positions demand hawkish personalities and are therefore filled by suitable agents, whose preferences can thus be predicted. This strikes us as an implausibly simple-minded view of what a position 'requires'. Let us instead consider 'hawkishness' not as an input but as a type of interpretation by an actor in taking decisions underdetermined by information and rules of calculation.

At this point it should be helpful to hand over to the Rational Actor model. But, in the standard version, it is not. There is no such thing as 'hawkish data-processing', because the calculating unit is universal. That is not good enough. For the group around the President's table at the key meetings there were large problems of interpreting the facts, of weighing their importance and of assessing likely reactions to any American move. These problems, we suggest, are wrongly described as those of calculating accurately in the face of uncertainties. The scope for pure calculation was too small and the results too sensitive to changes in the interpretations on which they could be based. Or, to put it the other way, the scope for judgement was too large. Personality types matter because they affect the sort of judgements which an actor makes, when trying to decide the course of action for which there are the better reasons. They need to be considered under the heading of 'belief' at least as much as under that of 'desire'.

The notion of rational judgement is thus to be detached from a limiting case of perfect computing with complete information and reworked as one of reasoned belief. 'Hawks' and 'doves' differ both in the reasons they give for their interpretation of evidence and in their reasons for expecting a course of action to lead to one result rather than another. The giving of reasons is itself, however, a part of a process of reasoned debate. A reworked Rational Actor model which had something substantial to say about this process would be a useful tool for the study of international relations.

An obvious feature of debate and discussion is that it affects the beliefs of those taking part. We do not mean that those present are rational innocents who always accept the better case. There are, for instance, pressures of 'groupthink' which can greatly influence perception and judgement in ways unmentioned in a logician's handbook.[16] Also, some debate is merely artificial in the sense that it is sheer manœuvre in a language of reason by persons who have no intention of budging from their pre-set, perhaps bureaucratically determined, views. But we certainly suppose that there is some genuine uncertainty among those who sit down to decide on foreign policy. Where it exists, the actors are in search of reasoned judgements, and personality has a legitimate part in shaping the collective decision. In the language of International Relations theory, personality is a crucial factor in the mind-sets or belief-systems of the individual decision-makers. Beliefs about what should be affect beliefs about what is. This is particularly the case when belief-systems are 'closed', so that information is processed in such a way as to reduce cognitive dissonance, thereby preventing information from challenging deeply held beliefs. This is also a source of misperception.

'Personality' can be incorporated, then, partly by showing how bureaucratic positions are suited to particular personalities, but more by reworking the relation of the models. Our role-player is not a self-contained processing device whose inputs are supplied by a bureaucracy. Roles call for judgement, which involves reasoned belief, self-monitoring of aims, and a general shrewdness. These elements are not covered by 'information processing'. So we propose amending the Rational Actor model to include them.

[16] See S. Smith, 'Groupthink and the Hostage Rescue Mission', *British Journal of Political Science*, 1985, 15(1), pp. 117–23.

Roles and Reasons

That also changes the relation of the models, since the bureaucratic and calculative aspects of role-playing now fuse. We do not insist that this move deals with the 'personality' variable completely, since it would be odd if psychology were left nothing substantial to say about international relations. But we do suppose that it is no longer an extraneous factor, with mysterious influence. At any rate, we now turn to the more awkward question of power.

In their opening versions the two models have markedly different views of the nature and workings of power. The Bureaucratic Politics model so far locates power in bureaucratic structures in varying amounts which show up in the ability of one bureaucracy to dominate another. In the Rational Actor model so far power is revealed typically in the price of actors' compliance, or, rather, in the system of prices within which bargains are struck to the greater or lesser advantage of particular actors. Neither approach seems to us sufficiently revealing, and an attempt to combine them creates a puzzle about their relation. The key questions are how power functions and how deep in the system to locate its sources. We shall treat them as queries about the ability of one agent or group of agents to impose an outcome on another.[17]

The clearest expression of power comes at the moment of a disputed decision. On 22 March 1980 Cyrus Vance's objections to a reconnaissance mission were overriden. On 11 April his objections to a rescue mission were dismissed *in absentia*. On 15 April his attempts to state them in person met with 'deafening silence'. But even this simple sequence makes the point that power is not confined to overt conflict. There was no overt dissenting vote on 11 April. Vance had been neatly removed to the sidelines beforehand and his deputy did not press the State Department's doubts to a vote. Even the fact that a rescue mission was on the agenda was off the agenda given to the losers. The power of the winners had been exercised even before the meeting started.

Attention moves to the earlier phase of manœuvre, during

---

[17] We gratefully acknowledge a large debt to Steven Lukes in *Power: A Radical View* (London: Macmillan, 1974) and his other writings on the subject. The next paragraph relies on his 'first dimension', where power is the ability to win in overt conflict. The following paragraph is about his 'second dimension', where the crux is the ability to keep opposing views off the agenda. But we diverge at the 'third dimension', which Lukes discusses in terms of real interests, whereas we are content to talk about the manipulation of opposing desires. (Against Lukes, we believe that people can exercise power contrary to their own real interests.)

which the presidential supporters came around to wanting a rescue mission. This shift spelt the defeat of the State Department, since it gave the hawks a majority to count on. The chief reason for it lay, however, in the changing mood of public opinion and not in the activity of the defence spokesmen. Since there is no theoretical obscurity about the idea of manœuvre and outmanœuvre, we shall not linger here.

The difficult aspect of power concerns the engineering of preferences. If the first test of power is in overt conflict between competing preferences and the second is in covert, pre-agenda conflict also between competing preferences, then the third is in conflict over the formation of preferences. Agent A has a distinguishable and important kind of power over agent B, if A, confronted with B's preference for x over y, can cause B to prefer y to x. Whether B's preference change is the result of A's power depends on how the change comes about. For instance, policy preferences respond to new information. In the main, that falls under the heading of rational deliberation and is not to be regarded as engineering from without; but where the trigger is deliberate misinformation, that is engineering. Had the outcome on 11 April hung on a single vote which Carter swung by wrongly telling Christopher that Vance had conceded the issue, this would have been an exercise of power.

With the focus on the formation of preferences, the Rational Actor model is at a disadvantage. Its earlier version works with an instrumental notion of rationality, where preferences are given and action results from rational deliberation. It is silent about the source of preferences and drifts into trouble as soon as it admits that preferences can be reshaped in or by the process of decision. The Bureaucratic Politics model is better placed. If one thinks of bureaucratic role-players as stewards of their offices, working chiefly in the permissive area between what the role definitely requires and what it definitely forbids, then the manipulative aspect of power is more readily understood. The actors' interpretation of their roles depends on their reading of the situation, which, like their judgement of how to act, is significantly influenced by the need to justify themselves on return to home base. If that makes the process too conscious, then it is also the case that preferences are formulated by the bureaucratic mind-set associated with particular positions. Since individual bureaucrats have to work within a given structure, and co-operate with others, they come to see the world in certain ways. These ways are not solely confined to the interpretation of evidence, but also relate to the determination of what issues are most important. Adherence to the bureaucracy's point of view and priorities is required in order to gain promotion.

We thus hope to tame the 'power' variable too. On a role-playing account it is not just stuff which some bureaucracies have more of. It is an ability which goes with different offices in varying degree, provided that the actor has the skill to use it. This skill is one of those involved in reasoned judgement and, because it is a skill, we can understand how the distribution of power among players of different ability can change during the game. If we may speculate, the initial distribution at the start of a game is at least partly the cumulative result of previous games. As with the 'personality' variable, we do not suppose that all questions thus disappear. We have not conjured the idea of power structures out of existence. The actor, after all, cannot fundamentally shift the distribution of power between bureaucracies. But we do suggest that our notion of role goes some way towards understanding changes in power.

ROLES AND PERSONS

Earlier we toyed with the idea of Brzezinski becoming Secretary of State and cooing like a dove. We called it an ornithological wonder, implying that it could not happen. Yet office-holders do change sides. Many British ministers, for instance, have found themselves appointed to the Treasury and arguing fervently against all that they had proposed under their previous hats. There remains a tantalizing query about the relation of offices to incumbents, despite the claims so far made for our notion of role.[18]

---

[18] See the discussion on this in G. H. Snyder and P. Diesning, *Conflict among Nations* (Princeton University Press, 1977), pp. 297–310; A. L. George, *Presidential Decision-Making in Foreign Policy* (Boulder, CO: Westview, 1980), pp. 55–80; and R. Betts, *Soldiers, Statesmen and Cold War Crises* (Cambridge, MA: Harvard University Press, 1977), pp. 174–82 and 209–12.

Return to the question of why hawks are hawks. That question is awkward if posed before the models have been reworked. While the Rational Actor model was all to do with 'economic' calculation and the Bureaucratic Politics model all to do with positions, there was a gap for awkward questions about personalities. Nor could the gap be closed simply by adding the unamended models together. It is false that policy is the output of information dictated, in the form of perceptions, by bureaucratic position and processed as in the pure theory of rational choice. It is also false that what passes for deliberation is at heart only the grinding of a bureaucratic system in which all officials are wholly *partis pris*. In other words, the notion of 'role' originally offered by the one model will not combine with the notion of 'reason' offered by the other, unless both models are reworked first. The reworking yields an idea of reasoned role-playing which explains why hawks are hawks.

The central point can be put most clearly as a gloss on the concept of role-distance. This usually refers to the sort of detachment from a role which goes with disenchantment, alienation, and covert private purposes. But we have a different sort of detachment in mind. Foreign policy is made, in our view, by persons in various offices, who need to juggle with the imperatives of office, to display skill in negotiation and readiness to concede one point for the sake of another, to ride the horses of role-conflict, and to interpret a changing situation with a mixture of impartiality and commitment. These are talents which, while being broad requirements of office, demand that roles be played with distance. Moreover, the exact ingredients and blend vary from role to role. The role of National Security Adviser in 1980 would have reduced any dove, carelessly appointed to it, to incompetence. Hawks are hawks, because only hawks can assemble the pieces of an office which needs a hawk with any consistency.

That also makes for a concept of rationality which philosophers will find more familiar than economists. We reject the 'economic' view that reasons for action reduce to correctly calculated expected utilities of means to unquestioned ends. Our actors *interpret* information, *monitor* their performance, *reassess* their goals. The leading idea is that of reasoned judgement, not of computation. The difference is that decision-making is not to be studied by decomposing groups into individuals and individuals into self-contained subprocesses. Instead, it is to be regarded as an interaction among disparate, intelligent role-players. Furthermore, decision-making does not occur at a single instant, as the timeless models of microeconomics seem to suggest. Today's interaction is steeped in yesterday's engagements. Officials bring with them powers, perceptions, and aims which were shaped in previous manœuvres. The student ignorant of yesterday's events will not understand the reasons for today's reasoned judgements, since those preferences may result from previous bureaucratic disputes. The same goes, we might add, for the role-players themselves.[19]

That, then, is our general line, to be pursued further in the next chapter. But there still remains an itch of curiosity about the persons who play the roles. Brzezinski stubbornly remains himself. We seem to catch glimpses of him in all his manœuvres. But to make him the unique, active individual which no doubt he rejoices in being is to pose a new threat to the enterprise. If foreign policy is finally the work of unique persons there will be nothing of systematic explanatory value to say about its ultimate workings.

To retain elements of structure, we shall invoke a fresh element: the language in which the process of decision is conducted. Return for a moment to the initial Rational Actor thought that foreign affairs resemble a market in which the firms are nation states pursuing, as an analogue of profit, their national interest. This image retains an important truth. The internal language of decision is the language of national interest. The meetings of 22 March, 11 April, and 15 April were called to decide what the American response should be. The State Department voice, for instance, spoke not of what would profit the State Department but of what was best for America. When introducing the Bureaucratic Politics model initially, we remarked dismissively that the 'national interest' can often be regarded merely as the name of the policy which wins in the bureaucratic power struggle. That is much too offhand. It implies that, if bureaucracies are the key unit, then talk of a larger body, like the nation, is mere words. Explanation, it might seem, truly operates only at the level upon which actors are sincerely engaged, as opposed to the levels at which they find it convenient to pitch their words.

There is a large *non sequitur* here. The language of decision-

[19] See L. Freedman, 'Logic, Politics and Foreign Policy Processes', *International Affairs*, 1976, 52(3), pp. 434–49.

making is also the language of manœuvre. It constrains and enables the actors, whatever their personal aims.[20] Whatever one's purpose in pursuing a policy, it will fail unless it can be presented as a legitimate and plausible policy in the forum where the collective decision is taken. A dove needs hawk's plumage in a colony of hawks, if doveish policies are to have a chance. Subtly, then, it was never a complete mistake to think in terms of states pursuing monolithic national interests. The same point recurs, if we drop down a layer and think of the actors in relation to the legitimating language of their own bureaucracies. State Department officials inhabit the State Department and speak a language there which embodies its aims and views, whatever their own. They have to speak it whether they are sincere or not. It therefore matters for our understanding, because it constrains and enables in the by now familiar way. But, given the latitude which we have discerned in the playing of roles, personal aims still make a difference. In the end, actors have to live with themselves. There has to be a personal consistency as well as an official one; so the itch of curiosity remains. But, by stressing the way in which roles have to be played within the terms of the prevailing language, we hope to leave the itch bearable and analysis-by-role systematic enough.

CONCLUSION

We began this chapter with the fundamental problem posed for any theory of foreign policy behaviour by the relationship between bureaucratic structure and individual decision-makers' perceptions. We have ended with a concept of role which allows a two-way process between structure and actor. As our discussion of power indicated, we cannot simply combine the standard Rational Actor

[20] The point has been excellently made by Quentin Skinner in his studies of history and political thought. See, for instance, his essay 'The Principles and Practice of Opposition: The Case of Bolingbroke versus Walpole', in N. McKendrick (ed.), *Historical Perspectives* (London: Europa, 1974), pp. 93–128. For further discussion see M. Hollis, *Models of Man* (Cambridge: Cambridge University Press, 1977), pp. 74 ff and 'Say it with Flowers', *Proceedings of the Aristotelian Society*, supplementary volume, 1978. See also J. Tully (ed.), *Meaning and Context: Quentin Skinner and his Critics* (Princeton: Princeton University Press, 1988).

and Bureaucratic Politics accounts as if, in some way, *homo economicus* could serve as the computer for *homo sociologicus*, since the concepts of power involved are not complementary. Nor have we wanted to reconcile them by holding that the key variable is personality, since, as we have argued, there is no need to grant that the sources of personality are internal to the actor. On the other hand, although the Bureaucratic Politics account seemed to have an advantage because it directs us to the external sources of policy preferences (via bureaucratic structure), this advantage was not to be bought at the price of postulating actors as mere puppets.

So we introduced a more sophisticated notion of role. Role involves judgement and skill, but at the same time it involves a notion of a structure within which roles operate. This combination of increased latitude for the individual with role-governed definitions of preference and judgement seems to us to represent a distinct advance on the standard Rational Actor and Bureaucratic Politics models. Such Rational Actor theories are vulnerable to the impact of bureaucratic structure on the formation of preferences; such Bureaucratic Politics theories have relied on over-mechanistic accounts of preference formation which result in actors being puppets. The decision to attempt to rescue the hostages is better analysed by having actors, not puppets, and by accepting that bureaucratic position was the prime cause of policy preferences. Our conception of role fulfils both requirements. It relates reasons to structure and allows for flexibility and judgement in the playing of the role: in so doing we bring the individual back in without reducing our explanations of foreign policy to the individual as the unit of analysis.

It will be very clear by now why opening the box does not resolve the level-of-analysis problem. On the contrary, it makes the problem more challenging. On the one hand, bureaucratic positions can be thought of as a system in which human rational individuals are the units. On the other hand, bureaucratic role-players can be thought of as the units in a system which is the nation state. In other words, the problem has several layers, each marked by system and units, and how the players are identified is a crucial point. Readers must decide for themselves. But it may help to add a further word about Explaining and Understanding.

Had we settled for a mechanical account of roles and reasons, where bureaucracies shape and shove and pre-programmed rational actors maximize the value of variables automatically, then Explaining would clearly have held the key. Had we settled for an account where creative individuals were uniquely themselves and roles were created in the playing of them, then Understanding would clearly have held the key. But we have in fact settled for elements of flexibility in roles and of judgement in reasons, which offer scope for both Explaining and Understanding. The scientific tradition must generalize but can accommodate flexibility by refining the conditions in which the same cause produces the same effect. The hermeneutic tradition must work from the inside but can regard rules and roles as powerful sources of determinacy. Although the chapter began to sound more hermeneutic towards the end, nothing in it resolves the argument between Explaining and Understanding.

To take this argument further, we must raise a pressing problem. So far we have concentrated on the process of decision-making within a single state. But the decision-makers cannot make rational choices without thinking about the process going on in other states. (It is an obvious merit of a Game Theory approach that each player considers the likely strategies of others. If the Bureaucratic Politics model failed to incorporate this feature, it would be doomed.) The problem is what each decision-making group is to assume about others. Should American decision-makers assume that Russians are moved by Russian interests (thus applying some version of a Realist or Rational Actor model) or should they be consulting flow-charts of Russian bureaucratic organization (thus applying a Bureaucratic Politics model)? Or, indeed, should they be thinking in terms of particular personalities, as a worried State Department seems to be doing currently in the face of the 'Gorbachev factor'?

This problem is peculiar to the social sciences. Any theory of how actors behave must reckon with what theory the actors themselves hold, since this is part of what produces behaviour. It follows that rational actors need to know what is in the minds of the actors with whom they are dealing. This emerged clearly in the previous chapter, since Game Theory makes a convincing point of it. But, while accepting the point, we did not accept that the games nations play are in accord with Game Theory. The players are motivated by reasons connected with their roles, if the present chapter is right, and so should think of other players as similarly motivated. Yet it may still be true and interesting that international relations consist of games which nations play, at any rate if there are games of a kind unknown to Game Theory. That is a cue for philosophical ideas from Wittgenstein, which offer fresh ways of connecting roles and reasons.

8

The Games Nations Play (2)

In the last chapter we argued that a critical concept in explaining and understanding foreign policy decision-making was that of role. We found that 'opening the box' did not automatically move us into a world of rational choosers, since the same issues apply within the state as applied on the international layer of the system–unit debate. Yet role is a key to international relations, since the preferences of even the most slavish and unreflective mouthpieces of a bureaucracy are not the only input to decisions. Decisions, after all, are aimed at something external to the state, however much there is an internal game to be played. This external arena not only provides some of the inputs to decision-making but also opens up the tricky question of how to understand the perceptions and intentions of the other actors in the international system. Since much of the impetus for decisions comes from the external environment of the state, and because international relations cannot be analysed simply in terms of the bureaucratic or rational decisions and motivations within states, we have to consider how each side perceives the aims and perceptions of the other.

THE 'OTHER MINDS' PROBLEM

That leads back to the idea that decisions are moves in the games nations play. Chapter 6 explored the idea with the help of Game Theory but was left with some awkward queries about its relation to the actual processes of decision-making. These queries become more urgent—and more difficult—as soon as the Bureaucratic Politics model is taken seriously. Role-players are certainly playing 'games' but, we shall find in a moment, in a sense at odds with the one defined by Game Theory. International relations set a fertile version of what philosophers term 'the problem of Other Minds'.

The philosophical problem arises because we are inclined to regard each person as a separate individual with a private 'mind', furnished with beliefs, desires, emotions, and experiences directly known only to its owner. Access to other minds then has to be by inference, it seems. Inferences are partly from behaviour, as when Juliet reads Romeo's feelings from his loving glances, and partly from words, as when he tells her what he feels. Either way, however, there is a gap, in that Juliet infers from his outward, public expressions to his inner, and private, state. Only Romeo can truly know whether her conclusions are correct, since only he has access to what they refer to. In comment on Weber's notion of *Verstehen* in Chapter 4, 'empathy' is not literally perception by one person of another's inner world, and 'explanatory understanding' by rational reconstruction cannot fully bridge the gap.

The problem with this way of thinking is that there can never be an independent check on the inferences. When a car makes a nasty noise and refuses to start, the expert can infer what is wrong with it by analogy with similar cases and can check the inference by taking the engine apart. Taking Romeo apart will not expose his private mind, and Juliet has no similar cases of direct contact with any other minds. One might suggest that she has similar cases where Romeo has made inferences about her which she can check, because she knows her own mind. But, if she is asked how she *knows* that Romeo or anyone else has a mind like hers, she has to reply that she does not. On this way of thinking, there is only behaviour (including language) to go on, and it does not guarantee a match between separate inner experiences which not even 'empathy' can compare directly. Hence the philosophical problem of Other Minds is how one mind can ever know what is in the mind of another. The answer might seem to be that, although no one can ever *know*, it is at least *likely* that Romeo feels the love which he expresses. But where there are no known previous observed cases, there is no basis for probabilities; and the problem stands.

This is an austere puzzle, and, before taking it further, we must show that it matters for international relations. Less austere versions certainly do. For instance, if one tries to think of nation states by exact analogy with human individuals, there is an obvious question of how Mother Russia can know the intentions of Uncle Sam. But attributing intentions to nations is only a figure of speech. Stated more carefully, the question for Russian policy-makers is what intention is embodied in American decisions and so can be correctly attributed to American policy-makers. Even so, it is a slippery question. Every decision gives a signal about its aim and about likely reactions to responses. But the signal can be very misleading. It may simply have been misread at the Russian end. It may have been correctly read but deliberately designed to mislead. Conversely, it may have been correctly interpreted but indirectly so, because the Russians understand the pressures on American decision-makers better than the Americans themselves do. Moreover, the behaviour may not be the same as the decision-makers decided. The implementation process, as we remarked in Chapter 6, may significantly affect the way in which a state behaves, to such an extent that there may be little resemblance between decision and outcome. All of this makes reading international signals particularly problematic.

These very practical possibilities call for theoretical reflection. Where basic Game Theory applies, there is no puzzle about intentions. Players intend to maximize the expected pay-off to themselves and choose the course of behaviour which best embodies this intention. The observer is puzzled only if the behaviour chosen seems to be an inferior solution to the maximizing problem. In that case one needs to ask what action the behaviour is meant to perform, and what beliefs and calculations led the agent to suppose it the best way to satisfy the preferences behind it. This rational reconstruction is made by reference to a simple ideal type of instrumentally rational action, modified to allow for subjective departures from perfect rationality.

But if Game Theory ever applies in so pure a form, it is only where decision-makers have been hypnotized by it! If a group of decision-makers is utterly convinced that they are playing Chicken against another group equally so convinced, then the observer can no doubt count on Game Theory too. But this very special case does not hold in the face of any uncertainty about its application, whether because the strategies and pay-offs are ill-defined or because the actors are not all thinking in Game Theoretic terms. Hence it is no surprise to find a more nuanced version of Game Theory in the work of those, like Thomas Schelling (cited in Chapter 6), who have applied it. In particular, Schelling's ideas on tacit communication and the manifestation of signals make it clear that the players are involved in bargaining as much as in fighting.

Bargaining is an area of manœuvre, where, for instance, it can pay to establish a reputation for strong nerves and hence to give signals intended to mislead.

This is exactly the problem underlying nuclear deterrence. The task is to convince an opponent that if attacked you would retaliate by using nuclear weapons even if the original attack was non-nuclear or only involved a limited strike. This is despite the fact that once you have to implement your threat your deterrent has already failed. The paradox of nuclear deterrence is that it is in neither side's interest to have the threat carried out: one side because it will receive the punishment, the other because its deterrent has already failed. This is particularly so when carrying out your threat will lead to retaliation from your opponent. Think of the basic logic of mutual assured destruction ('MAD'): each side, if attacked by even a small pre-emptive strike, will retaliate, but will be unable to defend itself against further strikes from the other side.

The most problematic example of this phenomenon is that of the US commitment to extend its nuclear guarantee to its allies. The cement that holds NATO together is the US commitment to use its strategic nuclear arsenal to attack the USSR if the Warsaw Pact ever attacked NATO. At the end of the day, this has to be a skilful exercise in signalling, since it is difficult to believe such US guarantees when the USA itself, by using nuclear weapons against the USSR, would invite retaliation in kind. Would the American leadership be willing to suffer this retaliation when the US mainland had not been attacked, let alone by nuclear weapons? Would the USA sacrifice Washington to save Bonn? This dilemma has been at the heart of NATO's crises over the years. It calls for a complex set of signals and ambiguities to keep the Russians out and the alliance happy. The essential problem for the alliance is how to do both simultaneously, since signals that suggest *détente* with the USSR tend to suggest a weakening of the US commitment to NATO to the Europeans. In cases of extended deterrence, when signalling is the name of the game, it is a very real practical problem to assess the intentions and perceptions of others.

There is thus a practical Other Minds problem which calls for theoretical flexibility without spoiling the general claims of Game Theory. But the uncertainties also go deeper. The image so far is, so to speak, one of postal chess between clubs in different countries, with each move by each club the result of a conference among its members. When the move transmitted by telex sets a trap, all the members who agreed to make it know what trap they have set. The members of the club at the receiving end are on the look out for traps and live in hope not only of detecting them but sometimes also of finding them unsound, seeming to fall into them and thus outplaying their opponents. In this image, uncertainties do not extend to doubts about the sense in which the clubs have intentions, or how the individual members' contributions relate to the aim of the club, or whether the activity is a strategic game, similarly regarded on both sides.

All these doubts can be raised for the games nations play. This is plainly true, but makes it sound as if they are practical doubts, to which the ready answer is that Game Theory is a useful abstraction whose merits do not depend on exactly what is in anyone's head, since states demonstrably conform to the analysis in their behaviour. We have more radical and subversive doubts in view, however, leading back to the philosophical problem itself.

Whereas the chess players in each club are narrowly but fully engaged in tackling a well-defined question about the club's best move, the agents of foreign policy decisions are incompletely engaged on several fronts, not all to do with the matter in hand. There is no defined game in which 'the national interest' is a clear, unifying concept. Hence not only is there no fictive 'Uncle Sam' to whom intentions can be ascribed as a useful shorthand, but nor are there any individuals whose intention is America's intention. The analogy with Juliet's attempt to infer Romeo's inner state from his outward expression breaks down for want of an American inner state. But the moral must be drawn with care. The language of action still applies and we can still attribute aims and motives, once we are clear about the role of signals in international relations. In reality, decision-makers have no choice but to engage in assessing intentions. The literature of international relations is packed with discussions of the kinds of problems that this causes, the two most important lines of argument being Robert Jervis's work on misperceptions and Raymond Garthoff's thoughtful article on the problems of imputing intentions from behaviour.[1]

---

[1] R. Jervis, *Perception and Misperception in International Politics* (Princeton: Princeton University Press, 1976); R. Garthoff, 'On Estimating and Imputing Intentions', *International Security*, 1978, 2(3), pp. 22–32.

To proceed, however, we need to take two philosophical steps sideways.

The first is to disconnect intentions from motives. Think of an intention as what is knowingly communicated by an action or utterance. This makes intentions like moves in a game, where the move has a conventional public meaning and to say that the player intended to make it is to say merely that it was not made by accident. The stress is on the public significance, secured by there being conventions for interpreting behaviour common to both parties to the communication. That still leaves room for intentions which are misunderstood, where failure to communicate occurs in a context of meaning-rules normally clear enough for success. In other words, think of intention as the outgoing aspect of what identifies the action in the behaviour and the message in the linguistic sign.

Now think of motives as inward reasons for action which agents can keep to themselves. They are thus distinct from the public, justifying reasons which often accompany the message. A diplomat was defined by Sir Henry Wotton with nice ambiguity as 'an honest man sent to lie abroad for the good of his country'. This catches the idea exactly. Diplomats lying abroad, in the sense of residing there, speak for their country and convey their governments' legitimate and honest-sounding reasons for their actions. But they do not always convey, and need not even be privy to, the inward reasons of state involved. In other words, public, justifying reasons belong, like intentions, in an official game, whereas motives raise a different kind of question of why it suits the player to play the official game and to make that move in it. This way of separating out the inward and outward aspects of actions is philosophically contentious, but it is familiar enough for the moment.[2]

WITTGENSTEIN AND GAMES

The second step is to think further about the notion of a 'game'. In Chapter 6, 'The Games Nations Play (1)', we followed the notion

---

[2] We remain indebted to Q. Skinner, 'The Principles and Practice of Opposition: The Case of Bolingbroke versus Walpole', in N. McKendrick (ed.), *Historical Perspectives* (London: Europa, 1974).

used by Game Theory. In essence, any interaction could be classified as a game if its outcome was a sum of independent choices whose pay-off to the chooser depended on the outcome. This yields a well-defined model, sharp and interesting in its implications and defensible as a useful, illuminating abstraction from human affairs. But it does not exhaust the senses in which interactions can be compared to games. With help from Wittgenstein, we shall next suggest another way of taking the analogy.

In *Philosophical Investigations* Wittgenstein likens language to a game and the learning of a language to learning to play a game.[3] 'Language' here is widely drawn, so that mathematics, for instance, is one. Learning a language is learning the rules of activities, like counting or measuring, or, in short, learning 'how to go on'. Games are a ready-to-hand example of the process, and one which suits Wittgenstein's contention that activities are not attempts to capture and define something which exists independently of them. It is not as if all games had something in common—amusement?—and any proposed new game could be judged by how well it served this purpose.

Don't say: 'There *must* be something common, or they would not be called "games" '—but *look and see* whether there is anything common to all. For if you look at them you will not see something that is common to *all*, but similarities, relationships, and a whole series of them at that.[4]

There is only a complicated network of similarities, overlapping and criss-crossing, best characterized as 'family resemblances'. Just try extracting anything more precise from the common features of 'board-games, card-games, ball-games, Olympic games and so on'.

The negative point is that there is no essential character common to all interaction, nothing prior and personal like 'thought' or 'meaning' which uses of language convey. For an illuminating example, contrast the Platonist view that mathematics is a mental voyage of discovery into the realm of numbers with Wittgenstein's view that we construct mathematics as we go along. What Plato presents as a search after truth, Wittgenstein presents as an evolution of uses for mathematical terms. Constructively

---

[3] L. Wittgenstein, *Philosophical Investigations* (Oxford: Basil Blackwell, 1953).
[4] Ibid. i. 66.

speaking, the rules of any 'game' create an arena and give sense to what is said and done in it. Such arenas are not figments of the imagination, however. The constraints and enablements are real features of public life. To that extent, one might say, there is after all something which all members of the games family share. For anyone learning to play a socially constructed game, there are rules to discover, even though these rules are not somehow a pointer to a hidden Platonic world. (At least this is how we take Wittgenstein. His text is hard to pin down and capable of many interpretations. It is also marvellously suggestive and we urge readers to try it for themselves.)

For present purposes we wish to focus on the idea that games are self-contained, and that playing them is a matter of making moves whose sense is given in the rules of the game. Think of chess again. The game is constituted by precise rules defining the pieces, their powers and legal moves, the alternating character of play, and what counts as a win, draw, or loss. Actions within the game are described by reference to these constitutive rules (e.g. as 'castling' or 'giving check', not as shifting bits of wood) and could not otherwise occur. Special chess notation (e.g. 'O–O' for castling) identifies what is done. When we ask *why* it is done, however, the constitutive rules do not hold the whole answer (except perhaps for checkmate or when there is only one legal move). Here it needs explaining why the player has chosen rationally, or could believe so. 'Why?' is a matter of the likely advantage gained (or disadvantage avoided), either clearly in this position or, if the position is too complex, by appeal to a general rule of thumb, like 'castle early because it gets the king out of the centre and the castle into play'. In other words, there are also useful rules which regulate play, in that they are sensible in themselves and that the other player can be expected to follow them too. These rules do not define the game but they are part of its internal workings and the observer cannot understand serious chess without knowing them.

Chess shows nicely how conventions can create an activity and thus set problems about what it is rational to do which would not otherwise arise and are hard to solve. It will not serve as an ideal type for international relations because its conventions, as given by its constitutive rules, are clear and complete. But, before pressing the disanalogy, it is worth noting one family resemblance.

The game is challenging enough to have prompted many rival theories of good play. For instance, Nimzovitch's 'hypermodern theory' proposed in the 1920s, was that it is a good idea to open not by occupying the centre of the board but by flanking moves, biding time until the other player's pieces are committed to positions where they can be attacked. The theory has never been definitively assessed but is interesting enough to have influenced later opening strategy. That raises an intriguing question about the relation of theorizing about chess to the actual moves and motives of players who are impressed. A similar question arises, as we noted, over the influence of Game Theory on policy-makers and hence over its merits as an explanation in relation to its merits as an abstract analysis.

But the disanalogy is large enough to make us ask whether international relations have *any* constitutive rules. Wittgensteinians will reply that *all* social activities must have some constitutive rules because actions have a meaning which behaviour lacks. Social action can occur only where there is a rule followed, thus identifying what is going on. Rules are constructed by agreement or convention, even if tacitly or, at the extreme, unconsciously. Hence social activity is possible only in so far as there are 'rules of the game' to go by. Moreover, although some conventions are regulative, there must always be some constitutive ones, because regulations presuppose an activity to regulate. Nations could not even try to regulate their affairs (except perhaps by physical violence) without at least a rudimentary set of conventions constituting 'moves' for them to make by signalling to one another.

In Peter Winch's bold version of this line of thought, which we met in Chapter 4, it is made to seem as if every game belonged to a self-contained 'form of life', so that all motives could be read off in terms of the proper conduct of the game. For instance, a monastery is an institution belonging to a religious form of life and we can understand not only what monks do by reference to the rules of their monastic order in its religious context, but also why they do it. But international relations do not seem to us to be self-contained in this complete way. The power of tanks and missiles is not the internal authority of an abbot; moving a nuclear submarine is different from moving a castle in chess. International anarchy remains too firmly the starting point of the international game for an analogy with fully constituted and self-contained games to be plausible. Yet there are interesting similarities. Nuclear submarines function as threats and bargaining counters: the abbot's authority may have something to do with threats of hell-fire. Unless some kind of international society had been constructed, there could be no United Nations, with its Assembly and its fragile but often effective agencies. The more the constructed arena of international diplomacy matters for what nations are enabled and constrained to do, the more it is worth thinking of the arena as a place where Wittgensteinian games are played.

Even if the international scene is anarchic, in the sense that nations pursue their national interest and will break the fragile international rules when it suits and is not too costly, there are still enablements and constraints. Isolation is a handicap. The opinion of neutrals often matters as much as the opinion of allies. Whatever the deeper motives for a policy, its success depends in part on how it is judged abroad—a fact which enables some policy choices and constrains others. This is an international analogue of what we said earlier about the importance of the fact that at home bureaucracies need to legitimate their manœuvres as contributions to the pursuit of the national interest.

The first sideways step was to separate intentions from motives and the second to introduce a Wittgensteinian notion of games. Taken together, they suggest a way of dealing with the Other Minds problem. The international arena is fragile but it is sufficiently developed to have a language in which nations can signal intentions to one another. To detect the motives behind what is said and done, we turn to the domestic game and, within it, the games which the agencies of state play. Thus the motives of foreign policy are the intentions of the strongest bureaucracies; and the inquiry ends with an analysis of the distribution of bureaucratic power. This, in effect, is a Bureaucratic Politics solution to the problem of interpreting the apparent behaviour of states. Motives are hidden, if one looks only at the international game itself, but can be found in the constitutive and regulative rules of the decision-making process within states. Of course, the structure of the international system may well be a major source of the distribution of power within a state, in that some bureaucracies will have more power in foreign and defence affairs than others. It will also set much of the agenda and dictate the problems that have

to be addressed. Within these constraints, the internal game will
be played.

The pros and cons of this suggestion can be seen with the help of a
case study. On 15 April 1986 the United States carried out a
bombing raid on Libya, attacking five military targets in Tripoli
and Benghazi. This deliberate act of force by a large nation against
a small one with which it was not at war sets problems of analysis
on several levels.

Start with the official account of US intentions. President
Reagan was quick to explain that the raid was a reprisal for what
he termed Libyan 'state terrorism'. Despite a series of warnings by
the USA, Colonel Gadaffi, the Libyan President, had been
conducting a campaign of terror against Americans abroad,
against American interests, and against the free world in general.
There had been several incidents where Libyan involvement had
been proved, notably a recent bomb explosion in a Berlin
nightclub in which American soldiers had been killed. Terrorism
was intolerable in all its forms and 'state terrorism' especially
intolerable. The raid was a justified retaliation and had taught the
'mad dog' Gadaffi a salutary lesson. Admittedly, the loss of some
seventy civilian lives, including that of Gadaffi's youngest child,
was a matter for regret. But the raid had to be by night, thus
making complete precision impossible, and some of its military
targets were in or close to civilian areas. Since the raid itself was
justified, Libya rather than America was responsible for any
regrettable consequences.

This official account answers some questions about what was
done and why. The intention was not only to destroy some Libyan
military hardware but also to give a symbolic warning in terms
which a 'mad dog' would understand. It was a legitimate action, by
reason of persistent Libyan offences against the code of decent
international conduct. Whether the official account answers other
questions about *motive* depends crucially on how satisfactory one
finds these official reasons. Thus, if the test is American public
opinion at the time, there is no puzzle. The overwhelming
domestic consensus was that America, in the symbolic person of its

President, had acted in a way which was both right and rational. In that case the raid can be taken at face value for purposes of the rational reconstruction of its motives. A well-defined problem, posed for the USA by Libyan antics, had been found an effective and legitimate solution, with no need arising to look for a gap between the official reasons and the real motives.

From a European angle, however, the official reasons covered much less of the ground. It was not at all clear that the raid was a legitimate reprisal. The evidence that Libya was behind previous incidents could be challenged and the Berlin bomb, in particular, seemed more likely to be of Syrian than Libyan origin (a belief since confirmed). Even granted that provocation, the raid was arguably in breach of international law and, indeed, an act of 'state terrorism' itself. Whatever the legal niceties (which included whether the concept of state terrorism had meaning or standing), one could also doubt the morality and wisdom of open aggression by a powerful nation. Although the ethics involved are, presumably, unclear, the mention of wisdom leads on to doubts about the effectiveness of the raid. Whatever the ethics, Libya is a small Arab and Third World country. Gadaffi's activities do not find favour with all Arab and Third World governments but, when it comes to a public matter of taking sides, the courts of public opinion are loyal. That meant a likelihood of further consequences, both for relations between the USA and, especially, Syria and Lebanon, which America wanted to improve, and for the safety of American citizens, four of whom were assassinated in the Middle East within a few days of the raid. There are—and were—in short, serious questions about whether the raid was either right or rational.

The questions become sharper if one focuses them on Britain, where Mrs Thatcher, as Prime Minister, had agreed to the use of British bases by some of the F–111 bombers involved. Why exactly had the raid required bombers from such distant bases, especially when France and Spain had refused permission to overfly their territories, thus necessitating a huge detour? The official US answer was that there were not enough ship-based bombers in the Mediterranean to tackle five targets simultaneously with precision and at night. But that raises more questions than it answers. The British-based bombers did not have equipment precise enough in a night attack to avoid the civilian casualties which occurred. In any case, if the object was to teach a mad dog a lesson, there was no need for as many as five targets or for any of them to be in or close to civilian areas. Meanwhile one can wonder about Mrs Thatcher's reasons, despite her expressed conviction that, America being clearly in the right, an ally could not refuse its request. In so far as national interests are what counts, the costly loss to the economy from American tourists cancelling holidays in a Britain which had almost invited Libyan reprisals was entirely predictable. Here too it seems that there must have been more to it.

Such questions spring from irrationalities in the official account. Officially, there is a single arena and the USA, in the person of its leader, has acted reasonably and rightly in terms of what is permissible within the arena. Critics, finding cause to demur, look for ways to restore rationality by enquiring outside the arena. They are looking for the sort of answers evidence for which has come to light since the raid, although we are not in a position to guarantee their truth. For example, there is some evidence that the CIA had planned to catch Gadaffi himself in the bombing and thus get rid of an inconvenient troublemaker. If this was so, it becomes easy to see why one target was in Tripoli itself. It would have seemed worth some civilian casualties to achieve this aim. Less controversially, the ship-based planes in the Mediterranean were all under the control of the US Navy, whereas planes flying from Britain belonged to the US Air Force. Inclusion in the action could have been the US Air Force's price for co-operating during the planning and decisions. Meanwhile, the State Department would certainly have pressed the case for directly involving at least one European ally—Britain—in the incident. Nor should one forget that every American President needs to keep their popular support at home. The raid took place at 2 a.m. Libyan time, which is also 7 p.m. or peak television time on the east coast of America, and the electorate had a grandstand view. It was the sort of active foreign policy which helps the President and his party when things are not going well at home.

As we have said, we cite these points only as possibilities. But true or not, they illustrate our theme instructively by locating possible motives outside the official arena. As it happens, they are all instances which suit the Bureaucratic Politics model. But, once attention shifts to the domestic scene, rational reconstructions soon involve more individual elements. Mrs Thatcher, for instance, takes her role as Prime Minister very personally. If one asks why she agreed to the use of British bases, contrary to what many advisers took to be British interests, a plausible answer is that she was repaying a debt to the US for crucial help at the time of the Falklands War, and that she regarded such an obligation as a personal matter of honour. This kind of element invites comment from both Bureaucratic Politics and Rational Actor models without exactly suiting either. We are not trying to settle this dispute at the moment.

Our present point is one about understanding intentions from the inside. In Chapter 4 we introduced a tension between an 'individualism' which accounts for institutional action by summing individual choices, and a 'holism' which accounts for choices as the following of institutional rules. This was a tension within the hermeneutic camp, on the *Verstehen* side of the distinction between Explaining and Understanding. The two notions of a game let us take the argument further. The Game Theory notion, with its stress on consequences as calculated in terms of pay-off by self-interested rational agents, is the obvious vehicle for individualism. The Wittgensteinian notion, with its stress on prior, constitutive rules to give meaning to what happens, is the obvious vehicle for holism. The Libyan example shows that both have their merits but suggests that they cannot readily be combined.

At each level of analysis there is a framework of rules which enable and constrain what may be done, thus letting the inquirer identify the action by finding the intention in the behaviour and by locating the legitimating reasons for it. This is a matter of reconstructing the moves in a Wittgensteinian game, together with their surface rationale. But the rules of the international game at international level are too nebulous to take us far. The enablements and constraints are genuine but leave a great latitude, within which nations, as individual units, calculate pay-offs in self-interested terms which do not belong to the official game. To note the American claim that the raid was a right and rational response to threats to world peace is not yet to understand why it occurred. But, when we move down a layer, the situation repeats. Again there is a framework of rules within which foreign policy decisions are made. Again the rules enable and constrain what the agencies involved may do. Again there is latitude, so that to identify the moves made, together with their rationale, is not to understand enough of the action. So there is the same case for seeking motives 'off the board' and in the hidden workings of units like bureaucracies. Here too, however, the reconstruction finds a further set of rules within which the bureaucrats must play their moves or their parts.

This sketch carries the suggestion that the lowest level is one of *Realpolitik* in some form, presumably in the end the *Realpolitik* of self-interested human individuals. But the suggestion is to be resisted. Even if it were right in theory, the framework of rules becomes stronger as we penetrate the more firmly organized world of domestic politics. Bureaucrats who play their moves are also playing their parts, and there remains good reason to remember that 'where you stand depends on where you sit'. More importantly, the self-interest involved in *Realpolitik* is not a neutral, universal currency but depends on the meaning and value which units attach to outcomes. This leads back into the Wittgensteinian family of games after all. Nothing in our discussion requires that, in stepping outside a framework of rules in order to understand what goes on within it, we are committed at some point to stepping out of all frameworks and into a world of Game Theory alone.

OTHER MINDS AGAIN

Now we can return to the Other Minds problem as traditionally posed. Juliet knows Romeo's intentions, because to do so she needs only to know the rules of courtship and understand his words. But to make intentions so explicitly a matter of what words and actions 'mean' in a public way is not to answer all her questions. Are his intentions honourable? It is only part of the answer to say that he knows how to express an honourable intention. The crucial question is about his motives, which he may not have expressed and, if one thinks of them as inherently private, perhaps cannot fully externalize. In its traditional form, at any rate, the Other Minds problem arises on the assumption that separate persons *cannot* be fully transparent to one another because each has a separate inner being. Hence the rational reconstruction of motive on the evidence of words and actions relies on an unsecured analogy between Juliet, as known to herself, and other persons, whom she can know only in some other way.

There are, basically, three ways to secure the analogy. The (apparently) simplest is behaviourism, which denies the assumption about the separateness of persons by denying the need for inner beings. People's behaviour indicates all there is to know about them. Although Juliet may have more information about herself than about Romeo, it is not a different sort of information. This line has often tempted social scientists, because it suits the application of the methods of natural science to the social world. Human behaviour may be complex but it is no less observable than the behaviour of anything else. Currently, however, behaviourism is on the retreat, at least as a theoretically simple claim that human action is predictable on the basis of our physical properties and previous conditioning. Perhaps that is due to the lack of behavioural analysis of language, which may be only a temporary obstacle. Meanwhile, there is no behavioural theory of international relations sufficiently strongly supported to divert us into a philosophical discussion of this approach.

That leaves two other ways of securing the analogy which fit the theme of the chapter. The second way is to attribute a universal set of motives or interests to human nature, as is done in one way or another by versions of the Rational Actor model. For a colourful example, here is David Hume, writing in the mid-eighteenth century in the course of trying to lay foundations for a science of the human mind:

It is universally acknowledged that there is a great uniformity among the actions of men, in all nations and ages, and that human nature remains still the same, in its principles and operations. The same motives produce the same actions: The same events follow from the same causes. Ambition, avarice, self-love, vanity, friendship, generosity, public spirit: these passions, mixed in various degrees, and distributed through society, have been, from the beginning of the world, and still are, the source of all actions and enterprises, which have ever been observed among mankind. Would you know the sentiments, inclinations and course of life of the Greeks and Romans? Study well the temper and actions of the French and English: You cannot be much mistaken in transferring to the former most of the observations which you have made with regard to the latter. Mankind are so much the same, in all times and places, that history informs us of nothing new or strange in this particular.[5]

---

[5] D. Hume, *Enquiries* [1777], ed. L. Selby-Bigge (Oxford: Oxford University Press, 1975), viii. i. 65.

Hume's aim was to reduce human actions to 'their simplest and fewest causes' (as he explained in the introduction to *A Treatise of Human Nature*) and, having identified the passions which are always at work, to account for the variety of actions by reference to the variety of situations. The 'source of all actions and enterprises, which have ever been observed among mankind' is constant. The example is perhaps too colourful for today, but the assumption of self-interest as a universal motive behind instrumentally rational action is directly descended from this approach. Meanwhile, it is instructive to consider Hume's list of basic ingredients. Why do his descendants hold on to 'self-love', while leaving ambition, avarice, vanity, friendship, generosity, and public spirit to, presumably, the working of socialization? The longer the list, if reliable, the easier the Other Minds problem becomes!

The sharpest answer is that rational reconstruction predicated on universal motives needs a unitary currency in which rational actors can assess pay-offs. Hence it looks attractive to propose a single measure, 'utility', which corresponds to a motive common to all actors and allows an ordering of all feasible outcomes. Sources of utility can then be filled in systematically, for instance by 'profit' in the case of firms in a market or 'power' for political units. Yet, as we have seen, each way of filling in the blank sets questions. Is it true that all firms aim at profit? Can we specify 'power' without exploring the ideologies of those who seek it? In general, the whole attempt is poised uneasily between a motive so universal that it threatens to be vacuous and instances of it so socially specific that social context threatens to do all the work. If this charge sticks—which adherents of rational choice theory and Game Theory of course deny—then the Other Minds problem is still unsolved.

The third way is to let the social context secure the analogy between actors in it. Just as all chess players have the same motives *qua* chess players, so Romeo and Juliet are players of a game which, in giving their actions a shared meaning, also allows inference about motives. This is the line which we have been exploring with the Wittgensteinian idea of games and, as noted, it too is disputable. But it does at least suggest another way to think of the rationality involved in 'rational reconstruction'. If membership of a social group is a source of reasons for action, and if actors engage in social events solely as members of groups, then access to other minds is through the rules constituting the groups. In that case, to be rational is to act from reasons taken from stock and applied to new situations which actors face in a social capacity. To reconstruct where people are going, we need to know where they are coming from.

This approach is especially fertile for anthropology, since it allows an outsider to find another culture rational without insisting that its members must be maximizing some kind of pay-off. It supposes that there is a great variety of social and intellectual frameworks, each allowing the members to make sense of their world and find their way about in it. By drawing on their cultural stock of rules and reasons, they know 'how to go on'. By identifying the stock, the anthropologist achieves 'explanatory understanding' (to recall Weber's term from Chapter 4). The anthropologist's problem of 'Other Cultures' differs from the philosopher's problem of 'Other Minds' by being posed for groups rather than individuals. Individuals feature as place-holders and the work of understanding is done by discovering what any holder of the same place would have reason to do. This, in essence, is what the Bureaucratic Politics model proposes when in hermeneutic vein. A rational player of a role acts according to the reasons which the role supplies.

It is as well to be clear whether to accept or refuse the implied relativism. The suggestion is that rationality is not a universal capacity for calculating the costs and benefits of actions which contribute to an outcome, but the applying of a local rule which supplies reasons for acting. Thus there are many religions, each with a cultural setting and each informed by its own beliefs about an unseen world. Each religion is a source of rules, roles, and reasons for belief and action. To understand religious behaviour from within we clearly need to trace the local rules, roles, and relations. But is the tracing to be described as '*rational* reconstruction', implying that there are as many 'rationalities' as there are organized forms of life, or is it a *further* question which religions, if any, exhibit rationality?

This is a huge and intricate topic, which we introduce only to show how one might avoid it. On the one hand, it is tempting to say that there are no a priori limits on the kind of sense which ideas and practices may make when viewed from within. On the other hand, it can be argued that there is only one kind of sense—an organized consistency of ideas, experience, and action—and that understanding can succeed only where a universal test for consistency succeeds. Either way, one must then decide how an internal and intellectual account of a world from within relates to the workings of the social order to which the inhabitants of that world belong. Readers wishing to pursue these themes might like to start with the essays in *Rationality and Relativism*, edited by Hollis and Lukes.[6]

Theories of international relations can avoid going deep into questions of relativism by restricting the range of organizations and ideologies which needs to be taken into account. Provided that the principal actors have aims and interests which they can communicate to one another, and organize their domestic business in ways which outsiders understand, there will be enough of a common core to work with. But this is only a rough and ready way of avoiding a genuine puzzle, and those who take it should remain sensitive to the risks of foreclosure. For instance, it is not plain that the emergence of fundamentalist Islamic republics, like Iran, leaves the game of nations as before. The sort of fairly stable expectations which have evolved to the mutual advantage of states as ideologically different as the USA and the USSR may not hold for the relations of either with some Middle Eastern countries. Similarly, it has been suggested that American policy in Asia, notably in Vietnam, long suffered from imposing Western interpretations on forms of culture which had their own rules, roles, and reasons. To the extent that such claims are well-founded, they count against rational reconstructions which rely on a universal motive of utility-maximization.

EXPECTATIONS

One way to pose the Other Minds problem for purposes of international relations is to ask what warrants one nation state in holding expectations about another. This question serves to extend the argument about the sense of 'rational' in a rational reconstruction. In the world of fully rational agents postulated in

[6] M. Hollis and S. Lukes (eds.), *Rationality and Relativism* (Oxford: Blackwell, 1982).

pure economic theory, each agent has rational expectations about what others will do in various circumstances. These expectations depend on knowing how the others rank the feasible outcomes and how probable they believe the outcomes to be. But probabilities here have a peculiarity not shared by the probabilities used in predicting natural events, like hurricanes. Rational expectations are often interlocked. What is rational for A to do often depends on what A expects B to do, which depends in turn on what B expects A to do. The interlocking threatens to make expectations indeterminate, because of the regression, and so to undermine the prospects of rational action.

This problem is well brought out by Game Theory and is a challenge especially to theories of rational bargaining. The standard way of dealing with it is to define an equilibrium as an outcome where no agent could make a more rational choice of strategy, given the strategies chosen by the others. Each agent is then assumed to be in search of an equilibrium strategy and thus predictable to other rational agents similarly in search of equilibrium. Strategies can be probabilistic where necessary (as when A chooses between x and y by, so to speak, throwing weighted dice) and can be reckoned on accordingly. Determinacy is thus restored.

But two complications need considering. One is that there is nothing to guarantee that any equilibrium, as just defined, is unique. Indeed, they are often plainly not. In a co-ordination game, for instance, there are standardly several outcomes, each of which, if reached, will be stable because no one has any reason to depart from it. In that case, no agent can, in the abstract, form rational expectations about which particular equilibrium others will aim for. In more complex games with many players, it may be that, while all players prefer all stable outcomes to all unstable ones, they also have different rankings of the stable outcomes. For example, all parties to an industrial dispute may be better off by reaching a settlement but also prefer those settlements which best serve their particular interests. This threatens to reintroduce indeterminacies and is a living source of unfinished argument among economic theorists.

The other complication arises because agents need to be credited with a model of the economy and how it works. What A can expect B to do depends on the economic theory held by A and on the economic theory held by *B*. It is not obvious that *A* and *B* must hold the same economic theory, even if one assumes that both are rational agents. For instance, *A* might hold a monetarist theory and *B* a Keynesian one about the likely effects of an increase in the money supply. Both theories may be self-justifying in the sense that in a world where all agents hold a monetarist theory, their expectations about what will happen are fulfilled, as will also occur in a different world where all agents hold Keynesian theories. If this is indeed possible—a further matter of unfinished argument—indeterminacies soon multiply.

Although we shall not venture further into economics, we can say that, at least while no economic theory is universally accepted, the Other Minds problem arises even in the ideal-type world where all agents are fully rational. It is then easy to see why this matters for rational reconstruction with the aid of models in the world of International Relations theory. Theoretically speaking, nations would not be rationally predictable even if one assumes that all apply Game Theory, and become even less predictable if one allows that Game Theory is not the only theory which ideally rational agents can have in their heads. Meanwhile, further problems arise as soon as we move from an ideal-type world to an actual one, where it matters what theories are in fact in the heads of decision-makers. The White House needs to know how the Kremlin believes that the White House conceives it.

These reflections threaten to multiply the possibilities unmanageably. To cut them down, think of *normative* expectations as a filter both on what decision-makers consider worth trying and on what they suppose that others will consider. That motives are enabled and constrained by the demands of office is a fact which influences the thinking of decision-makers about other decision-makers. Hence how the game is conceived is itself part of the game, not only of how it is regulated but also of how it is constituted. For instance, it is a game where the American President is normatively expected to heed American public opinion, and that is in turn a factor in Kremlin decisions.

Normative expectations are a genuine 'filter' in the sense that players ignore them at their peril. But they are not congruent with the 'rational expectations' of economic theory. 'Expect' can mean 'predict', as when we expect rain tomorrow, and this is its intended use in a Positive science. Normative expectations, however, are couched in a moral vocabulary of what is expected *of* people, what others are entitled to assume, and what criticisms are warranted by failure to perform. Office-holders do neither all nor only what is normatively expected of them. That does not make normative expectations idle. To predict what the Kremlin will do, one needs to know the normative situation of those involved, because that is a factor in the decisions even when it is not the sole determining factor. The players' interests, their conceptions of what they are undertaking, and their power to achieve their goals are all bound up with normative expectations, which enable as much as they constrain. By applying 'normative' as well as 'Positive' filters to what would otherwise be far too many possibilities to cope with, the games nations play may be manageable, in theory and practice, after all.

CONCLUSION

The Other Minds problem is serious for International Relations, as soon as one grants that it matters what decision-makers have in their minds. Game Theory, supplemented by a theory of rational bargaining, offers what seemed at first a neat solution. But we have by now found four broad reasons to think it insufficient and so to adopt a richer idea of the games nations play.

First, even in the ideal-type case where all agents can assume that all others are ideally rational, the games played are too rich for Game Theory. In the Prisoner's Dilemma and the Chicken Game, for instance, preferences and pay-offs are common knowledge, motives are transparent, and strategies, if opaque, can be explored in a series of games. International games, by contrast, call for a separation of intentions and motives. Intentions, and their public legitimating reasons, belong to a more or less formalized game where signals have meanings governed by conventions. But motives have to be sought, so to speak, 'off the board'. Thus American intentions in bombing Libyan targets were firmly signalled and publicly legitimated, but questions of motive led us to other games played outside the international arena. Internationally, America played Libya with world opinion as spectator; domestically, the Air Force played the Navy for a share of the action. Game Theory has something to say about each game separately but not about their relationship, given that neither is self-contained. So we invoked Wittgenstein's account of the 'games' of social life and of the overlapping, criss-crossing 'family resemblances' among them.

This led us, secondly, to challenge the Game Theory assumption that pay-offs are an objective measure of the satisfaction of a universal human motive like utility-maximization. What people value depends on the terms in which they think of themselves and their world. Motives therefore need to be understood in terms of what constitutes different people's self-respect, as anthropologists do when exploring other cultures. Here lies a contentious path, which we do not wish to pursue far. It leads to the suggestion that in the end there are no individuals but only 'forms of life', which include 'games' defining morality and self-respect. It is made attractive by the great variety of 'forms of life' which anthropologists seem to discover. But we were careful not to commit International Relations to any thorough relativism. That nations with different ideologies can still communicate and negotiate is a sign that local rules are not wholly local. We argued only that rational reconstruction must discover what is expressively, as well as instrumentally, rational.

Thirdly, we presented the difference between Game Theoretic games and Wittgensteinian games as one between two kinds of filter on possible moves. Game Theory deals in equilibria, which it identifies by assuming that rational players have *rational expectations* about one another. We argued that in the games nations play there are too often either no equilibria or several, thus rendering strategies indeterminate. *Normative expectations*, which enable and constrain the playing of roles, however, add another kind of filter. To understand Other Minds in social interaction, one needs to know what their roles require and forbid. Even when actors avoid doing what seems normatively expected of them, they are still constrained by a need to legitimate what they do. Rational reconstruction must use both filters, whereas Game Theory offers at most one.

Fourthly, there is the practical question of how to relate ideal-type models of action to actual behaviour. Comparison with frictionless motion does not help, because the coefficient of friction gives a clear and objective measure of departures from the model. There is no similar 'coefficient of irrationality'. Game

Theory abstracts from what decision-makers have in their minds.
But only in the special case where they have been influenced by
Game Theory can they be squarely said to be thinking in these
terms. Even then they do not have only Game Theory in mind,
granted what we have just said about normative expectations, and
they are dealing with other decision-makers who are not students
of Game Theory. For instance, what is the State Department to
make of Islamic fundamentalism in its dealings with Iran? It might
try supposing that the Ayatollahs are secret or unconscious Game
Theorists. But it seems to us more plausible to regard them in
Wittgensteinian spirit as players of an international game which
they insist on shaping as they go along. In that case, Game Theory
is not a suitable model for a part of the world which does not work
even approximately in ways idealized by Game Theory.

The four points taken together lead us to take stock of the level-
of-analysis problem. In Chapter 7 we 'opened the box' so that a
Game Theoretic Rational Actor model of the decision-making
state could be opposed by a Bureaucratic Politics analysis which
fragmented the state into bureaucracies. But we then found
ourselves opening a further box so that the Bureaucratic Politics
model could be challenged in turn from below by suggesting that
roles are what role-players make of them. Here, we seemed to say,
we reach the basement of the problem, where the final analysis is
to be conducted. But the present chapter, although supporting the
suggestion that we had reached a deeper layer, also shows that the
hunt is not ended. The discussion has reactivated earlier disputes,
which therefore prove to have been merely adjourned.

The problem now becomes one of how to put a stop to the
fragmentation of the games nations play into sums of local actions
performed for indeterminate reasons. The onus is initially on those
who advocate Understanding in a Wittgensteinian manner which
also separates rule-governed, public intentions from individual
motives. They need to show how International Relations can avoid
collapsing into a fragmented Diplomatic History which lacks all
rhyme and reason. To do it, they will need to insist that individual
motives have just enough structure for the normative filter to work
in the right sort of way. Consider, for instance, the part played by
judges in the evolution of law. Law based on precedent often
evolves, or might even be said to be made, in its application, as
judges bring their wits to bear on existing statutes and rule on what

they imply. A system of appeal courts filters out idiosyncratic judgements but accepts innovations which satisfy an (often imputed) test of what legislators intended. Legislators monitor the process in the course of playing the game of politics, which has a similarly soft structure. We can see how the stumbling emergence of international society might be understood as an evolving interplay which results in new games for old.

On the other hand, it is open to those who advocate a scientific approach to retort that fragmentation can be stopped only by reasserting the claims of a determining structure. If a Game Theoretic Rational Actor model cannot answer the four objections in this chapter, then structures must be sought outside the games which nations or individuals play after all, so that there is enough external shaping and shoving to explain how the games turn out. In that case, the deepest layer of the level-of-analysis problem will have been found to contain a missing argument which might have settled the dispute earlier and in favour of Explanation.

Hence this chapter offers only the limited conclusion that Game Theory is not enough. It needs supplementing either with normative filters which presuppose different notions of a game and of rationality or with renewed structural determinants. Which way shall we go? The answer will settle both which layer is crucial for the level-of-analysis problem and whether the key to method in International Relations is Explaining or Understanding. But since the authors of this book remain divided, we leave the denouement to the final chapter.

9

Explaining and Understanding

We began this book by saying that International Relations is heir to two traditions, the scientific and the hermeneutic. The discipline has not been equally grateful to both. Since the eclipse of Idealism it has been largely dominated by Realism—especially if one includes Behaviouralism and Neo-Realism under that title—and Realism is avowedly scientific in intent. But we have also considered objections to Realism, some of which advance the claims of hermeneutics and suggest that the international world makes sense only if understood from within. The reader no doubt expects us to have a view on the respective merits of the two traditions as guides to unresolved problems in the subject. Indeed, we do have a view and that is why we have written the book. But it is not the same view and we shall end by airing our differences.

Before launching into dialogue, however, we shall take fuller stock of the problems which have emerged so far and of the approaches which might plausibly be taken to them. We shall again use two dimensions. One is marked by the familiar 'level-of-analysis' problem, the other by our theme of 'explaining and understanding'. The former is a summary of some unfinished debates in the discipline, the latter an invitation to an unfinished debate of our own.

The 'level-of-analysis' problem was filled out in Chapter 5 with the aid of David Singer's analogy between theoretical levels and map projections. The levels were those of system and unit, the problem being somehow akin to that of relating different two-dimensional projections of a three-dimensional object. We let the analogy pass at the time, but it is interestingly questionable in a way which, in a moment, will let us set up our debate about understanding and explaining. First, however, we should again stress that the problem itself is not uniquely one of whether the international system or its units (nation states) holds the key to analysis. We noted in Chapter 1 that it is a problem with three layers and four possible contenders, as Figure 9.1 (replicating Figure 1.2) reminds us. On each layer the debate is about whether analysis is to proceed 'top–down' or 'bottom–up' and, less obviously but no less importantly, whether the aim is to explain or to understand.

In Singer's own posing of the problem 'the system' refers to the entire international system and 'the unit' to the nation state. Here, to proceed 'top–down' is to try to show that the states behave wholly as the system requires and not at all according to their individual peculiarities. To proceed 'bottom–up' is to counter by contending that 'the system' is a fiction except in so far as the term refers to relations and interactions among the units. Here, as with the other layers too, we have a particular case of a general dispute throughout the social sciences between holists and individualists, which tends to be fought to a draw. We wish only to make one general and two specific comments on it.

In general, it is wise to be clear whether the dispute turns on the 'reality' of systems or on the need to feature them in explanations. That they are 'real' is an ontological claim (from the Ancient Greek word for 'existence') raising questions about the relations of wholes to parts and inviting further (epistemological) questions about how knowledge of wholes could be grounded in what, it seems, could only be knowledge of particulars (or units). We have been careful not to pronounce on either kind of question and want only to point out that, with applied social science at present in hard-headed, broadly empiricist mood, the onus is on the holist to

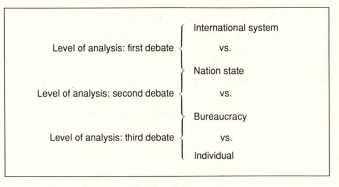

FIG. 9.1

persuade sceptics both that wholes are more than their parts and that science is capable of establishing such a proposition. On the other hand, to social theorists who are less empirically inclined systemic explanations certainly have their charms, and we gave a good deal of space to Waltz's advocacy of them. Besides, as we have seen, traditional empiricism is in theoretical trouble, both from Quine's attack on the very idea of theory-neutral facts of observation and from Kuhn's case for saying that scientific thought is always governed by paradigms. This means that 'methodological individualism' is by no means an obviously right explanatory strategy. The book has carefully given no conclusive reason to rule out explanations which turn on systematic properties and which present the behaviour of units as functional in a bipolar (or multipolar) system.[1]

In International Relations in particular, however, it seems to us that 'top–down' cannot do all the work on the explaining side. When even Waltz concedes that structures only 'shape and shove', and that their influence can be resisted, then we have also to look at the units. The anarchic character of the international system, which marks out international politics in sharp contrast to domestic politics, strongly suggests that the units affect the shape of relations, however firm the shove. The suggestion is also central to any account of how the system changes its structure. Even if the polarity of the system, bipolar or multipolar, explains something about its normal functioning, it seems to us impossible to account for change from one type of system to another only at the level of the system. Purely functional explanations are bound to be suspect, unless they include a causal contribution from the units. Hence not only change of all sorts but even normal functioning owes something to the character of the units.

Our other particular comment concerns the 'individual' involved, while the level-of-analysis problem is pitched at this great height. The unit is the nation state, not the agencies, and still less the individual human decision-makers within it. There is a parallel here with economic theories which treat firms as the units and refuse to enquire into their internal organization. This is not

---

[1] For a clear and helpful, if intricate, discussion, which separates ontological from methodological issues, see D.-H. Ruben, *The Metaphysics of the Social World* (London: Routledge and Kegan Paul, 1986).

stupid, provided that 'market forces' see to it that only firms of a profit-maximizing character survive, since, in that case, all successful internal organizations are functionally equivalent. But there are plenty of sceptical economists who believe neither in the analogy between market forces and, say, the laws of gravity nor in the utter dominance of profit-seeking. For them, the variety of internal organizations and goals does matter. Similarly, we have found several reasons to doubt whether 'national interest' is well enough defined to serve as a plausible and compulsive goal for the units of international relations. At the very least, it must be possible to debate the question.

To do so we need to consider the state not as the 'unit' of the dispute on the highest layer but as the 'whole' or 'system' on the next. This is to open the box. The question becomes how much the state's organization matters in analysing its behaviour. An incidental advantage is that it is then easier to discuss whether the state is truly the unit, or the only unit, which matters. Transnational corporations and revolutionary groups are among the rival candidates which seem to be growing in importance and which have no place in the rarefied dispute between system and states. But we shall continue to avoid this topic, on the grounds that some level-of-analysis problem applies, whatever the units deemed significant. Corporations and groups have organizations too. So let us stick to the question as posed for the state and its agencies. Do the agencies simply conform to the functional demands of the state's interests? Or is the state's behaviour the outcome of relations and interactions among the agencies? 'Top–down' proceeds in one direction, 'bottom–up' in the other. The best 'top–down' strategy we have found is to apply the theory of rational choice and Game Theory directly to the state as individual unit, thus using a 'Rational Actor' model. The best counter is a 'Bureaucratic Politics' model to show how interaction within and among bureaucracies sums to the behaviour of the state.

But debate on this layer of the problem cannot proceed without considering the individual men and women who engage in the process of decision. Both sides must find a way to make them unimportant. The Bureaucratic Politics model suppresses them by invoking the proposition that 'where you stand depends on where you sit'. It is inclined to add that bureaucratic learning procedures of selection, training, promotion, and, in periods of decision, 'groupthink' iron out any individuality. The Rational Actor model suppresses them by invoking a situational determinism, rather as economists ensure that individual economic agents do the bidding of their firms. It makes the human actors into maximizing machines which compute their choices entirely predictably, given their situation. If they cannot be suppressed in one way or the other, a further opening of the box is required.

We forced this further opening by objecting strongly to both ways of suppressing the decision-makers, and by rejecting also the obvious compromise, which accepts the Rational Actor mechanism but includes bureaucratic positions in the account of the situational determinants. Our chief objection was that role-play is neither pure calculation within parameters set by the role, nor automatic obedience to definite rules, nor yet a mixture of the two. This objection took us down to the lowest layer, where human individuals are the units, and did so in a way which also opposed Understanding to (at least mechanical) Explanation by suggesting that the actors may make situations and outcomes as they see them. That led us to think further about 'the games nations play', this time with the help of Wittgensteinian ideas of social life as 'games' in a new sense. Crucial to this sort of 'game' is the notion of constitutive rules which give moves in the game a meaning and motive internal to the game. Moreover, the rules are not fully specified in advance of all situations which will arise. So, whether we are thinking of constitutive rules which define the game or of regulative rules which facilitate it, the players are, to some degree, constructing the rules as they go along. Here Understanding starts to compete with Explaining.

We did not draw firm conclusions, because this is where we begin to disagree between ourselves. But, before setting to, we would like to sum up the 'level-of-analysis' problem. It is well enough defined for the opening two rounds. The first is marked by taking the state as the unit, the second by taking the state as the system. Both are conducted within a scientific canon of explanation and a central issue is whether the causal explanations are to proceed 'top–down' or 'bottom–up'. By 'causal' is meant at least the generalizing character of an appeal to laws of nature in the natural sciences and perhaps a reference to productive mechanisms whose presence is inferred as the best explanation of the regularities observed. But this central issue becomes complex if the individualist side then affirms that the natural 'individuals' of the social world are human beings.

One complication is the old problem of free will, since any moral concern with international relations seems to depend on the actors having a moral responsibility for choices which could have been different. But we can skirt the issue by pointing out that there is a philosophical line which reconciles freedom and determinism. 'Compatibilism' defines free action as action which is performed because the agent preferred its expected consequences. Since a rational agent needs a predictable world, in order to know the likely consequences, freedom presupposes determinism. This, if soundly argued, disposes of the problem. In pointing it out, however, we do not mean to claim that the line is sound. Indeed, one of us thinks it unsound. We mean merely to set aside the problem of free will in its traditional form.

The complication which we have pursued is that human beings have an insider's view of their world. This poses a question for a canon of scientific explanation designed to deal with molecules, molluscs, and mice. It may not be deeply awkward, granted that mice and more complex animals have some sort of inside view too and biology is no less of a science for that. But one reason often given for behaviourism (or Behaviouralism) is that it removes any awkwardness and, since we have firmly refused to endorse behaviourism, we must say something about causal explanation in a world of insiders. Morgenthau's Realism firmly included assumptions about human motivation, and later Realists, especially those applying Game Theory to foreign policy, employ a notion of rational choice. Any focus on small group decision-making also involves perceptions and intentions, language and ideology, far beyond any such concern in biology.

The crux, we suggest, is the interchangeability of actors. If their perceptions are predictable, given the psychology of small groups, and if their intentions are predictable, given the Theory of Games and given knowledge of their preferences, and if any ideological colour in perceptions and preferences is predictable, given the selection procedures which gave them their position, then the complications are merely complications. Although decision-makers are perhaps not completely interchangeable, personality and other changes involved in replacing one actor with another will, in principle, make a predictable difference. If so, a third round of the level-of-analysis problem can be conducted as before, with the group as the system and its members as the units. 'Top–down' again vies with 'bottom–up' and there is the standard prospect of a compromise or draw.

This says nothing to identify the most fertile level for conducting the argument. There are boxes within boxes. Theories favouring 'top–down' open as few as possible; those favouring 'bottom–up' are willing to seek the smallest relevant building blocks. For the purposes of this book the most fertile argument turns out to be between Rational Actor and Bureaucratic Politics models, with individual human decision-makers shuffled uneasily between them on the second layer and giving trouble to both on the third layer. Here the other dimension becomes crucial and our own disagreement breaks out in earnest. So we now turn to our dispute about the scope for *understanding* international relations. For the dialogue which follows it may be as well to bear it in mind that Martin Hollis is a philosopher, who believes that the social sciences are relevantly different from the natural sciences and claims no expertise in International Relations, whereas Steve Smith is an International Relations scholar, who inclines to level-of-analysis compromises which somewhat favour the structural side and claims no expertise in philosophy. Our intellectual concerns therefore intersect but do not coincide.[2]

---

[2] M. Hollis, *Models of Man* (Cambridge: Cambridge University Press, 1977), presents a general case for taking 'Autonomous Man', rather than 'Plastic Man' as the focus of social science and argues that 'action' is a concept foreign to the methods of natural science. *The Cunning of Reason* (Cambridge: Cambridge University Press, 1988) develops the line of thought by examining the scope and limits of rational choice and Game Theory analyses of social action. Both books contend that instrumental rationality is not the only or even the primary concept of rationality that is of service to the social sciences. Also relevant is Hollis's essay 'The Social Destruction of Reality', in M. Hollis and S. Lukes (eds.), *Rationality and Relativism* (Oxford: Blackwell, 1982). Steve Smith has mainly been concerned to look at how foreign policy behaviour is the result of structural forces. Commonly, this involves looking at the pressures on individual decision-makers and the impact of processes of implementation on foreign policy behaviour. For discussion of the former see his 'Groupthink and the Hostage Rescue Mission', *British Journal of Political Science*, 1985, 15(1), pp. 117–23, 'Policy Preferences and Bureaucratic Position: The Case of the American Hostage Rescue Mission', *International Affairs*, 1985, 61(1), pp. 9–25, and 'Allison and the Cuban Missile Crisis', *Millennium*, 1981, 9(1), pp. 21–40. See also his essay 'Belief Systems in the Study of International Relations', in R. Little and S. Smith (eds.), *Belief Systems and International Relations* (Oxford: Blackwell, 1988), pp. 11–36. For a discussion of the latter see S. Smith and M. Clarke, 'Introduction' and 'Conclusion' in their

MH   Could we start from our remark that David Singer's analogy between the 'level-of-analysis' problem and different map projections of the globe is interestingly questionable? I question it because it seems to me to beg an absolutely central issue. It embodies a Positivist presumption that there is a world awaiting the map-maker. This world is as it is and the alleged snag is only that the map is two-dimensional. Yet, although projections distort, they do so in unpuzzling ways and, despite what Singer says, there is not the slightest difficulty in combining them. Even if use of a third dimension is disallowed, the information given in one projection can readily be translated into information in the other. I firmly reject this Positivist presumption for the social world. International relations are what the rules (such as they are) and the decisions of foreign policy-makers (and others) create. The 'level-of-analysis' problem still arises, but now as one about whether the rules and roles constitute the moves made in the games nations play and, ultimately, the players themselves, or whether understanding should proceed in the opposite direction. But it is a problem about the method of *understanding* and I take the insider view to be fundamental. I wonder whether your doubts about Singer's analogy go as deep as mine and whether you think of 'understanding', in so far as it differs interestingly from 'explaining', as more than a preliminary and heuristic device.

SS   There are two issues here. First, the level-of-analysis problem. I, too, reject the Positivist notion that there is a world waiting to be mapped. There may be regularities in human affairs but I do not accept the idea that we can construct a neutral theory, valid across time and space, that allows us to predict in the same way as occurs in the natural sciences. I do not see that as only a matter of complexity, but as a fundamental feature of the social sciences. Our theories are always for some purpose and cannot be presented as in some way neutral and determined in some simple way by the 'facts'. The level-of-analysis debate is a methodological not an ontological debate: it refers to how best to explain and not to how the world really is. Indeed, Singer in framing the level-of-analysis problem thought that there was no way of combining the two levels. This was because the two levels had biases which were

edited volume, *Foreign Policy Implementation* (London: Allen and Unwin, 1985), pp. 1–10 and 166–80. See also Steve Smith, 'The Hostage Rescue Mission', in ibid. pp. 11–32.

mutually exclusive. His map analogy was meant to show that it was just as impossible to combine theories couched at the two levels as it would be to represent accurately a three-dimensional object on a two-dimensional map. But this suggests that both levels say something about behaviour. Therefore, I accept the possibility of analysing the actor's views; so, to turn to your second issue, I am prepared to consider Understanding as a way of analyzing human action. However, in contrast to you, I do not consider the insider view to be fundamental. I think that the view from the inside makes actors appear to have more freedom of manœuvre than they do, and it ignores the possibility that their perceptions and understandings are themselves caused by factors external to them. Thus, I can see that an account based on Understanding rather than explaining is a contender, but I do not think that it can do as much as you think it can.

MH Before we argue about how much 'Understanding' can contribute, we had better try to pin down what it involves. Throughout the book we have glossed it as 'rational reconstruction', rather than struggling with the several concepts of meaning which might be the key to discovering what situations and actions 'mean' to the actors. I suggest that we continue to speak of Understanding as reconstruction which proceeds on the assumption that actors are rational, thus applying an ideal-type yardstick and regarding departures from it as irrational (rather than non-rational because beyond the scope of rational assessment). In other words, the approach is to regard foreign policy decisions as the actors' solutions to problems. These solutions apply policies, for which we can also ask the reasons, to situations as the actors themselves understand them. Especially important is the actors' own understanding of what is in the minds of other actors. In the ideal-type case all problems are as rationally solved as is possible. Real-life departures from rational solutions are traced to actors' misunderstandings.

This sketch of the method is non-committal about the sense of 'rationality'. In Chapter 6 it meant the instrumental rationality (*Zweckrationalität*) favoured by economists and Game Theorists. 'The games nations play' were at first played for the sake of their pay-off. But, having explored the Bureaucratic Politics model in Chapter 7, we decided that reasons for action are not only of this instrumental kind. In Chapter 8, Wittgensteinian games were introduced and found to be both constituted and regulated by rules which furnished at least some reasons for action internal to the game, rather than external because furthering the pursuit of external goals. Understanding here requires reconstructing the rules on the one hand and seeking the actors' intentions, legitimating reasons, and underlying motives on the other.

Is this a fair summary of our idea of Understanding?

SS   Yes, although it is important to note that the explaining side also claims to be able to account for Understanding. But your outline of Understanding is also mine. We agree on what it is, but disagree as to its importance.

MH   Then may I take you up on your belief that the actors' 'perceptions and understandings are themselves caused by factors external to them'? I agree, of course, that rational actors are guided by how things are, or, where situations are opaque, by how they rationally take them to be. But you seem to have a mechanical picture of their minds and one which, if accepted, will reduce the actors to a throughput between what causes their 'perceptions and understandings' and their output. This picture makes sense to me only if, despite what you say about Singer's map projections, you are assuming a neutral, external, and causal set of facts. Conversely, the reason why the analogy does not hold, in my view, is that the furniture and events of the social world are identifiable only by reference to the rules which constitute and regulate the social world. The actors' understandings are therefore not a link in a causal chain but the stuff of the world which their understandings also reveal to them. That is why an insider view is fundamental.

SS   In the first place, I think that your comment about 'how things are' gives you some problems. That is to say, I do not think that resorting to an argument about forms of life allows you to escape from the problem that there is something going on apart from the actor's own thoughts. Forms of life themselves reveal patterns, and, of course, the Wittgensteinian notion of a game, so central to your conception of understanding, still involves rules. Thus, your charge that there is something causing perceptions applies on the understanding side as well. In fact, these rules which constitute and regulate the social world may be so powerful as to take out the actor as fast as you introduce him or her, thus becoming functional to an extent. Your actors, after all, are born into a world in which the rules of the game exist, and although they may be able to influence those rules, the rules remain, in a critical sense, external to them. Your main point, though, is about the existence of a causal chain, with Understanding *merely* a link in that chain. I do not see Understanding in this way, as I accept that the actor's own understanding is an area of underdetermination. Actors interpret, filter, and assess; they perceive and misperceive. Their perceptions are not completely determined; but this does not mean that perceptions are not caused. The central point for me is that perceptions are best understood as conditioned to a large extent. Again, this is a methodological, not an ontological, claim. I see actors as inhabiting a world in which their interpretations, filters, and assessments are all largely socially constructed. Focusing on the insider view overemphasizes the realm of choice and underemphasizes the realm of constraint. Even when there seems to be choice, remember that the language and concepts an actor uses are themselves socially constructed. In essence, then, I believe that reality is a social construct; it is in this sense that I see perceptions and understandings as largely determined, and why I see Understanding as secondary and not fundamental.

MH   Games, in the sense of rules and moves within them, are, we agree, socially constructed but no less real for that. I take this as equivalent to saying that they are external to each player but internal to the players collectively (and over time). Each inherits a stock of games, which enable and constrain and can only rarely be changed by one individual. Games can evolve, however, partly because their rules can come into conflict and be modified, especially in unforeseen situations, and partly because groups of players can combine to amend them. Language is one of these games, deeper and external to more players than most, but still mutable, rather in the spirit of what Otto Neurath once said about science, that it is rebuilding a boat while at sea. That is part of an answer to your remark about 'how things are' being a problem for me. It is not a complete answer, I grant, unless one espouses a form of idealism so strong that there is nothing social going on apart from the actors' own thoughts. Perhaps we should return to this.

   Meanwhile, if games are socially constructed in this sense, then the natural world certainly is not. You believe that natural and social worlds are all of a piece and call, in the end, for the same scientific method. So, consistently, you hold that 'reality is a social construct', meaning, I presume, the reality of both natural and social worlds. Really? Could we keep dry in a storm by all agreeing to amend our theories about what is real? Luckily for the umbrella industry, it seems to me that you do not even wish to suggest it. So why assimilate social structures to natural structures, rather than go the other way? Perhaps the crux is who or what constructs the framework of social actions. If it is *actors*, then I shall be quick to invite further concessions. But you may have it in mind that structures generate both structures and actions. At any rate, what notion of structure do you wish to set against my view that social structures are sets of rules and practices (and their—often latent—implications)?

SS My conception of structure is that used in the realist (in the philosophy of science, not the International Relations sense) notion of science. This includes the claim that science concerns the explanation of causal mechanisms, which may involve non-observable structures. Positivists dispute the notion of science as including non-observable structures, and your comment about the nature of structures implies a criticism that they do not exist in the social world as they do in the natural world. Yet there is a lengthy debate on this issue within the philosophy of science, with one side claiming that structures exist, and cause behaviour, and are unobservable. Thus, I do not think that I have a particular problem merely because I see structures in the social world and yet cannot prove, in a Positivist sense, their existence. Rather, my notion of structure is that positing their existence gives us the best explanation of social action. To use a phrase familiar in the philosophy of science, we are involved in 'inference to the best explanation'. To be explicit, then, I think that social action can best be explained as behaviour caused by structures. I cannot prove the existence of these structures, but I think that we get the best explanations by inferring their existence. These structures may be as specific as the bureaucratic structure of a state, or as general as the structures of racism, patriarchy, and class. That I cannot take you and show you a hard, solid structure of, say, patriarchy, does not mean that inferring the existence of such a structure is not the best way of explaining the patterns of inequality and dominance between the genders. What is more, I am sure that to many minorities or suppressed groups (such as women, gays, blacks, and the poor) there are very real structures of dominance at work, including one that determines how they see themselves.

But let me turn to your own view of social action. I have two main worries about it. First, how do you avoid the difficulty of seeing society as only the sum total of what goes on inside the heads of individuals? Do you really want to accept such an idealistic (again, in its philosophical not its International Relations guise) position? At times, it seems to me that you have no way of explaining the material world. The second problem for you is that I want you to say something about your conception of an actor. You make great play with the important difference between each actor and all actors, yet I sense sometimes that your individual actors are very empty vessels. In short, I feel that your view of an active actor applies only to a certain type of person, one relatively free from constraints, and occupying a position of power or influence in society. Does your view of the actor allow us to explain the lives of all individuals or only those on the apex of society?

MH   I agree that (philosophical) realists in the philosophy of natural science can maintain that structures and mechanisms are the best explanation of what we observe, and so can be inferred even though they cannot be themselves observed. I do not mean that the realist side wins—only that it has a defensible case and should not be scared off by Positivists or pragmatists. By that token, however, I too can take a realist line on natural and material processes and thus explain the natural world.

That leaves it unclear where the boundaries between natural and social and between ideal and material fall. For instance, the spread of AIDS is a natural and material fact, if one thinks about human physiology, and a social and ideal fact, if one thinks about the apocalyptic images which spread with it. But the two boundaries do not always fall neatly in the same place. The power of group over group is a social fact and depends on what people have in their heads. But it depends also on threats and fears being materially enforceable—an aspect which is both 'social' and 'material'. That is awkward for me but also, I think, awkward for you. Domination does not work through physical force alone. Patriarchs have an authority, legitimated rather than legitimate no doubt, without which they could not function as patriarchs.

So we both need to be very clear about 'structure'. I hope that you are not thinking in literal terms, as if institutional structure were literally like the hidden structure of a building. Institutional structure is a metaphor which needs cashing in. I am happy to cash it in (partly) in terms of 'power', defined as the ability to bring about a desired outcome and traced to the enablements and constraints which institutional rules create. This gives a sense of structure suited to, indeed calling for, a method of Understanding.

It is an ability which suitably placed actors have, but only in so far as they have the skill to use it. Here we start to disagree in earnest, I fancy. *All* actors are enabled as well as constrained by institutional rules, in my view. Although they may vary in endowments, all can learn the skills which often enable them to ease the constraints. This is a general proposition about humans as social beings. But, of course, power varies with context and not everyone is equally placed. People who have some power in their domestic lives may be largely at the receiving end in their public and workplace lives. In the context of bureaucracy, the power of those who work for, say, a Foreign Office waxes and wanes depending on what is going on at home and abroad. But I see nothing odd in holding that, in general, rules always enable and constrain and that, for the particular case of international relations, most decisions depend on a few actors as members of élite groups thanks to their official positions.

Crucially, my actors are not interchangeable. Enablements and constraints are initially like a hand of cards one is dealt. But in social life not all the enablements or constraints are fully specified in advance of play. How the game turns out depends on how well one plays the hand. That is one reason why International Relations cannot abolish history in the name of a timeless science, and why therefore Understanding is not a species of Explaining.

To put it in my terms, you seem to think that situations, being structured, always have outcomes which were fully determined in advance, rather as if the actors were speaking lines from a fully scripted drama. Do you really think this? It seems to me a metaphor gone mad.

SS   I do not believe that actors have fully scripted lines, nor do I think that outcomes are fully determined. However, I want to make a couple of comments about your own assumptions. The first is about your notion of social life as a hand of cards that each is dealt. That analogy can be read in two ways. Your way is that the way one plays the hand determines, in part, the outcome. My worry is that another reading of the analogy seems far more relevant to social life. This other reading is simply that an awful lot of people get dealt very poor cards, hands so bad that no matter what their skill they cannot do much to improve their lot. As soon as they pick up the hand they begin to lose heart, especially if they live in a society that worships the high cards and treats a poor hand as in some way the fault of its holder. My view of society (both domestic and international) sees actors as having little ability to change their lot. Talking about skill seems to me to place responsibility on individuals for changing their lot, whereas, in reality, they cannot do so. What sense is there to say that the downtrodden and dominated have an ability to play their hands skilfully? Surely to the battered economically dependent woman, to the unskilled unemployed black in Harlem, or to the economically poorest nation states, such an analysis of social life as yours seems irrelevant. You risk portraying society as the sum total of individual activity, and opposing structures because you can think of them only as fully determining. More saliently, your view of actors is such an individualist one that I have to note the comments of many Critical Theorists that knowledge is a reflection of its social and political context.

So, I do not think that because I believe in the existence of structures as providing the best explanation of social life I am committed to seeing them as 'fully determining' or as 'timeless'. Now, of course, a tempting compromise is for both of us to accept that individuals have some room for manœuvre but are also constrained, and that we differ 'only' about the degree of latitude individuals have. That is to say, we accept that individuals are subject to external influences but can still use skill and judgement to make actual choices. This is tempting, but I do not think that either of us can accept this compromise; and I think it is important that we make it clear to the reader why we cannot. At the end of the day I think we have two very different views of social action: mine fits broadly within the 'Explaining' mode, yours within the 'Understanding'. These different views entail fundamentally distinct (and mutually exclusive) views of the individual and of the social world. These views cannot simply be combined because one sees Understanding as the key to analysis, and debates whether that should be analysed 'top–down' or 'bottom–up', while the other sees no need to resort to Understanding as a necessary constituent of analysis, preferring instead to analyse by Explaining, with, again, the debate being whether to go 'top–down' or 'bottom–up'.

The implication of this is that in all discussions of social life there are *always* and *inevitably* two stories to be told, one concentrating on Understanding, the other focusing on Explaining. My view fits on the 'Explaining' side, seeing structures as operating to cause vast areas of social action. I am reminded of a quotation from Louis Althusser who, writing from an even more deterministic position than myself, wrote:

The structure of the relations of production determines the places and functions occupied and adopted by the agents of production, who are never anything more than the occupants of these places, insofar as they are the supports (*Träger*) of these functions. The true 'subjects' (in the sense of constitutive subjects of the process) are therefore not these occupants or functionaries, are not, despite all appearances, the 'obvious-ness' of the 'given' of naive anthropology, 'concrete individuals', 'real men'—but the definition and distribution of these places and functions.[3]

Thus, contrary to 'commonsense' and the 'obviousness' of our existence, the intentional subject (whose desires, beliefs, and natures are seen as the explanation of social events) is not the starting point for analysis.

Turning to international relations, I believe that you and I agree that there are always two stories to be told, in each of the three layers of the level-of-analysis debate discussed earlier. To restate, the typical disputes are: (a) the international system versus its units (states); (b) the monolithic state versus its constituent bureaucracies; (c) the bureaucracy versus its individual members. Each of these disputes occurs within each method of analysis, so that you can use 'Explaining' and 'Understanding' at each level. In fact, of course, even when it comes to the individual we still disagree, and the reason why we cannot finally reconcile our differences is that we actually see a different individual. My individuals come in as members of bureaucracies, dominated by their role and with little freedom for manœuvre. This puts me firmly on the 'Explaining' side at each of the three layers of the

[3] L. Althusser and F. Baliber, *Reading Capital* (London: New Left Books, 1970), p. 180.

level-of-analysis debate. Specifically, I explain international relations primarily in terms of the impact of the system and the bureaucracies on the state: that is to say, I see the foreign policy of states as resulting from two sets of structural causes, the system and the bureaucracies. At the first level I see systemic pressures considerably affecting the context for foreign policy-making; at the second level I see policy as the result of bureaucratic bargaining; and at the third level I see bureaucracies largely determining the actions and beliefs of individual role-players. More generally, I see such structural accounts as the most productive in the analysis of social life. You prefer Understanding as the best way of analysing social life. How, precisely, do you use such an approach to analyse international relations?

MH   I wholly agree that millions of people are dealt very poor cards. This is all too plain where life is drudgery or starvation. It is also true often enough even for the domestic life, where romantics like to fancy that the poor and dispossessed are enabled to live at least as happily as the rich. But the other side of this thought is that other people are dealt good cards. You seem to suggest that poor cards anywhere are a reason for structural explanation everywhere. That seems to me a manifest *non sequitur* and wholly implausible for international relations in particular.

But it does usefully bring out a point about the notion of 'Understanding' as used in this book. It has been a modest notion, addressed to decision-making and its context, not to the hidden dynamics of history. Its source has been Weber, rather than the hermeneutics favoured by Absolute Idealism in the nineteenth century or by Critical Theorists today. A serious attempt to understand the distribution of power and the persistence of op-presion, and to use that understanding in search of emancipation, needs to be more ambitious. I am not sure attempts can succeed before collapsing in their own fog; but that is a topic for another day. For the purposes of this book, we have taken a modest but clear notion of rational action and worked with a proposal that international relations can be understood as the sum of actions in an institutional context and their (often unforeseen) consequences. To compare the games of Game Theory with Wittgensteinian games is only a modest exercise, although one which seems to me useful for thinking about method in International Relations.

At any rate, I am clear as to what I want to say about

Understanding and the level-of-analysis problem. On the highest layer, Understanding can proceed 'top–down' only if one defines the system in ambitious terms like 'international interests' rather than the more modest 'international society'. The latter refers to something too fragile and too plainly in the tentative process of construction to give 'top–down' a chance. This is, I confess, how I see it myself, thus siding with 'bottom–up' in the first dispute and understanding international relations through the actions of the units.

In the second dispute (nation states vs. bureaucracies), I find the state important too. This may be because I am more impressed than you are by the legal enablements and constraints which arise because the state has supreme coercive *authority* in its own domain of domestic politics. I think of bureaucracies as players in the state's game (not vice versa), more as lesser authorities under licence than as confederated baronies. But, unlike you, I regard it as crucial that the actual players are bureaucrats, not bureaucracies. That prevents the advantage of the state in the second dispute being the whole answer to the problem.

The third dispute, which we classified as bureaucracy vs. individual, is the most subtle. It turns on what one is to think about role-players. I will not try to repeat what was said about creative latitude in earlier chapters, but you see where it tends. Micro-economic 'individuals' seem to me a misleading abstraction from men and women as social beings, who can shape their own identity in their relations with others. How bureaucracies, within the enablements and constraints set by the state, act is a matter of how role-players combine to decide that they act, given that they interact with members of other bureaucracies (and other organizations) similarly propelled. The role-players, as institutional selves, hold the final trumps.

I thus favour an Understanding which gives most of the bureaucratic game to its players, where you favour an Explanation which largely subordinates the players to the demands of the bureaucratic structure. In broader summary, the theoretical weight, which you place on the international system and bureaucracy, I place on the nation state and the role-playing bureaucrats.

So we have a lively disagreement about the level-of-analysis problem. But it is not a simple collision, since you believe finally in Explaining and I in Understanding. As you rightly say, there are always two stories to tell and they cannot be merely added together. Nor, by the same token, does an umpire have any easy perch from which to decide on their relative merits. We cannot hope to settle our disagreement on the spot and I do not think that we should try. We would both rather leave it to readers to make up their own minds.

CONCLUSION (BY BOTH AUTHORS)

Our unfinished debate threatens to ramify into areas where we earlier spoke with a single voice. Yet the stories do not always conflict—otherwise we could not have written the earlier chapters— and we shall end by charting some common ground. It is easier to find, if one appreciates that the debate is not between the disparate disciplines of international relations and philosophy but between disparate views within each discipline. Someone who inclines to a Structuralist view in International Relations will be best suited by some kind of realism in a unified philosophy of science and hence by taking the main task to be one of *explaining* international relations. Someone who inclines to a hermeneutic view in philosophy will be best suited by an International Relations theory which works from the inside and tries to *understand* international relations in terms of rules, actions, and their (often unforeseen) results. Although neither of us advocates what would best suit the other, each sees how it could be done.

To chart the common ground, we need to abstract from the three layers of the level-of-analysis problem. In place of three layers involving respectively international, national bureaucratic, and human elements we shall be content with two poles, the holist and the individualist. Crossed with 'Explaining' and 'Understanding', they give Figure 9.2 and a 2 × 2 matrix (as in Figure 1.1). With the help of the intervening chapters we can now characterize the leading idea in each of the four cells. The circle in the middle, which represents the core of our debate, should be thought of not as a position of four-way compromise but as a movable counter to be manœuvred to whatever place on the chart the reader finds most satisfactory.

In summary, then, Singer's level-of-analysis problem is classically one of whether to *explain* top–down or bottom–up, whatever quite

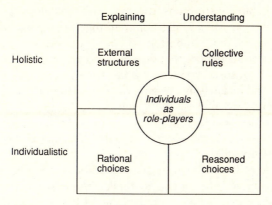

FIG. 9.2.

one identifies for the purpose as 'system' and as 'unit'. To give it an uncompromising answer is to affirm or deny the legitimacy of inferences to external social factors or forces. The holist affirms it, as Waltz did until he made concessions. The individualist denies it and, we suggest, does best to uphold the claims of rational choice theory and Game Theory to account for social institutions as well as for interactions. There is, however, also a level-of-analysis problem in the 'Understanding' column. Here an uncompromising answer affirms or denies that to understand the rules governing action is to understand action. To affirm it is to hold that rules (or institutions) make the actors; to deny it is to hold that actors make the rules. In both columns there are compromises to consider, whose effect would be to move the 'Individuals as role-players' counter on to the dividing line, or close to it, on one side or the other. In our dialogue Hollis tried to manœuvre it to just below the line in the 'Understanding' column, Smith to just above the line in the 'Explaining' column.

Which column is the more promising? That is a hard question even to summarize. For, although placings on the vertical axis are perhaps a matter of degree, we have emphatically said that the horizontal dimension spans two irreconcilable stories. Yet some kind of dispute among holists is possible about whether, for instance, economic relations of production owe more to productive forces or to legal, political, and ethical relations. Some kind of dispute is possible among individualists about the relative import-ance of instrumental and expressive rationality in analysing action, interaction, and institutions. Indeed, our dialogue offers some compromises, as when Hollis admitted that social facts are not all or wholly ideal and Smith granted that it makes some difference what bureaucrats believe that other bureaucrats have in mind. But there is a limit to how much of a fair summary of the riddles of social life and its analysis can be given with a simple 2 × 2 matrix. Let us merely say that we think the counter impossibly placed in the exact centre and leave it to the reader to decide whether it can be stably positioned elsewhere on the dividing lines and how close to the centre itself.

We hope to have shown that both traditions, the scientific and the hermeneutic, offer much to think about. Idealism in International Relations has been undervalued by treating it as starry-eyed and woolly-minded moral optimism. Its implications for *understanding action* remain fertile and in instructive contrast to the claims of Realism to *explain behaviour*. Realists may have the stronger case in the end; or, then again, they may not. We have no final word on that. But we do suggest that the electrifying issues in International Relations repay tracing throughout the social sciences and that, in the present state of intellectual upheaval, to say nothing of the upheavals in Eastern Europe, philosophy is both an aid and an element in the exercise.

Guide to Further Reading

INTERNATIONAL RELATIONS

Many of the major works in the subject of International Relations have been mentioned already in the survey of the subject which we undertook in Chapter 2. Having said that, anyone wanting to read a general overview of the theory of the subject could look at J. Dougherty and R. Pfaltzgraff, *Contending Theories of International Relations*, 2nd edn. (New York: Harper and Row, 1980). This has chapters on the main areas of theory. An alternative introduction to the theory of the subject is P. Viotti and M. Kauppi, *International Relations Theory* (New York: Macmillan, 1987). There are a host of general introductions to the subject, both empirical and theoretical, the most popular of which are, in the US, K. Holsti, *International Politics: A Framework for Analysis*, 5th edn. (Englewood Cliffs, NJ: Prentice-Hall, 1988), and in the UK, P. Reynolds, *An Introduction to International Relations*, 2nd edn. (London: Longman, 1980).

We have divided the subject into three main phases: Idealism, Realism (including Neo-Realism), and Behaviouralism. For good brief discussions of the history of the subject see H. Bull, 'The Theory of International Politics, 1919–1969' and W. Olson, 'The Growth of a Discipline', both in B. Porter (ed.), *The Aberystwyth Papers: International Politics 1919–1969* (London: Oxford University Press, 1972), pp. 30–35 and 3–29 respectively. The latter paper has been updated and published as W. Olson and N. Onuf, 'The Growth of a Discipline: Reviewed', in S. Smith (ed.), *International Relations: British and American Perspectives* (Oxford: Blackwell, 1985), pp. 1–28. The development of theory in the subject is also summarized in S. Smith, 'The Development of International Relations as a Social Science', *Millennium*, 1987, 16(2), pp. 189–206, and M. Banks, 'The Evolution of International Relations Theory', in M. Banks (ed.), *Conflict in World Society* (Brighton: Wheatsheaf, 1984), pp. 3–21.

The best example of Idealist writing is Sir A. Zimmern, *The League of Nations and the Rule of Law* (London: Macmillan, 1939). The main attack on Idealism is by E. H. Carr in *The Twenty Years' Crisis 1919–1939* (London: Macmillan, 1939). The classic Realist text remains H. Morgenthau's *Politics among Nations: The Struggle for Power and Peace*, 1st edn. (New York: Knopf, 1948), and its five subsequent editions. But, of course, Idealism and Realism are rich in their diversity and the reader is referred to the general surveys listed above for detailed references to other writers. The debate between the traditionalists and the Behaviouralists is contained in the collection of essays edited by K. Knorr and J. Rosenau (eds.), *Contending Approaches to International Politics* (Princeton: Princeton University Press, 1969); see especially the essays by Bull, pp. 20–38, Kaplan, pp. 39–61, Singer, pp. 62–86, and Levy, pp. 87–109.

We characterized the current state of the discipline as being divided into three main theoretical approaches: Realism, Pluralism, and Structuralism. For a collection of readings that is similarly divided, see M. Smith, R. Little, and M. Shackleton (eds.), *Perspectives on World Politics* (London: Croom Helm, 1981). This division is also used by Michael Banks in his excellent summary of the current scene, 'The Inter-Paradigm Debate', in M. Light and J. Groom (eds.), *International Relations: A Handbook of Current Theory* (London: Pinter, 1985), pp. 7–26. This is a most useful little book, since it contains summaries of the state of all the main sub-fields in the discipline, as well as excellent bibliographies. It is very difficult indeed to nominate a single representative for each of these current approaches, because they are quite diverse. The literature on Neo-Realism is focused on the one book that we discussed in depth in Chapter 5, Kenneth Waltz's *Theory of International Politics* (Reading, MA: Addison-Wesley, 1979). Also important are R. Gilpin, *War and Change in World Politics* (Cambridge: Cambridge University Press, 1981), S. Krasner, *Defending the National Interest: Raw Materials Investments and US Foreign Policy* (Princeton: Princeton University Press, 1978), and R. Keohane, *After Hegemony: Cooperation and Discord in the World Political Economy* (Princeton: Princeton University Press, 1984).

Pluralism is best represented by the works of Robert Keohane and Joseph Nye; see, for example, their edited volume, *Transnational Relations and World Politics* (Cambridge, MA: Harvard University Press, 1972), and their *Power and Interdependence: World Politics in Transition* (Boston: Little, Brown, 1977). Also important are S. Brown, *New Forces in World Politics* (Washington, DC: Brookings Institution, 1974), and E. Morse, *Modernization and the Transformation of International Relations* (New York: Free Press, 1976). A very good collection of essays dealing with the main claims of the Pluralists is R. Maghroori and B. Ramberg (eds.), *Globalism versus Realism: International Relations' Third Debate* (Boulder, CO: Westview, 1982).

Structuralism is the most difficult of the three to deal with. Its roots being in Marxism, there are many different versions of it. Good examples are J. Galtung, 'A Structural Theory of Imperialism', *Journal of Peace Research*, 1971, 8(1), pp. 81–117; T. Skocpol, *States and Social Revolutions* (Cambridge: Cambridge University Press, 1979); I. Wallerstein, *The Capitalist World Economy* (Cambridge: Cambridge University Press, 1979); and S. Brucan, *The Dialectics of World Politics* (New York: Free Press, 1978).

In the last few years several alternative approaches have begun to attack the dominance of these three. The three that the reader should be aware of are Soviet theory, Critical Theory, and feminist theory. Each poses a challenge to the orthodoxy, which, we should remind readers, is still dominated by Realism and Neo-Realism. Soviet theory is well covered in two books: A. Lynch, *The Soviet Study of International Relations* (Cambridge: Cambridge University Press, 1987) and M. Light, *The Soviet Theory of International Relations* (Brighton: Wheatsheaf, 1988). Critical Theory's contribution is summarized in Mark Hoffman's very good article, 'Critical Theory and the Inter-Paradigm Debate', *Millennium*, 1987, 16(2), pp. 231–50. See also A. Linklater, 'Realism, Marxism and Critical International Theory', *Review of International Studies*, 1986, 12(4), pp. 301–12. Feminist views of international relations theory are discussed in a special number of the journal *Millennium, Women and International Relations*, 1988, 17(3); see especially, the articles by Halliday, Brown, and Tickner, pp. 419–28, 461–76, and 429–40 respectively. See also J. B. Elshtain, *Women and War* (New York: Basic Books, 1987).

Finally, readers might like to follow up on the discussions of the methodology of the subject. The links between the study of international relations and the study of history are dealt with in Chris Hill's excellent essay, 'History and International Relations', in S. Smith (ed.), *International Relations: British and American Perspectives* (Oxford: Blackwell, 1985), pp. 126–45. See also the explicitly methodological essays in P. Lauren (ed.), *Diplomacy: New Approaches in History, Theory, and Policy* (New York: Free Press, 1979). For a view that attacks the scientific pretensions of International Relations, preferring instead a more historical method, see C. Reynolds, *Theory and Explanation in International Politics* (Oxford: Martin Robertson, 1973).

As for literature dealing specifically with the issue that has been the concern of this book, namely, the link between International Relations and the philosophy of social science, there is a useful guide by Michael Nicholson, 'Methodology', in M. Light and

J. Groom (eds.), *International Relations: A Handbook of Current Theory* (London: Pinter, 1985), pp. 90–9. For Nicholson's own view of the linkage, see his *The Scientific Analysis of Social Behaviour: A Defence of Empiricism in Social Science* (London: Pinter, 1983). Within the subject of International Relations, there have been many debates about methods, as one would expect from a subject dominated by quantitative approaches; but there have been very few attempts to discuss the philosophy of social science questions underlying the discipline. The most interesting of these has been the debate on the value of quantitative analysis between Young and Russett; see O. Young, 'Professor Russett: Industrious Tailor to a Naked Emperor', *World Politics*, 1969, 21(3), pp. 586–611 and B. Russett, 'The Young Science of International Politics', *World Politics*, 1969, 22(1), pp. 87–94. For two interesting, and rare, essays on the philosophy of social science, see R. Spegele, 'Deconstructing Methodological Falsification in International Relations', *American Political Science Review*, 1980, 74(1), pp. 104–22 and R. Gorman, 'On the Inadequacies of a Non-Philosophical Political Science: A Critical Analysis of Decision-Making Theory', *International Studies Quarterly*, 1970, 14(4), pp. 395–411. See also the essays dealing with philosophy of social science questions in Part II of J. Rosenau (ed.), *In Search of Global Patterns* (New York: Free Press, 1976). But, of course, this very dearth of material is what has led us to write this book.

PHILOSOPHY

Readers unfamiliar with philosophy may find it best to start with the philosophy of natural science. A. F. Chalmers, *What is this Thing called Science?*, 2nd edn. (Milton Keynes: Open University Press, 1982) is an excellent guide. Its main focus is on issues made central by Popper, Kuhn, and Lakatos but it is also helpful more generally, for instance about realism and instrumentalism. R. Harré, *The Philosophies of Science* (Oxford: Oxford University Press, 1972) is clear and lively. For the story at first hand, begin with Logical Positivism as conveyed by R. B. Braithwaite, *Scientific Explanation* (Cambridge: Cambridge University Press, 1953) and, if brave, follow up the references to Carnap, Nagel, and Hempel which we gave in the footnotes to Chapter 3. A. J. Ayer, *Language, Truth and Logic* (Harmondsworth: Penguin, 1971 and several other editions) was first published in 1936 and brought the broad message of Logical Positivism to English readers with panache.

Karl Popper's most commanding essay is 'Conjectures and Refutations', in the collection of his essays published under that title (London: Routledge and Kegan Paul, 1969). Also classic is his *The Logic of Scientific Discovery* (London: Hutchinson, 1958). His views start to shift interestingly with *Objective Knowledge* (Oxford: Oxford University Press, 1972). For Quine see 'Two Dogmas of Empiricism', in W. v. O. Quine, *From a Logical Point of View* (New York: Harper and Row, 1961)—it is marvellously clever and subversive. T. Kuhn, *The Structure of Scientific Revolutions*, 2nd edn. (Chicago: University of Chicago Press, 1970) has become a landmark. Recent discussion has been stimulated especially by Imré Lakatos's idea about research programmes in his *Collected Papers*, Volume I (Cambridge: Cambridge University Press, 1980), by P. K. Feyerabend, *Against Method* (London: New Left Books, 1975), and by R. Bhaskar, *A Realist Theory of Science* (Brighton: Harvester, 1978). Ian Hacking's edited collection, *Scientific Revolutions* (Oxford: Oxford University Press, 1981) is well chosen.

A guide to these themes which also offers a transition to the philosophy of the social sciences is R. Keat and J. Urry, *Social Theory as Science* (London: Routledge and Kegan Paul, 1975). A simpler, if more Positivist, introduction is A. Ryan, *The Philosophy of the Social Sciences* (London: Macmillan, 1970). Two evergreen attempts to apply science to social life are definitely still to be read. They are T. Hobbes, *Leviathan* (first published 1651) and D. Hume, *A Treatise of Human Nature* (first published 1739), both available in many editions. J. S. Mill, *A System of Logic*, Book VI, ed. A. J. Ayer (London: Duckworth, 1988) was first published in 1843 and remains a clear and robust statement of scientific method applied to this purpose.

On the other hand, the social sciences may have a special character which calls for a philosophy of Understanding rather than of Scientific Explanation. An introduction which explores this line is L. Doyal and R. Harris, *Empiricism, Explanation and Rationality* (London: Routledge and Kegan Paul, 1986). The case (or rather a Wittgensteinian version of it) was stoutly made by Peter Winch in *The Idea of a Social Science* (London: Routledge and Kegan Paul, 1958), as we noted in earlier chapters. For Max Weber's (ambivalent) views of meaning and rationality see the start of *Economy and Society* (New York: Bedminster Press, 1968; first published in 1922). The opening pages have often been reprinted. One useful source is G. Runciman (ed.), *Weber: Selections in Translation* (Cambridge: Cambridge University Press, 1978). Another is F. Dallmayr and T. McCarthy (eds.),

Understanding and Social Enquiry (Notre Dame: University of Notre Dame Press, 1977), which includes, among other useful readings, Charles Taylor's essay 'Interpretation and the Sciences of Man', originally published in *The Review of Metaphysics*, 1971, 25 and also reprinted in his fertile *Collected Papers* (Cambridge: Cambridge University Press, 1985).

Those drawn to Critical Theory might begin with R. Geuss, *The Idea of a Critical Theory: Habermas and the Frankfurt School* (Cambridge: Cambridge University Press, 1981). For Habermas himself there are English translations of *Knowledge and Human Interests* (Boston: Beacon Press, 1971) and *Legitimation Crisis* (Boston: Beacon Press, 1975). T. Adorno *et al.*, *The Positivist Dispute in German Sociology* (New York: Harper, 1976) is an instructive confrontation between the Positivist and German hermeneutic traditions. In so far as issues of social realism (in one of its philosophical senses) are involved, readers might like to grapple with R. Bhaskar, *The Possibility of Naturalism* (Brighton: Harvester, 1979).

The waters run much clearer for topics in rational choice and Game Theory. Jon Elster has contributed much lucid and ingenious philosophical discussion, notably *Logic and Society* (New York: Wiley, 1976), *Explaining Technical Change* (1983), *Sour Grapes* (1981), *Ulysses and the Sirens* (1983), and *The Cement of Society* (1989) all published by Cambridge University Press. *Explaining Technical Change* opens with a helpful sketch of three basic approaches to social analysis. For a reflective review of this area see S. Hargreaves-Heap, M. Hollis, B. Lyons, R. Sugden and A. Weale, *Choice: A Critical Guide* (Oxford: Blackwell, forthcoming).

Finally, there may be merit in recommending a few general works. For those unacquainted with philosophy we venture to suggest Martin Hollis, *Invitation to Philosophy* (Oxford: Blackwell, 1985), if only to show where the wind in this book has been blowing from. Similarly, his *The Cunning of Reason* (Cambridge: Cambridge University Press, 1988) contains deeper reasons for the philosophical lines in this book. For the theory of knowledge, B. Aune, *Rationalism, Empiricism and Pragmatism* (New York: Random House, 1970) is a good general starter. For the philosophy of mind and action, so is L. H. Davies, *Theory of Action* (Englewood Cliffs, NJ: Prentice-Hall, 1979). By now, however, the whole landscape of philosophy is coming into view and this is not the place to map it out further.

Index

Adorno, T. 222
Alker, H. 40
Allison, G. 13, 54, 147, 150 f.
Althusser, L. 211
analytic statements 57
anarchy 7, 102, 108, 179
Anti-Ballistic Missile Treaty 69
appeasement 63
arms control and disarmament 123 ff., 136
Aune, B. 222
Axelrod, R. 132, 136
Ayer, A. J. 12, 220, 221

balance of power 24, 29, 38, 47, 97, 103 f.
Banks, M. 217 f.
Bay of Pigs Invasion 81
Bayesian 121
behaviouralism 12, 17, 28–32, 45, 53 f., 67, 71, 73, 97 f., 101, 196, 201
behaviourism 12, 71, 73, 186, 201
belief systems 86, 146
Bhaskar, R. 61, 221, 222
Biersteker, T. 40
bipolarity 101–4, 110
Braithwaite, R. B. 220
Brams, S. 132 f.
Brown, H. 150
Brown, Sarah 219
Brown, Seyom 35, 218
Brucan, S. 219
Bruck, H. W. 30, 145
Brzezinski, Z. 150, 154, 156 f., 164, 166
Bull, H. 20, 31, 35, 217 f.
bureaucratic politics model 13 f., 44, 60, 63, 89, 143, 146–9, 150–70, 180, 183, 184, 188, 194, 199, 202, 204
Buch, G. 1, 3

Carnap, R. 50, 220
Carr, E. H. 20 f., 45, 217
Carter, J. 150, 152 ff., 162

causation 49, 81
Chalmers, A. 220
Chicago School 113
chicken game, see games
Christopher, W. 154, 162
compatibilism 201
Comte, A. 11, 66
Condorcet, M. 49, 63
Cuban Missile Crisis 54, 148

Dallmayr, F. 221
Davidson, D. 91 n.
Davies, L. 222
deterrence 130 ff., 135, 174–5
Dougherty. J. 217
Doyal, L. 221
Dunne, T. v
Durkheim, E. 11, 74

Einstein, A. 59
Elshtain, J. 219
Elster, J. 222
empathy 78
empiricism 48, 55, 61, 66
escalation dominance 131
expectations 70, 189–93
    normative 191, 193
    rational 190, 193
expected utility 75, 121
explaining, explanation 1, 3, 10, 16, 41, 45–67, 71, 86, 89, 144, 168 f., 196–216

Falklands Conflict 138, 184
Feyerabend, P. 221
First World War 16–20, 22, 28, 33, 40, 133
focal points 132
foreign policy analysis 38, 74, 145
form of life 179, 193, 205
Fortes, M. 108
free-rider problem 125
Freud, S. 53
Friedman, M. 58, 62

Gadaffi, M. 1, 139, 181 ff.
Galtung, J. 219
games, theory of 13, 64, 79 f., 88, 90,
    93, 118, 119–42, 169, 171, 173,
    174–5, 177, 179, 184, 185, 187,
    190–5, 199, 201, 204, 212
  assurance game 123
  chicken game 64, 126–7, 130, 134 f.,
    139 f., 141, 173, 192
  coordination game 123
  prisoner's dilemma game 64, 124–6,
    129 f., 132 f., 135 f., 139 f., 141,
    192
  truth game 134
games, Wittgensteinian 176–81
Garthoff, R. 175
Geuss, R. 222
Gibraltar 136
Giddens, A. 6
Gilpin, R. 218
Gorbachev, M. 1, 3, 84, 102, 136, 169
Gorman, R. 220
Green, P. 131
Grenada 136
Groom, J. 218, 220
groupthink 81, 161, 200

Haas, E. 34, 99
Habermas, J. 222
Hacking, I. 221
Halliday, F. 219
Hargreaves-Heap, S. 222
Harré, R. 220
Harris, R. 221
hegemonic stability 37
hegemony 37
Hempel, C. 50, 220
hermeneutics 71, 74 f., 87–91
Herz, J. 33, 99, 104
Hill, C. 219
Hobbes, T. 94, 102, 129, 132, 158, 221
Hobson, J. 105
Hoffman, M. 219
Hoffmann, S. 28
holism 5, 9, 184, 196, 215
Hollis, M. 222
Holsti, K. 217
Hume, D. 48 f., 158 f., 186 f., 221

ideal type 76, 193
idealism 11 f., 17–20, 22, 26 f., 42, 44,
    60, 93 f., 135, 196, 216
ideology 70, 84, 85

individualism 2, 9, 90, 128, 184, 196,
    215
interdependence 32–6
interest 25
Iran–Contra Scandal 86
Iranian Hostage Crisis 149–54

Janis, I. 81
Jervis, R. 175
Jones, D. 150
Jordan, H. 150

Kahn, H. 130, 132
Kant, I. 159
Kaplan, M. 30 f., 87, 98 f., 107, 218
Kauppi, M. 217
Keat, R. 221
Keohane, R. 36, 110, 133, 218
Khomeini, Ayatollah 84
Knorr, K. 218
Krasner, S. 36, 218
Kuhn, T. 55, 57–61, 66, 198, 220 f.

Lakatos, I. 61, 66, 220 f.
Lauren, P. 219
League of Nations 20, 96
Lenin, V. 105
level-of-analysis problem 7–9, 10, 32,
    82, 89 f., 99–101, 118, 143, 168,
    194, 196, 200, 203–16
Levy, M. 218
Libya 1, 181–4, 192
Light, M. 218 f.
Linklater, A. 219
Lipsey, R. E. 50, 52 f., 55, 59
Little, R. 218
Locke, J. 94, 128
logical positivism 12, 50, 61, 63, 66
Lukes, S. 110, 162 n. 189
Lynch, A. 219
Lyons, B. 222

McCarthy, T. 221
Machiavelli, N. 22
Maghroori, R. 218
Mansbach, R. 36
Marx, K. 5, 11, 53, 90
Masters, R. 99
materialism 11
Mill, J. S. 62, 221
Mondale, W. 150
Morgenthau, H. 10. 22–30, 32, 37,
    41 f., 45 f., 63, 76, 85, 87, 97, 101,
    107, 201, 217

Morse, E. 218
multipolarity 101–4, 110

Nagel, E. 50, 220
national interest 24, 29, 63, 66, 85, 147,
     151, 166, 175, 180, 183, 199
NATO 174
neo-realism 36–8, 93, 104–10, 196
Neurath, O. 206
Newton, I. 46, 48, 50, 59, 92, 111
Nicholson, M. 219 f.
Nixon, R. 69, 86
Northedge, F. 35
Nye, J. 218

Olson, W. 217
Onuf, N. 217
organizational process model 148
other minds problem 171–6, 185–9, 192

paradigms 57–61, 64, 198
personality 158, 160–2
Pfaltzgraff, R. 217
pluralism 38, 60, 65
polarity 101–5, 108–9
Popper, K. 52 f., 56, 65, 220 f.
Porter, B. 217
positive economics 12
positivism 11, 46, 58, 66, 88, 203, 207
Powell, J. 150
power 25 f., 29, 42, 97, 102, 110, 118,
     158, 209
pragmatism 55–7
pre-theory 58
prisoner's dilemma, *see* games
prominence 132
psychology 4, 5

Quine, W. 55–7, 59, 61, 65, 198, 221

Ramberg, B. 218
Rapoport, A. 130 f.
rational actor model 14, 53, 60, 94,
     119, 143–7, 150–70, 184, 186,
     196–7, 199 f., 202
rationality 75, 77, 120, 204
rational reconstruction 90, 172 f.,
     182 f., 185, 187 ff., 191, 193
Reagan, R. 1, 4, 181–3
realism 10 f., 17, 20–8, 29 f., 38, 40,
     50, 60, 64 f., 66, 76, 85, 88, 92 f.,
     135, 144 f., 147, 196, 201, 216
realpolitik 64, 85, 86, 185

reductionism 37–8, 105, 107, 109, 115
regime 37
Reynolds, C. v, 219
Reynolds, P. 217
role-distance 165
roles 155–70
Rosecrance, R. 99, 107
Rosenau, J. 58, 218, 220
Rothstein, R. 27 f.
Ruggie, J. 114, 115
Runciman, G. 221
Rushdie, S. 84–6
Rusk, D. 140
Russell, B. 220

Sapin, B. 30, 145
Schelling, T. 130 f., 136, 173
Second World War 23, 28
Shackleton, M. 218
Singer, D. 32, 89, 100 f., 107, 196 f.,
     203, 205, 214, 218
Skinner, Q. 167 n., 176 n.
Skocpol, T. 219
Smith, M. 218
Smith, S. 217, 219
Snyder, R. 30, 145
Spegele, R. 220
Star Wars 69
state of nature 94, 128
structural-functionalism 92, 111–13,
     118
structuralism 38, 60, 65
structuration 6
Sugden, R. 222
synthetic statements 57
systems theory 85, 89, 92–118, 119

tacit communication 132, 173
Taylor, C. 22
teleological explanation 47
Thatcher, M. 1, 4, 5, 182–4
Tickner, J. 219
tit-for-tat 132
traditionalists 31
transnationalism 32–6
Turner, S. 150

understanding 1, 2, 10, 16, 41 f.,
     68–91, 144, 168 f., 196–216
  direct 78, 172
  explanatory 78, 172, 188
United Nations 180
Urry, J. 221

Vance, C. 150, 153 f., 157, 162 f.
Vasquez, J. 31. 35 f.
Vietnam War 63, 81, 86
Viotti, P. 217

Wallerstein, I. 40, 219
Waltz, K. 13, 36 f., 87, 93, 98 f., 104–18, 143, 146, 198
Warsaw Pact 174
Weale, A. 222
Weber, M. 11. 71–82, 88, 90, 121, 159, 172, 188, 212, 221

Wilson, W. 20
Winch, P. 73, 82–8, 90, 179–81, 221
Wittgenstein, L. 8, 82–4, 170, 176–81, 184 f., 193 f., 200, 204 ff., 221
Wootton, H. 176

Yom Kippur War 69
Young, O. 220

Zalewski, M. vi
Zimmern, A. 217